Praise for *Wall Street's War on Workers*

"*Wall Street's War on Workers* is incisive, infuriating, and yet inspiring. Leopold upends conventional wisdom, not only pinpointing the causes of mass layoffs but providing a blueprint for what we can do about them. This is a highly readable and thoroughly researched analysis; it should be required reading for workers, organizers, and policy makers alike."

—**Rebecca Givan,** associate professor, Labor Studies and Employment Relations, Rutgers University

"Les Leopold cuts through a lot of myths and explains the dynamics of mass layoffs and the reality that the white working class did not desert Democrats—the Democrats deserted them. Leopold also offers ingenious and practical solutions to take back our politics from the plutocracy."

—**Robert Kuttner,** founding co-editor, *The American Prospect*

"After reading Les Leopold's vivid description of how two little words ['stock buybacks'] affect factory closings, mass layoffs, income shifts, and polarized politics, I've come to think of stock buybacks as the key, not just to why things have gone wrong, but how, if we choose, we can make them go right. . . . This book gave me a new lens to see the world."

—**Robert Krulwich,** former co-host of WNYC's *Radiolab*

"Les Leopold's latest book, *Wall Street's War on Workers*, is a must-read for anyone concerned with income inequity and employment instability in the US economy. Leopold locates the growing disaffection of the white working-class voter with Democratic candidates in the mass layoffs that have been characteristic of American capitalism since the 1980s. Yielding to the predatory demands of Wall Street, leading Democrats have failed to confront the prime cause of mass layoffs: trillions upon trillions of corporate dollars devoted to stock buybacks to jack up stock prices. Leopold lays out a comprehensive policy agenda for Democrats to stop the mass layoffs and win back the white working class."

—**William Lazonick,** professor emeritus of economics, University of Massachusetts

WALL STREET'S WAR ON WORKERS

Also by Les Leopold

Defiant German, Defiant Jew:
A Holocaust Memoir from
Inside the Third Reich
(2020)

Runaway Inequality:
An Activist's Guide to Economic Justice
(2018)

How to Make a Million Dollars an Hour:
Why Financial Elites Get Away with
Siphoning Off America's Wealth
(2013)

The Looting of America:
How Wall Street's Game of Fantasy Finance
Destroyed Our Jobs, Pensions and Prosperity,
and What We Can Do About It
(2009)

The Man Who Hated Work and Loved Labor:
The Life and Times of Tony Mazzocchi
(2006)

WALL STREET'S WAR ON WORKERS

HOW MASS LAYOFFS AND GREED ARE DESTROYING THE WORKING CLASS AND WHAT TO DO ABOUT IT

LES LEOPOLD

Chelsea Green Publishing
White River Junction, Vermont
London, UK

Project Manager: Rebecca Springer
Project Editor: Matthew Derr
Copy Editor: Deborah Heimann
Proofreader: Angela Boyle
Indexer: WordCo Indexing Services, Inc.
Designer: Melissa Jacobson
Page Layout: Abrah Griggs

Printed in the United States of America.
First printing February 2024.
10 9 8 7 6 5 4 3 2 1   24 25 26 27 28

Our Commitment to Green Publishing
Chelsea Green sees publishing as a tool for cultural change and ecological stewardship. We strive to align
our book manufacturing practices with our editorial mission and to reduce the impact of our business
enterprise in the environment. We print our books on chlorine-free recycled paper, using vegetable-
based inks whenever possible. This book may cost slightly more because it was printed on paper that
contains recycled fiber, and we hope you'll agree that it's worth it. *Wall Street's War on Workers* was
printed on paper supplied by Sheridan that is made of recycled materials and other controlled sources.

Library of Congress Cataloging-in-Publication Data
Names: Leopold, Les, author.
Title: Wall Street's war on workers : how mass layoffs and greed are destroying the working class
    and what to do about it / Les Leopold.
Description: White River Junction, Vermont : Chelsea Green Publishing, [2024] | Includes
    bibliographical references and index.
Identifiers: LCCN 2023046364 | ISBN 9781645022336 (hardcover) | ISBN 9781645022343 (ebook)
Subjects: LCSH: Working class—United States. | Labor demand—United States. | Capitalism—
    United States. | United States—Economic conditions—2009-
Classification: LCC HD8072.5 .L46 2024 | DDC 331.0973—dc23/eng/20231005
LC record available at https://lccn.loc.gov/2023046364

Chelsea Green Publishing
White River Junction, Vermont, USA
London, UK

www.chelseagreen.com

In memory of Jeff Dreyfuss:
My vivacious and gifted cousin—more like a brother—
who passed far too soon

CONTENTS

The Destructiveness of Mass Layoffs

"When I first lost my job, it was kind of scary thinking of where I could go to work. You almost felt like you're paralyzed because, especially at my age and you didn't have the [Covid] vaccine yet, it's like . . . Where do I go to work where I won't die?" —Diane, age 61, laid off after 17 years of service

"How do you keep going, feeling this depressed or this sad? That's what it was like. When you knew that this was definitely going to happen, it was like grieving." —Mary, age 60, laid off after 18 years of service

"It still hurts. I mean, even though I say I'm over it, I don't really know if I am or not. I don't think I ever will be, honestly. You know, that was a long part of my life, and to lose it is kind of like losing a family member. It's like grieving. You know, you can grieve forever. . . ." —"Susan Carroll" (pseudonym), age 50, laid off after 26 years of service

"It was like suffering through a death, and I went through a deep depression. I think that's another reason why I didn't want to go searching for a job. I felt, I don't know, [it] just made me feel unappreciated and worthless. I had no confidence in myself after that." —Lori, age 57, laid off after 26 years of service

"[W]hen I have a medical issue I have to seriously think about, do I even want to go to a doctor? . . . So my medical care is coming basically from the CVS MinuteClinic. . . . If something major happens, this insurance I have now, it covers crap. So financially, a major medical issue would wipe me out." —Pat Baker, age 55, laid off after 8 years of service

THESE GUT-WRENCHING ACCOUNTS FROM THE VICTIMS OF MASS LAYOFFS in 2020 echo the pain and suffering of America's laid-off workers over the last four decades.[1]

The first mass layoff wave in the post–World War II era focused on manufacturing workers as the Rust Belt formed and corroded during the 1970s and 1980s. Then, in the 1990s, white-collar professionals found that their shiny offices were not immune. Now, workers in the tech industry are under assault: 1,060 companies dumped 164,744 workers in 2022, and another 213,298 in the first half of 2023.[2]

The disturbing statements above, however, do not come from the business sector. Rather, these are voices from among the 113 unionized food service and cleaning workers terminated by Oberlin College, my alma mater, six months into the pandemic. (Around 50 of these workers managed to find employment with one of the subcontractors.)*

This nonprofit progressive college—"the first college in America to adopt a policy to admit Black students (1835) and the first to grant bachelor's degrees to women (1841) in a coeducational program," according to the college's website[3]—chose to cut costs by terminating these workers, many with decades of service, and replacing them with lower-wage subcontractors. In doing so, Oberlin adhered to the Wall Street employee handbook. Rule #1: Workers must be reduced to mere numbers. Rule #2: Workers are expendable. Rule #3: Loyalty is irrelevant. Finally, the most sacred rule of all, Rule #4: Bottom-line financial calculations trump all other considerations.

And so, Oberlin saw absolutely no reason to factor into their decision-making calculus the harm done to these workers, nor the consequences to the surrounding town, which was already saddled with a 24.9 percent poverty rate.[4]

---

* Approximately fifty of the laid-off Oberlin workers (mostly food service plus a few custodians) were rehired by an Oberlin subcontractor, AVI, which negotiated a contract with the workers' union, the United Auto Workers (UAW). When Oberlin announced it was pursuing outsourcing, workers had no idea that the vendor ultimately selected would already have a positive relationship with the UAW elsewhere and want to maintain it by rehiring these workers and signing a new union contract. The rest of the janitorial workers were less fortunate. Scioto Services, the new contractor, hired only one laid-off worker—and then only at the insistence of the College's art museum, which wanted to retain an experienced custodian to protect the museum's priceless collection.

The harm so studiously ignored is considerable.

Layoffs upend people's lives. They cause extraordinary levels of stress, loss of confidence, and financial insecurity, including depleted savings and, often, increased debt. Medical studies have shown that the trauma of unemployment causes disease.[5] Sandra Sucher and Marilyn Morgan Westner, writing in the *Harvard Business Review*, reported on additional research that reveals the vast extent of the personal suffering caused by unemployment:[6]

- Losing your job is the seventh most stressful life event, ranked more stressful than "divorce, a sudden and serious impairment of hearing or vision, or the death of a close friend."
- Recovery from the psychological trauma of job loss takes two years on average.
- Even for those without preexisting health conditions, "the odds of developing a new health condition rise by 83 percent in the first 15 to 18 months after a layoff, with the most common conditions being stress-related illnesses, including hypertension, heart disease, and arthritis."
- The stress of a layoff "can increase the risk of suicide by 1.3 to 3 times. Displaced workers have twice the risk of developing depression, 4 times the risk of substance abuse, and 6 times the risk of committing violent acts including partner and child abuse."
- Stress from layoffs can "impair fetal development."
- For many layoff victims the loss of income "can last for the remainder of their careers: Workers who lost their jobs during the 1981 recession saw a 30 percent decline in earnings at the time of their layoff. Twenty years later, most still earned 20 percent less than workers who retained their jobs—the cumulative effect of unemployment, underemployment, and an inability to find work commensurate with their skills."

As mass layoffs devastate rural areas, they become opioid death zones, supplying a disproportionate number of the nation's overdose victims, now totaling more than 100,000 deaths per year.[7] Little wonder that even the US Department of Labor recognizes that "being laid off from your job is one of the most traumatic events you can experience in life."[8]

The enormous harm caused by mass layoffs has been known for decades. Yet, we do little to stop them.

There are no laws in the United States to protect working people from "mass layoffs" (defined by the Bureau of Labor Statistics as 50 or more workers losing their jobs at a single company during a five-week period). Public outrage about layoffs is, at best, localized, while new mass layoffs are announced without much fanfare each day across the country. Layoffs have become so commonplace, so normalized, so routinized, that for-profit and nonprofit executives alike do not hesitate to slash jobs whenever they feel it necessary—and they alone have the authority to define "necessary."

There's always a justification. Costs need to be cut because competition demands it. Nonprofit colleges lay off workers to keep tuition increases down as they compete for students. Budgets must be balanced, "structural deficits" addressed, and endowments protected.

A half-century earlier, it would have been difficult for Oberlin to find less expensive workers to replace those they had laid off. At that time, a booming industrial economy surrounding the college in northeast Ohio depended on well-compensated labor. Steel mills and auto factories, refineries, and chemical plants were working three shifts to meet demand spurred by the war in Vietnam and the War on Poverty. And trade unions, about four times the size of today's labor organizations, were powerful enough to cripple companies—or colleges—that dared to engage in union-busting activities.*

But the Reagan revolution, which attacked unions and deregulated Wall Street, led to a dramatic shift in how corporate capitalism functioned, and eventually how nonprofits would as well.

In short order, hostile corporate takeovers became routine, massive debt was piled onto corporate balance sheets, and stock buybacks—using corporate money to repurchase the company's shares to raise their price—became legalized. (In times past, stock buybacks were considered stock manipulation, and stock manipulation was considered a contributing cause of the 1929 stock market crash.) The deregulation of Wall Street in the name of free-market ideology made it possible for investment bankers and corporate raiders (that we now politely call private equity companies and hedge funds) to strip wealth away from corporations and their employees. This

---

* For example, the United Auto Workers had approximately 1.5 million workers in the late 1960s and has fewer than 400,000 today.

slash-and-burn mentality increasingly moved wealth into the hands of the few while leading to devastating job losses again and again, especially in manufacturing areas like northeast Ohio.

The Democratic Party, pressed by labor unions, considered legislation to inhibit corporate shutdowns and mass layoffs. Its 1984 presidential platform urged that workers should have "actual ownership of the company, employee representation on corporate boards, quality work circles, and greater worker participation in management decisions." In addition, the platform called for the government to "encourage employee participation and ownership, particularly as an alternative to plant shutdowns."

"It is destructive of labor-management relations when concessions extracted from labor to preserve jobs are converted after the restoration of profitability into management bonuses, rather than restoring the concessions that the workers made," said the Democratic Party presidential platform statement of 1984. "Such practices offend our sense of fairness, as does the Reagan Administration–inspired union-busting."[9]

Rather than fulfill these pledges, the next Democratic administration, under Bill Clinton, doubled down on financial deregulation—from deregulating derivatives to allowing risky investment banks to merge with commercial banks, leading to more mass layoffs. In effect, both parties were competing for Wall Street's favor. The victims of mass layoffs were political orphans.

Of course, there was always a lofty excuse, packaged as a bold new vision that claimed the job carnage was necessary to modernize our economy, meet the foreign competition, and create a better future for us all.

The unleashing of Wall Street, and the reasoning to justify it, became so prevalent for so long that few can remember a time when job destruction was not routine.

But before financial deregulation, corporate leaders considered mass layoffs a sign of their own failure—an indication that they had misread markets, failed to anticipate competitive needs, and didn't invest enough in research, development, and worker training to build thriving, long-lasting enterprises. To be sure, during recessions they might be forced to cut jobs, but not during periods of general economic expansion. Today, in good times and bad, jobs are cut. What formerly was considered failure is now considered smart management, the coin of the realm in every MBA program. It has become axiomatic that cutting jobs is what smart managers must have the guts to do.

As Wall Street has routinized the financial strip-mining of productive enterprises, more than 30 million of us have experienced mass layoffs.* And even more have felt the pain and suffering as our family members lost jobs.

Most mass layoff victims experience it as one of the most traumatic events of their lives. For people in rural areas, where many layoffs have occurred, the trauma is even more extreme, since decent jobs there are scarce. When jobs do open up, scores of colleagues, friends, and neighbors line up and compete for them. This cruelty—this mass destruction—is baked into modern financialized capitalism, including at nonprofit colleges like Oberlin. And it is rarely questioned, now that financialized management has oozed into college administrations, boards of trustees, and their endowments.

The mass layoffs at Oberlin served as a wake-up call for me and other concerned alumni. We organized, fundraised, investigated the college's finances, and created a fund for the displaced workers. The Oberlin layoffs also illuminated for us at the Labor Institute, where I've worked since 1975, how pervasive mass layoffs have become as a management technique. It triggered our team's investigation into the whys and wherefores of this profound economic and social disruption, its impact on politics, and how mass layoffs might be mitigated.†

To claim that massive job dislocation is the price we must pay for a modern economy is to ignore the political price we also are paying. A volcano of disappointment among working-class people has erupted throughout our country as political elites of all stripes ignore the devastation that job loss has left behind. One result is apparent: Working people—especially rural white working people in the border states as well as in the North and Midwest—are walking away from the Democratic Party, their historic champion. And if

---

* Bureau of Labor Statistics' mass-layoff database records 20.2 million layoffs for the years 1996–2012 (2012 was the last year this statistic was calculated). If layoffs continued at that rate through 2022, the total number of layoffs would be 32.8 million.

† When using terms like *we*, *us*, and *our*, I'm often referring to the committed team of Labor Institute staff, consultants, and interns who worked tirelessly on this book (see the acknowledgments). However, the responsibility for all of the writing, the factual content, and the expressed opinions falls solely on me.

nothing is done to provide more stable employment, they may walk away from democracy as well.*

Similar trends are emerging for Black and Hispanic working people. There are signs that Republicans are gaining ground among these groups.[10] The alienation of working-class voters continues today as the Democrats fail to intervene even when doing so would require very little political capital. We will report on how, unlike then-President Donald Trump, who bombastically forced a reduction of mass layoffs at the Carrier air-conditioning facility in Indiana in 2017,† the Democrats have shied away from interfering with the prerogatives of corporate America and Wall Street even during the presidency of pro-labor Joseph Biden.

The ultimate question, however, is whether either political party has the courage to curtail mass layoffs. Will the political establishment continue to cower before the prevailing view that such efforts would cripple capitalism and harm US competitiveness, thereby leading to more job loss? Will they continue to blame supposedly unstoppable forces like globalization and technology, now led by AI? Will they continue to avoid challenging the power of corporations to conduct mass layoffs, while instead showering them with subsidies to "grow the economy," "bring jobs home," and "invest in new infrastructure"? In short, will they time and again tell the victims of mass layoffs, "tough luck"?

Or will working people build a movement either within the two parties or outside of them to fight for basic job security?

At the start of our project, we thought that halting mass layoffs might prove too great a challenge, and that perhaps for us—and others working for economic justice—the focus would have to be on creating new jobs and expanding the social safety net for those left behind. But then we looked at what German trade unions have been able to achieve—including forcing Siemens Energy, a large global conglomerate, to reverse its decision to lay

---

* We define white working class as those who identify themselves as white, are in the bottom two-thirds of the income distribution, and have less than a four-year college degree. For further discussion, see "Why Focus on Race and Ethnicity?" (page 13) and "The Most Commonly Used Definitions of Class Focus Entirely on Education" (page 16).

† Approximately half of these workers are people of color.

off 3,000 workers in Germany, even as it terminated more than 1,700 workers in the United States. In Germany, Siemens agreed to eliminate jobs only through *noncompulsory* buyouts and attrition.

Why there and not here?

Answering that question may well help us save our democracy. Unless steps are taken to bring stable employment to the tens of millions of people who have suffered and will continue to suffer mass layoffs, democracy could very well lose a significant portion of its legitimacy. If the two parties continue to shy away from addressing mass layoffs, authoritarians will inevitably fill the breach. In fact, they already have.

It's time to break free from four decades of groupthink that insists that the mass slaughter of jobs is natural and necessary. It doesn't have to be this way if we are willing to reregulate Wall Street and limit its financial control of corporate life.

This book, which was inspired by the laid-off Oberlin workers and includes the contributions of Oberlin students and graduates, is dedicated to all those working people who have lost their livelihoods in mass layoffs. We hope in some small way our exploration can help make sense of their plight and contribute to building a more just society.

Here's our case:

Democratic leaders have been writing off the white working class because of a fatalistic understanding of our modern economy.
From Bill Clinton to Barack Obama to Chuck Schumer, there is a shared belief that the growth of the knowledge economy makes mass layoffs inevitable. Rather than taking responsibility for the ensuing economic devastation, too often they blame the white working class for turning economic despair into increasing racism, sexism, xenophobia, and homophobia. (Chapter 1)

White working-class defections from the Democratic Party are concentrated in rural areas that have been hit hardest by mass layoffs.
We provide new data and analysis showing how the rise of mass layoffs in rural counties corresponds with the decline of the Democratic presidential vote. We suggest that the failure of the Democrats to counter the

estimated 30 million job losses in mass layoffs that have ripped through the economy since 1996 is a primary reason for working-class defections from the Democratic Party. (Chapter 2)

White working-class attitudes on social issues (abortion, LGBTQ+ rights, immigration, gun control, affirmative action, and the like) have not become more illiberal even as mass layoffs increased and the Democratic vote declined. By analyzing three large national surveys, we have found compelling evidence that upends the media's negative portrayal of the white working class. Our new data shows that, as a group, the white working class has become significantly *more* liberal, not less, on a majority of these divisive social issues. (Chapter 3)

There actually are very few illiberal white working-class populists. When Hillary Clinton described half of the more than 69 million Trump voters as racist, sexist, homophobic, and xenophobic, she implied that a vast number of people hold these views across the board. Former President Obama also saw these working people as "clinging to their guns and religion." However, our original research finds that only a minuscule number of respondents answer five basic social issue questions illiberally. Similarly, the data show that the white working class is becoming less, not more, involved with religion, while a majority favors a ban on assault rifles. Also, we demonstrate that when it comes to extreme illiberalism, there is very little difference between the white working class and the white professional-managerial class. Reactionary "populism" should not be viewed as a white working-class phenomenon. (Chapter 4)

The conventional wisdom about white working-class populism is wrong. The white working class does not form the rabid reactionary base that dominates Republican Party primaries. Yet the populist negative meme, so often repeated in the media, conflates the white working class with reactionary populism and turns that word into a negative epithet. We need to understand the origins of this conventional wisdom and why it is erroneous. (Chapter 5)

The epidemic of mass layoffs, impacting working people of all colors and ethnicities, flows directly from concrete public policy choices, not inevitable economic "laws," or new technologies like AI. Policy choices enabled a new virulent, financialized version of American capitalism. As financial deregulation swept through the Reagan and Clinton administrations, mass layoffs became part of the process by which Wall Street entities extracted wealth from productive enterprises—a practice that had been rare before 1980. That millions of working people oppose financialization and free-trade agreements—and hold politicians accountable for these policies—is a sign of a healthy class interest, not populist irrationality. (Chapters 6, 7, and 11)

The Democrats have refused to interfere with mass layoffs even when they have the power to do so. Joe Biden, Chuck Schumer, and Bernie Sanders had golden opportunities during the pandemic to stop two significant mass layoffs, one in Morgantown, West Virginia, and the other in Olean, New York. Their failure to act contrasts starkly with Trump's strikingly symbolic and partially successful effort to prevent the Carrier Global Corporation from moving jobs from its Indiana facility to Mexico in 2017. (Chapter 8)

Surviving and thriving in a competitive global economy does not require mass layoffs. Siemens Energy, a German company with more than 90,000 global employees, adapted its complex operations to a no-layoff demand from its empowered German unions. We share an interview with one of those German union officials. In the United States, where there are no structures to inhibit mass layoffs, Siemens proceeded to slash its workforce like any other US firm. (Chapter 9)

To stop mass layoffs, we must challenge Wall Street's domination of our economy. For democracy to endure, our nation must provide stable livelihoods for working people. Stock buybacks must be eliminated. Corporate raiders must be removed from boards of directors and replaced by employees and their representatives. Workers should be free to join labor unions without corporate interference. And the federal government itself needs to create jobs, as it did through the New Deal programs and the Marshall Plan. That is what it will take to revive communities and regions that have been left behind, from old industrial and coal-mining counties to depressed urban areas. (Chapters 10, 11, and 12)

CHAPTER 1

White Working-Class Blues

Who Is the White Working Class and Why Are the Democrats Abandoning Them?

"I went from about $60,000 in savings to zero. Absolute zero. I'll never forget the day my wife came to me and she says, 'Jack, we're out of money.' I said, 'That's impossible.' She said, 'No, it's not. Because, you know, the house payment, the car payment, the insurance, the regular living bills.' That money went fast. It put me in a very deep state of depression. . . . When you have no money to fall back on, no savings left, no money coming in, you feel really hurt and disappointed with yourself and your life because you can't help your children when they need help anymore. And that's really hard. And I'm not that kind of person, me and my wife, to ask my kids for anything.

"But yet, my oldest son, and my middle son, actually my daughter, too, they've actually had to, a couple times, help us out with the bills. And you know that hurts. I don't know. I hope we never have to go through that. So you know, it's really hard. You're supposed to be the person that is there for them. Not the opposite way . . . Nobody really wants to hire somebody on the edge of retirement. It's not in the cards for me. I've looked, I've put things out there. Nobody wants to hire somebody 59 years old." —Jack Kubicki, age 59, laid off after 12 years of service

For many labor educators and researchers, "white working class" is a jarring construct. We prefer to think of this group as members of the working class who happen to be white.

Most workplaces are diverse, especially in metropolitan areas, but often in rural areas as well. For example, the workforce at the Indiana Carrier Global Corporation facility (made famous in 2017 when Trump intervened in a mass layoff) is 50 percent Black.[1] Every labor union on a national level is integrated and preaches racial solidarity. Each strives to build a more unified class awareness to protect and enhance the lives and livelihoods of their members. The last thing labor organizations want, or need, is a specifically *white* working-class consciousness.

The promotion of a separate white working class goes all the way back to Bacon's Rebellion in Virginia in 1676, during which Black and white indentured servants joined together under the leadership of Nathaniel Bacon to enhance their rights (as well as to pilfer more Native American land). The plantation owners, fearful of growing common demands from Black and white workers, then passed Virginia's first color laws, creating legal distinctions between Black and white residents.[2]

For the next two centuries, racial laws and brute force were used to prop up slavery and keep white and Black working people apart. After the Civil War, Southern elites again used race and overt violence as tools to undermine a rising progressive Populist movement—a movement that had significant success in forming coalitions between Black and white farmers.[3] (More on this in chapter 5.)

Race and class entanglements were further exploited during the early 20th century as pseudoscientists conjured up an elaborate array of "races" that corporations used to undermine worker solidarity and strikes. As shown in figure 1.1 (from the Pittsburgh Central Tube Company in 1926), the goal was to divide the workforce into as many groups as possible by deploying preposterous "objective" skill assessments.[4] Nationality was a race. Religion was a race. Skin color was a race. By birth, your blood and culture supposedly produced immutable skills that fit you neatly into a stratified corporate hierarchy and determined what you were worth. Your heritage was your inescapable destiny.

(Why were Jews placed on the bottom? Because they were believed to be more sympathetic to unions and more likely to be organizers sent from New York labor organizations who were seeking to unionize the steel industry.)

Even though this corporate chart mixes race, religion, and nationality into a neat hierarchy, skin color has always been treated differently. Every time the word *race* is used, it conjures up biology—the idea that genetically, we really are separate species. If darker skin makes someone Black, isn't it likely there also are many deeper biological differences as well?

After 150 years of trying, however, race pseudoscientists have utterly failed to find a basis for separate biological races. They have looked hard, very hard, into every nook and cranny of our bodies and souls—bone structure, brain size, strength, hair type, lips, intelligence, and even lust. But no one has found the differentiating line, because biological races do not exist. Without question, race is a social construct—the invention of human beings who seek to justify the subjugation of others based on their supposed racial inferiority.

Nevertheless, we still live in a color-coded society where everyone soon learns that they are white, Black, or something else. As much as we wish it weren't so, those identities matter in the overall distribution of money and power in our society. Even the official Census reports on five "races," none of which exist biologically, but all of which make a significant difference socially and economically.[5] We can't escape racial identification.

Why Focus on Race and Ethnicity?

This book has uncovered information that casts doubt on the notion that white members of the working class are substantially less tolerant than other groups. The data in chapters 3 and 4 show that the white working class has become more supportive of the rights of immigrants, LGBTQ+ communities, and racial minorities, and is becoming ever more so.

By challenging the negative stereotypes about the illiberal white working class, we hope to encourage more solidarity among all working people. Our goal is to bring more precision and clarity to understanding what working people, especially in rural areas, experience and believe. These working people, we have found, share a common reality with all workers across the country: Millions upon millions have suffered through devastating mass layoffs and the other consequences of Wall Street's domination of our economy. It is likely that this devastation will continue until working people of all shades and colors organize around a common program for economic justice and fairness.

To be sure, white members of the working class are not free of right-wing populism. There are plenty of racists among them. Our research strongly suggests, however, that the white working class does not have a monopoly on illiberalism. It's coming from managers and professionals as well, and also from Black and Hispanic workers and managers. At the very

Figure 1.1. Racial adaptability to various types of plant work

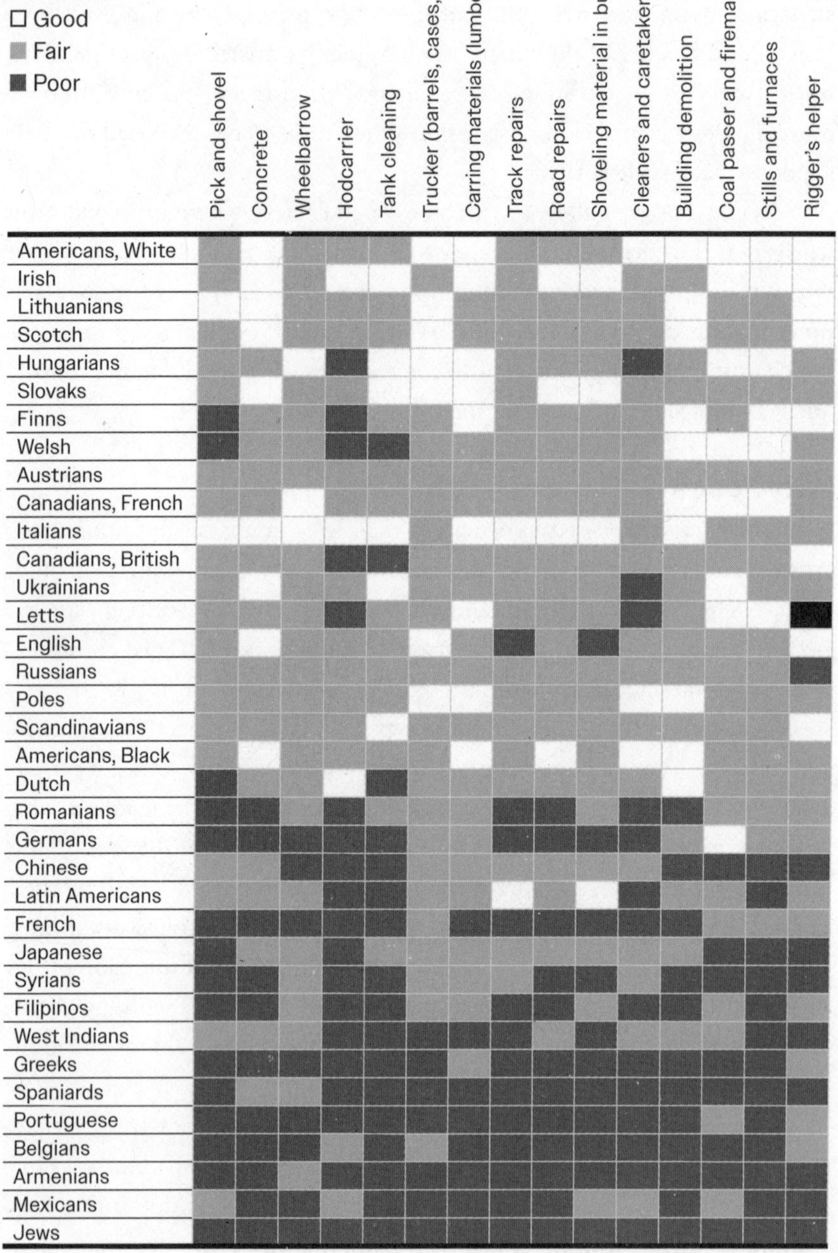
□ Good
Fair
Poor
Pick and shovel
Concrete
Wheelbarrow
Hodcarrier
Tank cleaning
Trucker (barrels, cases, etc.)
Carring materials (lumber, steel, etc.)
Track repairs
Road repairs
Shoveling material in bulk
Cleaners and caretakers
Building demolition
Coal passer and fireman
Stills and furnaces
Rigger's helper
Americans, White
Irish
Lithuanians
Scotch
Hungarians
Slovaks
Finns
Welsh
Austrians
Canadians, French
Italians
Canadians, British
Ukrainians
Letts
English
Russians
Poles
Scandinavians
Americans, Black
Dutch
Romanians
Germans
Chinese
Latin Americans
French
Japanese
Syrians
Filipinos
West Indians
Greeks
Spaniards
Portuguese
Belgians
Armenians
Mexicans
Jews

Source: Pittsburgh Urban League Archive[6]

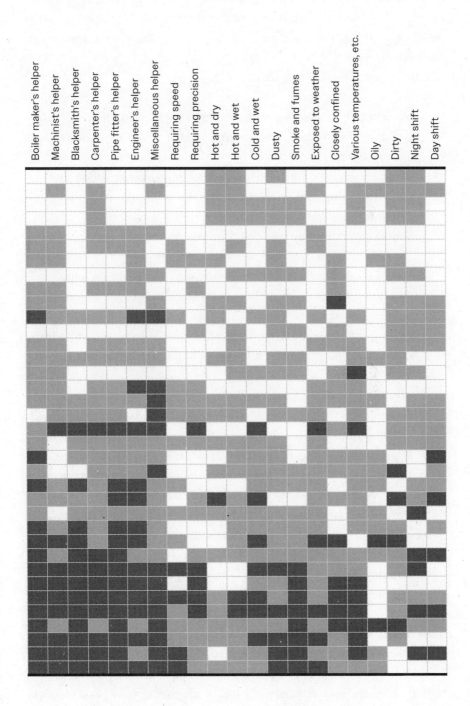

least, our research suggests we should be very cautious when using gener-alizations like "populist," or relying on stereotypes like "deplorables." More refinement is badly needed if we are to better understand the threats posed to our democracy.

How do we define *working class*?

- Is it based on whether someone says they are working class?
- Is it composed of those who are members of labor unions or would like to join one?
- Are you working class if you are a plumber on a construction site but not working class on the weekends when you run your own plumbing business?
- Should we define it by those who are less educated? If so, then where do teachers and nurses fit in?
- Should we include only those in the bottom part of the income distribution? Then in what class are low-income adjunct professors and graduate students?
- What about expanding the definition to include anyone who isn't a man-ager or supervisor, which includes about 85 percent of the labor force?

To conduct our research, we needed to decide on, and then put a circle around, some group of people and see where the data led us. Otherwise, each of us would be grabbing for anecdotes like "I know this guy who believes that . . ." or "Union leaders tell me they think that . . ." or "I've seen enough to sense that . . ." and so on. The anecdotes and our intuitions certainly give us crucial hunches to test. They send us to look in certain directions and help us interpret the data we find. But on their own, they don't provide the solid ground we need to reveal significant trends. By coming up with a consistent definition, we hoped to better describe the values and collective ideas of the white working class, and potentially counter negative stereotypes that hide more than they reveal.

The Most Commonly Used Definitions of Class Focus Entirely on Education

Democratic pollster Stanley Greenberg, for example, defines *working class* as "those without a four-year degree."[7] Nearly all pollsters and pundits agree.

Apparently, that's your automatic escape hatch from the working class, no matter what you earn, no matter where you work, no matter whether you are a boss or a worker or have power over your work, or power over others. (It's the modern-day version of the old union ditty, "The working class can kiss my ass / I got the foreman's job at last!")

Researchers like to use education as a proxy for class because it's easy to extract this information from public opinion polls. It also seems to capture what many of us feel—that there really is something different between college graduates and nongraduates.

This shorthand definition of the working class is a conceptual disaster. First of all, it makes no distinctions among college graduates. Are those who graduate from a fly-by-night for-profit college really in the same socioeconomic class as Ivy Leaguers?

Furthermore, using education as a class identifier places in the working class millions of business owners without college degrees. Of the 32.5 million small business owners in the United States today, approximately 62.2 percent[8] do not have four-year college degrees.[9] That means there are about 20.2 million small business owners who are counted in a "no degree" definition of the white working class. If the white working class is defined as white people who lack a college degree (about 87.1 million Americans), then almost a quarter (23.2 percent) are likely to be small business owners—bosses to be sure.[10] Are these business owners really in the same class as those who clean their offices? Are construction contractors without college degrees in the same class as the immigrant day-laborers they hire on street corners?

Defining "bosses and workers" as "educated and less educated" makes it next to impossible to understand how working people—not bosses—think about the world. It also makes it all too possible to write off the less educated as irrelevant cogs in our modern, high-tech economy.

In this study, education alone won't be used as a proxy for working class. Instead, our primary definition combines income and education. Education is a critical variable because it does provide one path into management and better-paying jobs. But we believe there must be a connection between income and class that transcends the degrees you have.

Therefore, members of the white working class are defined as those *who are labeled as white in public opinion and census data, who do not have four-year college degrees, and who are in the bottom two-thirds of the income distribution.*

We recognize this definition excludes some of the higher-paid skilled workers, including many teachers and nurses, who should be considered part of the working class. It also excludes low-income but highly educated workers, like graduate students and adjunct faculty. Nevertheless, we think our classification system helps pierce the fog surrounding white working-class politics and economics.[11] And it allows for a clearer focus on national working-class attitudes as well as the shift in political orientation in more rural areas within key presidential electoral states like Michigan, Pennsylvania, and Wisconsin.

Why not add "rural" to our definition of the white working class? Certainly, mass layoffs have had a disproportional impact in rural areas where alternative employment is hard to find and where the declining number of family farms means they no longer provide a fallback to laid-off workers. However, our research has found no discernable pattern on divisive social issues like race that distinguish white working-class attitudes in rural, suburban, and urban areas.

Why Are the Democrats Writing Off the White Working Class?

From Franklin Roosevelt to Lyndon Johnson to Jimmy Carter, working people have thrown their support to the Democrats for the most part because the party was perceived to champion the common man and woman. (This was less so in rural farming areas that had long-term Republican affiliations. Many family farmers viewed themselves as businesses with seasonal itinerant employees.)

The Democrats legalized unions, passed and enforced the National Labor Relations Act (1935) that made collective bargaining possible, and thanks to pressure from workers and their organizations, passed unemployment insurance, Social Security, Medicare, and the eight-hour workday, as well as an assortment of job-creation programs during hard times.

In return, working people consistently propped up the Democratic Party, showing more support for its presidential candidates than the country as a whole. Even after Richard Nixon's "Southern Strategy" drew more Southern white working-class voters into the Republican party, Jimmy Carter still got 52.3 percent of the total white working-class vote in 1976.

But from there we can see in figure 1.2 the steady white working-class shift away from the Democrats—even Democratic presidents who won their elections. This trend predates Trump's election in 2016.

Figure 1.2. Democratic presidential vote among white working-class voters

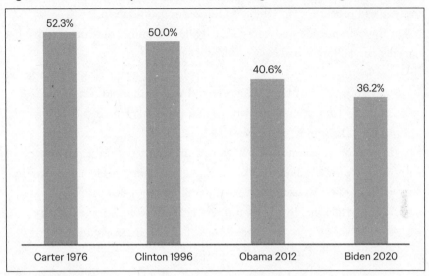

Source: ANES VCF0704[12]

The change is particularly acute in the all-important "Blue Wall" states of Pennsylvania, Wisconsin, and Michigan. Historically, Democratic presidential candidates always could count on working-class voters in these states to keep them in the race. But in 2016, Hillary Clinton lost all three states to Trump, and with it the presidency. Biden narrowly recouped these states in 2020, but clearly the Blue Wall is turning purple.

Why did these working people abandon the Democratic Party? Or did the Democrats abandon them?

James Carville, the "Ragin' Cajun" Democratic strategist, cut to the chase in 2006: "Pennsylvania is Philadelphia and Pittsburgh with Alabama in between," he said.[13] To be sure, Carville was not referring to Alabama's Black voters, who account for nearly 30 percent of its electorate. Instead, he was conjuring up an image of a rural white working class soaked in racist, sexist, homophobic, and xenophobic beliefs who are turning against liberal Democrats.

By 2016, Senator Chuck Schumer (D-NY) enthusiastically welcomed this alleged new reality. More votes, he believed, would be gained by letting the white working class go and instead reaching out to more culturally akin suburbanites: "For every blue-collar Democrat we lose in western Pennsylvania, we will pick up two moderate Republicans in the suburbs in Philadelphia, and you can repeat that in Ohio and Illinois and Wisconsin."[14]

During her presidential campaign, Hillary Clinton said out loud what Carville and Schumer had only implied:

> You know, to just be grossly generalistic, you could put half of Trump's supporters into what I call the basket of deplorables. Right? [Laughter/applause] The racist, sexist, homophobic, xenophobic, Islamophobic—you name it. And unfortunately, there are people like that. And he has lifted them up. He has given voice to their websites that used to only have 11,000 people, now have 11 million. He tweets and retweets offensive, hateful, mean-spirited rhetoric. Now some of those folks, they are irredeemable, but thankfully they are not America.[15]

Clearly, the "basket full of deplorables" will haunt her for the rest of her days. However, the next part of her statement contained a much deeper admission of Democratic Party failure.

> But that other basket of people are people who feel that government has let them down, nobody cares about them, nobody worries about what happens to their lives and their futures, and they are just desperate for change. It doesn't really even matter where it comes from. They don't buy everything he says, but he seems to hold out some hope that their lives will be different. They won't wake up and see their jobs disappear, lose a kid to heroin, feel like they're in a dead-end. Those are people we have to understand and empathize with as well.

Hillary Clinton was lamenting the failures of a federal government often run by Democrats, including the eight years her husband was president and she played a prominent public role in shaping policy. She recognized that someone like Trump offers hope—even if it's a false hope—that one day soon these workers "won't wake up and see their jobs disappear."

FDR and his immediate Democratic successors distinguished themselves from Republicans by confronting every major unemployment crisis with proposals to use government as the employer of last resort. But since the election of Bill Clinton, direct job creation has been taken off the table. No more New Deal Works Progress Administration. No more War on Poverty. No more public works programs like the one even centrist Jimmy Carter implemented in the late 1970s, which provided more than 750,000 government sector jobs for the unemployed.[16]

Ironically, in her comments about workers' loss of faith in the Democrats, Hillary Clinton was only echoing the analysis put forward by Barack Obama in 2008 when he took aim at the policies of Bill Clinton. Once again, Pennsylvania drew the attention:

> You go into these small towns in Pennsylvania and, like a lot of small towns in the Midwest, the jobs have been gone now for 25 years and nothing's replaced them. And they fell through the Clinton administration, and the Bush administration, and each successive administration has said that somehow these communities are gonna regenerate and they have not. And it's not surprising then they get bitter, they cling to guns or religion or antipathy toward people who aren't like them or anti-immigrant sentiment or anti-trade sentiment as a way to explain their frustrations.[17]

The media attention, of course, focused on the "cling to guns or religion" and ignored the economic underpinnings. But taken together we see more clearly why Schumer and so many in the Democratic Party establishment have given up on the white working class, especially in rural areas, and instead are playing to suburban voters.

Mass-Layoff Fatalism

This economic transformation did not happen by accident. The Democratic Party placed its bets on a newly globalized knowledge economy. They expected it would make America the leader in high value-added jobs that required, at the very least, a four-year degree. These jobs would mostly be found in metropolitan areas, which appealed to the young college-graduate professionals who filled them. The Clintons, Obama, and Schumer, along with many other post–New Deal Democrats, stoked this new economy through the deregulation of Wall Street and through trade deals that expanded global markets.

They knew that those without college degrees, especially in lower-skilled jobs in rural manufacturing areas, would see their work flee to low-wage areas all over the world. But these Democratic leaders saw the expansion of the economy as an overall win that would produce more economic activity and lower-priced goods, even as it caused some pain—pain they believed would be manageable.

These policies, even though humans created them, were in some ways so successful they took on the force of natural law—an unrelenting and unstoppable force that could not be altered. Despite noble rhetoric and some inadequate political efforts to mitigate the pain, working-class job dislocation was seen as nothing more than collateral damage from the tidal waves of globalization and technological innovation. Just like you can't defy gravity, you can't stop mass layoffs.

However, natural laws created neither the man-made Reagan revolution nor the "trickle-down economics" his administration espoused, which sent rural and urban Americans in opposite directions.

No leading Democrat would ever openly embrace Reaganomics, of course. But the fact is that Democratic leaders bought into a "free-market" ideology, which claimed that somehow the new prosperity that was gushing upward to elites after 1980 would also find its way downward to those who had been left behind. And that areas that had been decimated would "regenerate," as Obama said.

Rather than reflecting on the possibility that maybe, just maybe, "free-market" trade deals would harm millions of Americans, Obama instead placed "anti-trade sentiment" on the same hit list of negative working-class attributes as "antipathy toward people who aren't like them." Think about the connection. You fight to keep your job from fleeing abroad and somehow that makes you a bigot? Surely that kind of logic from the leader of the Democratic Party didn't sit well with many working people.

Obama did have the guts to admit publicly what few other Democrats would admit even to themselves—that the magic of the free market would never spread to the nation's economically depressed rural areas. "Regeneration" was supposed to come as market forces rushed in to tap relatively inexpensive labor pools and build on cheap rural land. But year after year, that just didn't happen. Obama could not have been clearer: "Somehow these communities are gonna regenerate and they have not."

By saying "somehow," Obama also hinted that free-market ideology is more like pixie dust—you sprinkle it into the policy conversation and "somehow" wish the problems away. (Actually, free-market magic *did* come to these depressed areas—in the form of opioids! See the story of Mingo County, West Virginia, in chapter 2.)

Neither Hillary Clinton nor Barack Obama owned up to the enormity of the problem. Instead, with a sleight of hand, they subtly blamed the victims, in effect saying, "Yes, it is understandable that you white workers are angry. However, you have free will and individual responsibility. No one is forcing you to channel your suffering into guns and religion and anti-immigrant hatred to explain away your economic decline and to emotionally compensate for your loss. That's on you, not us."

So, here's the Schumer-Carville-Clinton-Obama analysis in a nutshell: The modern knowledge economy has wiped out lower-skilled, decent-paying jobs in places like Pennsylvania, Michigan, and Wisconsin. As a result, the white workers left behind have lashed out against liberal ideas on a vast array of social issues—from abortion to immigration to minority rights to guns. Regretfully, most members of the white working class are a lost cause politically.

Why a lost cause?

Because these leaders firmly believe that's just not how modern capitalism works. Most of the good jobs today are in metropolitan areas and require significant personal investments in higher education, especially in science and technology. Government can help with education, but it doesn't, and shouldn't, create jobs directly. And even if leaders wanted to, the "populist" masses so hate government that such policies would never pass. As Bill Clinton said, "The era of big government is over." End of story.

Furthermore, the growing intolerance—the racism, sexism, homophobia, and xenophobia—is like a one-way switch, nearly impossible to reverse. Even if, by some miracle, the rural economies began to regenerate, those reactionary beliefs would continue to fester. These people, who once overwhelmingly voted Democratic in places like West Virginia, will not come back to a party focused on educated and multiracial voters.

It's not a pretty picture: Economic turmoil leads to white working-class racism, sexism, and xenophobia. And basically, there's nothing to be done about it because of the profound global economic forces at work and the raw facts of life about human nature. Once job destruction is accepted as an unalterable given, our options for effecting change are diminished.

In this view, the best we can do is to refrain from looking down our noses at those whose circumstances are increasingly so alien to ours. As Hillary Clinton put it, "Those are people we have to understand and empathize with."

Understanding and empathy, however, are no match for mass job destruction (and forced "empathy" can often feel like a patronizing insult). Unless working people experience substantive interventions that produce decent livelihoods, autocrats will be able to use workers' frustration and anger to fuel a formidable, resentful "populist" phalanx.

Why have so many political leaders become so fatalistic about mass layoffs? Why have they failed to acknowledge that the deregulation of Wall Street, started by Reagan, then accelerated ever since by corporate-oriented Democrats and Republicans, is a death sentence for working people, especially in rural America? Why aren't more Democrats fighting harder on behalf of these working people?

Virtually every Democrat would claim that they are indeed fighting for working people of every shade and creed. There are infrastructure bills, bills to reduce prescription costs, bills to provide day care and child support, and more. But, like Schumer, they also know that their efforts are not selling in rural white America.

Why that's the case is the subject of this book.

Next stop, the very white state of West Virginia.

CHAPTER 2

Mingo Capitalism

How Wall Street Destroyed Jobs in West Virginia, Pennsylvania, Michigan, and Wisconsin, and How That Cratered Support for the Democrats

"[The college] is taking valuable resources from a community and exporting it as a product in the form of high-priced degrees at the cost of local people. There wouldn't be much difference between a coal-mining extraction company town and Oberlin College."　　—Geoff, age 35, three years of service

MINGO COUNTY, WEST VIRGINIA, POPULATION 22,573,[1] EARNED ITS place at the heart of labor union history. The great Coal Wars started in the small Mingo County town of Matewan in 1912, when mine workers went on strike and the Baldwin–Felts Detective Agency—working for the mine owners—beat up or shot at just about any miner who dared join the United Mine Workers of America. After six months of pitched battles, the state militia occupied the Mingo area and broke the strike.

On May 19, 1920, the company again used Baldwin–Felts to evict union-friendly miners from Stone Mountain Coal Company housing. All hell broke loose, leading to several dead detective agency guards and two dead townspeople. The sheriff, Sid Hatfield, and the mayor, Cabell Testerman, sided with the miners, and some claim they initiated an attack on the Baldwin–Felts enforcers that day. Hatfield was later acquitted of charges in the case. Then Felts sued him, and the Baldwin–Felts guards killed the sheriff and his deputy in revenge on the courthouse steps in August 1921. Things went further downhill from there:

In response to the assassination, an army of miners 10,000 strong began a full-on assault against the coal company and the mine guards.

While miners shot at their opponents, private planes organized by the coal companies' defensive militia dropped bleach and shrapnel bombs on the union's headquarters. The battle only stopped when federal troops arrived on the order of President Warren Harding.[2]

Hundreds of miners were indicted for murder and treason, and the union suffered a stark decline in membership. For the next dozen years, the area was basically an occupied zone. The federal siege was finally lifted in 1933 by the Roosevelt administration, when for the first time the government acted on behalf of these working people. The United Mine Workers union blossomed and its members, their families, and their communities attained a modicum of economic and social stability. It seemed that they would forever be grateful to the New-Deal Democrats who came to their rescue.

Mingo County didn't forget, at least not for a long time. As late as 1996, with more than 3,200 coal miners still at work,[3] Mingo County gave Bill Clinton a whopping 69.7 percent of its vote. But every four years thereafter, support for the Democrats declined, going down and down, and down some more, as figure 2.1 shows. By 2020, Joe Biden received only 13.9 percent of the vote in Mingo, a brutal downturn in a county that once saw the Democratic Party as its savior.

Figure 2.1. Mingo County Democratic presidential vote

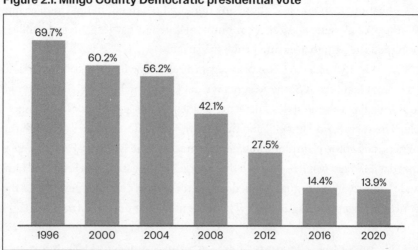

Source: US Election Atlas[4]

This precipitous decline for the Democrats paralleled the decline of coal jobs in Eastern coal-mining areas. Several major developments caused the collapse of coal-mining jobs. The shift to "mountaintop removal" (blasting mountaintops with vast machinery to get to coal seams) required fewer workers than extracting coal through deep shafts did. Competition grew from Western coal, which ate into profits. Demand shifted from coal to cheaper (and somewhat more environmentally friendly) natural gas as fracking expanded. As jobs were slashed, Democrats took much of the blame because of their support for environmental controls on fossil fuels—something Republicans and many locals called the "War on Coal."

Mingo County, in fact, has the distinction of losing more coal jobs than any other county in West Virginia. Between 1995 and 2020, coal employment fell from 3,257 to only 322,[5] erasing memories of how the Democrats helped the coal miners back during the Depression. Little wonder that the Democratic presidential vote cratered during that same period.

The same story is told all over coal country. In 1996, Bill Clinton received 51.5 percent of West Virginia's vote. In 2020, the state vote for Biden collapsed to 29.7 percent. The seven West Virginia counties with the most coal jobs lost 59.2 percent of jobs between 1996 and 2012. During that time, the Democratic vote total fell by an astounding 41.4 percent.

President Obama admitted in 2008 that neither the Democrats nor the Republicans had much to offer the rural areas that had suffered such declines. In 2016, Hillary Clinton put the nail in the coffin for Democrats in coal country when she said, "We're going to put a lot of coal miners and coal companies out of business."[6]

That "deplorable"-like gaffe was in the middle of a talk in which she also said, "I'm the only candidate who has a policy about how to bring economic opportunity using clean energy as the key into coal country." In fact, she proposed a massive $30 billion plan with investments in education, job retraining, new business development, housing, broadband, health, wellness, and the arts to help coal communities survive and potentially thrive again.

But no one in coal country believed her. For good reason: 16 years of Democratic administrations under Bill Clinton and Barack Obama had done nothing to rebuild these areas. Instead, the party increasingly focused its energy on urban and suburban areas, where engagement with the financial industry of banks and investment funds stoked both political contributions and increasing vote totals. Mingo County and all coal country were left starkly behind.

Sadly, these political leaders seemed unable to appreciate the deep connections between these voters and their environment. Hunting, fishing, and just moving among the forests, streams, and lakes are fundamental to the lives of rural Americans. Conservation and environmental protection should have created organic bonds between the Democratic Party and Appalachians. Instead, the opposite occurred.

Invasion of the Opioids

When federal public investment never materialized for the miners, the business sector filled the breach. The magic of the free market brought to Mingo County a highly profitable and growing industry: *opioids*!

By 2019, Mingo County's tiny Tug Valley Pharmacy, along with the Hurley Drug Company store a few blocks away and the Family Pharmacy across the river, were filling prescriptions for millions of opioid pills a year in a town of 3,000 people. Up the road in the town of Kermit, population 280, the Sav-Rite Pharmacy was doing 30 million pills a year.

To be sure, big businesses like Purdue Pharma, Johnson & Johnson, and other firms were doing all they could to push these addictive painkillers into the mouths of down-and-out populations. It was the local businesses, however, that provided the distribution, aided and abetted by doctors who churned out prescriptions by the millions. People drove hundreds of miles to line up at pharmacy drive-through windows. The seamy side of modern capitalism was at work in Mingo County. A 2019 exposé in *The Guardian* reported on the operations of Williamson Wellness Center there:

> Each day, hundreds of people lined up outside an old animal feed store where a group of doctors were set up by a former pimp, just out of federal prison for running a gay prostitution ring in Washington, DC, to churn out opioid prescriptions faster than West Virginia's major hospitals.[7]

Next came an Economics 101 textbook example of how free markets encourage competition and reward the industrious. James Wooley, the owner of a low-volume drugstore in Kermit, showed the kind of entrepreneurial passion that drives our economy. *The Guardian* continued:

> Wooley decided to follow the Williamson model by setting up a doctor to churn out opioid prescriptions for him to fill. . . . [T]hey recruited a doctor more than an hour away at Marshall University's medical school, Dr. John Tiano. All he had to do was lend his name to the prescriptions and one of the nurses at the clinic would fill it out.
>
> Within a few months, Wooley was filling an opioid prescription a minute. . . . The pharmacy . . . ranked 22nd in the nation among retail pharmacies for hydrocodone purchases.[8]

Not surprisingly, abandoning West Virginia to the pharmaceutical drug pushers gave the state the hideous distinction of leading the nation in overdose death rates—81.4 per 100,000 in 2020. The next highest state, Kentucky (at 58.1), has also hemorrhaged coal jobs. The 2020 national average was 29.6 overdose deaths per 100,000.[9] Coal mining always was a dangerous industry, but not as dangerous as the opioid epidemic unleashed by unmitigated laissez-faire economics.[10]

Drug Capitalism

The pattern of drugging up a population suffering from severe job loss had already become the economic development model for urban Black and Hispanic communities. As early as the 1960s, civil rights leaders Martin Luther King Jr., A. Philip Randolph, and Bayard Rustin recognized that decent-paying manufacturing jobs were leaving major metropolitan areas, making it increasingly difficult for inner-city residents to climb out of poverty. At the same time, poverty was rediscovered in rural America through Michael Harrington's explosive 1962 exposé, *The Other America*. To deal with both white and Black/Hispanic poverty, Rustin put forth "A Freedom Budget for All Americans" (1967), which called for *"full employment* for all who are willing and able to work, including those who need education or training to make them willing and able."[11] Unfortunately, the effort failed to gain traction as the Vietnam War engulfed the political moment.

As in Mingo County, the inner-city economic vacuum was filled by entrepreneurial drug activity. Heroin hit these communities hard in the 1960s and '70s, followed by crack cocaine in the '80s. But there were critically important differences. Unlike the barely legal rural oxycodone distribution networks sponsored by Big Pharma, heroin and crack cocaine were severely criminalized in the War on Drugs, initiated by Nixon in 1971 and carried forward by every president since. Instead of gaining access to decent jobs, millions of Black and Hispanic city dwellers gained access to jail in disproportional numbers.[12]

Differences between urban and rural drug capitalism also appeared in the political rhetoric used to blame the victim. The Black and Hispanic urban communities supposedly were filled with "crack babies" and "predators."[13] For the people in rural areas, accounts like J. D. Vance's *Hillbilly Elegy* offered a somewhat more compassionate view of the demoralized rural white working class. Nonetheless, in both rural and urban areas, explaining the negative behaviors of those left behind focused on their individual failings as well as the cultural instability of their communities. It's far easier to blame those harmed by job destruction than to guarantee decent-paying jobs for all, as called for in the "Freedom Budget."

The Wall Street Vultures

As if the coal miners didn't have enough problems, Wall Street added to their grief. What they don't teach in Econ 101 is how financialized capitalism zooms into distressed areas to squeeze out any remaining wealth. The collapse of coal mining isn't just about new climate regulations and plummeting demand for fossil fuels. It's also about how very wealthy Wall Street banks and hedge funds have profited from the situation. The people of West Virginia were financially strip-mined.

As we see again and again, working people suffer when Wall Street sinks its claws into markets with distressed properties. In 2010 or so, financial speculators believed that China would become a major market for the coal used to feed its ever-expanding steel industry. "Bankers helped coal companies to borrow billions of dollars for expansion, and to shed unprofitable mines and obligations, and earned a percentage on every deal," according to another exposé by *The Guardian*.[14]

Loading companies up with piles of debt is the first step. The next step is to cut costs, which usually means screwing the workers, especially vulnerable retirees. The trick is to set up another corporation and then stick it with the liabilities, which is what the world's largest coal company, Peabody Energy, did:

> The new company, named Patriot Coal, was born at a disadvantage: it contained 40 percent of Peabody's healthcare liabilities, and only 13 percent of its productive coal reserves. In a call with investors, Peabody's CFO, Rick Navarre, said: "Our legacy liabilities, expenses and cashflows will be nearly cut in half."[15]

The new and weakened Patriot Coal, along with much of the region's energy sector, had been pushed to the brink by Wall Street's financial engineering. The risk grew catastrophic when the Chinese market failed to appear. By 2016, crushed by billions in debt, six major coal companies declared bankruptcy, destroying 33,500 jobs and removing billions in tax revenue from schools, hospitals, and other public services.

Then, after all that carnage, and just when you'd think that Wall Street would have had enough, they come in again to feast on the carcass. Some hedge funds, called *vultures*, make a killing by buying up failing corporations. The game takes place in bankruptcy court, where hedge funds are allowed to shed the worker liabilities and walk off with profitable assets. Their apologists say they are just saving what can be saved. But in reality, it's all about siphoning off whatever wealth remains from the vulnerable to fill the pocketbooks of the connected few.

Patriot Coal attracted Mark Brodsky, "a prominent vulture investor nicknamed 'The Terminator,' whose critics called him a 'bully,' an 'extortionist,' and a 'suppository.'" Brodsky maintained that firms like his "do a lot of constructive things." Somehow, The Terminator convinced the bankruptcy court to "abandon the union contract that provided [health benefits] to 23,000 retired miners and dependents."[16]

Miners, already accustomed to seeing their benefits terminated when companies collapsed, were scheduled to lose $1.3 billion worth of health care so that The Terminator could keep his financially extractive company alive. Fortunately, the United Mine Workers union was able to prevent some of this theft through its negotiations with the company. But in 2015, Patriot Coal went belly up anyway, causing 12,500 retirees to see their health care coverage vanish.

It's not known how much Brodsky raked in on his investment. We do know, however, that his victory paved the way for more vultures to feast on the decaying coal carcass. And all the theft was legal, a product of a deregulated finance system that has polluted our economy since 1980 or so. *The Guardian* put it this way:

> [T]o the men and women affected, Patriot and the cases that followed its pattern were the perfect illustration of a growing crisis: the laws and values of modern capitalism had been honed by lobbyists and political donors to advantage those with the most power already—to ensure that the winners kept winning. The looting of Patriot Coal was not illegal; the scandal, as the saying went, was that it was legal.[17]

Legalized Looting Through Stock Buybacks

There are two prominent features of financial strip-mining. The first is borrowing money to buy up companies and sticking that debt on the company. The second is stock buybacks, which allow CEOs and large share-sellers to move money out of the companies and into their own pockets. West Virginia miners, and working people everywhere, have been the victims of these modern financial maneuvers that now form the heart and soul of modern capitalism.

In a stock buyback, a company uses its cash, or borrows more money, to buy back its own shares. It then usually retires the shares.* Because most of those shares no longer exist and there are fewer shareowners in the company, all the other shares of that company still in the stock market become more valuable, benefiting existing shareholders—especially those with big stakes who time their sales. Buying shares in the marketplace requires getting others to sell them, and this, too, usually drives up the share price.

The big winners of stock repurchases are company executives, Wall Street bankers, and hedge fund activists who time their buying and selling of shares

---

* The company does not always retire the shares. It may keep them in the corporate treasury for future use as, for example, stock-based compensation, but while in the treasury the shares have no votes and pay no dividends.

to take full advantage of the process. It should not come as a shock that these players have access to insider information not available to the rest of us.*

From the New Deal in the 1930s until 1982, corporations seldom engaged in stock buybacks. Why? Because it could be viewed by the Securities and Exchange Commission (SEC) as *stock manipulation*, which was widely believed to have led to the 1929 stock market crash. (The SEC under Sections 9 and 10 of the Securities Exchange Act of 1934 has the power to curb market manipulation.[18]) But when the Reagan administration promoted deregulation as the cure-all for every economic ill imaginable, the SEC created a new rule, 10b-18, which facilitated the expansion of stock buybacks. The new regulation helped to achieve the Reagan administration's deregulatory mission of unleashing corporate initiative . . . and greed. In effect, the new rule allows corporations to use as much money as they want on stock buybacks. William Lazonick, professor emeritus of economics at University of Massachusetts, has called 10b-18 a "license to loot."[19]

Contemporary corporate executives, hedge funds, and other major shareholders in US industry now make their money through stock purchases, stock investments, stock grants, and stock options. Before all this, corporate executives received 90 percent of their income from salaries and bonuses. Today more than 85 percent of their income comes from stocks granted to them by the corporation.[20] This allows corporate raiders and hedge fund vultures, along with top corporate executives, to make a killing via stock buybacks, or in plain language, legalized stock manipulation.

Because of this, corporate executives and their big shareholders have irresistible incentives to squeeze all the cash and capital they can from a company to buy back its shares and thus raise the price. Making and selling products is hard. Stock buybacks are a much easier path to riches. In 2018, nearly 68 cents of every dollar of corporate profit went to stock buybacks. (See chapter 7.)

Even the Department of Defense (DOD) understands that the business model of defense contracts focuses on stock repurchases. A DOD study on

---

* Stock repurchases always increase the stock price because of the increase in the demand for the shares. If, however, the company subsequently has difficulty sustaining its earnings because of buybacks, the stock-price increase will falter. Hence, the importance of timing the buying and selling by the major players as the key to realizing gains from open-market repurchases.

defense contractor finances asks a simple question: "When industry has generated additional profits and cash, what has it chosen to do with it?" The answer should make us nervous about the trillions we are spending on national defense:

> The data in this study points to one answer: Industry did not choose to spend it on IR&D [industry research and development] and CapEx [capital expenditures]. It chose instead to significantly increase the percentage of cash paid to shareholders in the form of cash dividends and share repurchases, thereby reducing the amount of invested capital for the corporation.[21]

How big an increase? The defense contractors increased their stock repurchases and dividends to shareholders by 73 percent in the last decade compared to the decade before that.

Where to get all that money? For defense contractors it's a no-brainer—take it from our tax dollars. For the business sector, it is often extracted from the troubled companies through cost-cutting—including mass layoffs, wage and benefit cuts, shifting production to low-wage areas, and cutting spending on things like health, safety, environmental safeguards, and research and development.

Even as the coal companies they bought were cratering, the corporate vultures shamelessly engaged in one stock buyback after another. Peabody, the coal company that created Patriot Coal to get rid of its retiree obligations, had a $1.5 billion stock buyback program.[22] Arch Coal, the second largest US coal supplier, did $500 million worth of buybacks to enrich its executives and Wall Street share sellers.[23] They were sucking their companies dry of cash while decimating the jobs and benefits of their workers.

Financial Strip-Mining and the Blue Wall

The Appalachian coal seams that run through West Virginia also head north into Pennsylvania. So, too, do mass layoffs and financial strip-mining. In fact, the killing of jobs and the fattening of Wall Street coffers extend through the rest of the so-called Democratic Blue Wall of Michigan and Wisconsin as well.

More than 1.36 million Pennsylvania workers (out of a total labor force of 6.65 million) suffered mass layoffs between 1996 and 2012, according to the

Bureau of Labor Statistics's mass layoff database.[24] In Michigan, 1.11 million out of 4.94 million workers. And in Wisconsin, 689,000 out of 3.08 million. (These layoff figures count the number of layoffs, not the number of workers laid off. Some workers were laid off multiple times.)

The mass layoff rates (total mass layoffs divided by the workforce) were:

Pennsylvania   20.5 percent of workforce experienced mass layoffs
Michigan   22.5 percent of workforce experienced mass layoffs
Wisconsin   22.4 percent of workforce experienced mass layoffs

Job destruction was common to nearly every industry that dotted the countryside throughout these states. Mass layoffs were particularly severe in the vast network of auto and steel facilities and their suppliers, which formed the backbone of the region's manufacturing sector.

Nationally, the only states with higher rates were Illinois and California, which have much larger and more diverse economies to cushion the blow. (These states also have very large construction sectors, which have periodic mass layoffs when major facilities are completed.)

Research shows that mass layoffs often are driven by stock buybacks and debt-driven mergers and acquisitions. Mass layoffs are inevitable when top corporate officers, hedge funds, and other larger shareholders milk these companies instead of reinvesting in them. Mass layoffs enable corporations to accumulate more cash to spend on stock buybacks that enrich top officers and wealthy Wall Street shareholders. As William Lazonick writes:

> Since the mid-1980s, stock buybacks have become the prime mode for the legalized looting of the business corporation. I call this looting process "predatory value extraction" and contend that it is the fundamental cause of the increasing concentration of income among the richest household units and the erosion of middle-class employment opportunities for most other Americans.[25]

From 2010 to 2019, an astronomical $6.3 trillion went to stock buybacks, largely benefiting the rich.[26] That $6.3 trillion could have been used to upgrade facilities, fund research and development, create new products, raise wages and benefits, upgrade workers' skills, and invest in health, safety, and environmental controls. Instead, the stock buybacks led to cost-cutting and job destruction.

We are told that companies must lay off workers to remain competitive. If they don't cut costs now, even more workers will lose their jobs in the future. We also are told that a company has to move its plants abroad to cut labor costs, or else the corporation will succumb to the competition. But these are rationalizations used to hide the fact that most companies cut costs to pay for all the debt they've accumulated and to fund stock buybacks. As that money is siphoned away from the company, it grows weaker and more likely to fail, leading to more job destruction.

Wall Street hedge funds and other investment firms pressure companies to conduct stock buybacks again and again and again. It is no exaggeration to say that mass job carnage is the direct result of Wall Street's efforts to enrich itself and its wealthy allies.

In 2022, the Blue Wall states lost 15,676 jobs through mass layoffs. Table 2.1 shows a selection of companies that laid off workers in 2022 and also engaged in stock buybacks.

Democratic Carnage

Since the Reagan years, the stock buyback phenomenon has devastated manufacturing jobs in Blue Wall states. In 1990, Pennsylvania, Michigan, and Wisconsin had more than 2.3 million manufacturing jobs. By 2021, 31 percent of these decent-paying jobs (712,600) had evaporated.[27]

The presidential vote tally in 1996 shows why the Democrats call it "the Blue Wall." Bill Clinton won Pennsylvania by 9 percentage points, Michigan by 13.2 percent, and Wisconsin by 10.4 percent. By 2020, we can see the big cracks in the Wall: In 2020, Biden won by only a 1.2 percent margin in his home state of Pennsylvania and by 2.8 percent in Michigan, and he squeaked by with a 0.6 percent margin in Wisconsin.

Our research finds a strong correlation between the decline of the Democratic Party vote and mass layoffs, especially among white working-class people. The mass layoff information we used comes from a comprehensive Bureau of Labor Statistics (BLS) database that covers the years between 1996 and 2012. (Unfortunately, the Obama administration discontinued the program that year due to sequestration budget cuts.)

Table 2.1. Mass Layoffs in Blue Wall States, 2022

Company	Jobs eliminated	Stock buybacks
PENNSYLVANIA		
Argo AI	679	$97 million (2016)
Armstrong Flooring	606	$50 million (2019)
Zulily	504	$250 million (2015)
GEO Group	390	$40.2 million (2018)
FedEx	213	$1.46 billion (2022)
Radian Group	166	$300 million (2023)
Wal-Mart	129	$20 billion (2022)
Peloton Interactive	102	$130 million (2018)
WISCONSIN		
Phillips-Medisize	269	$200 million (2008)
Foot Locker	210	$1.2 billion (2022)
Pentair	210	$50.1 million (2022)
Gannett	181	$100 million (2022)
Briggs & Stratton	162	$50 million (2018)
Collins Aerospace (Raytheon Technologies)	90	$5 billion (2022)
DHL Supply Chain	72	$800 million (2022)
MICHIGAN		
Warren Truck Assembly (Stellantis)	1,215	$1.5 billion (2023)
Penske Logistics	572	$250 million (2022)
Faurecia	268	$1.6 billion (2023)
Booking.com	226	$3.1 billion (2023)
DHL Supply Chain	202	$800 million (2022)

Source: State WARN notices[28]

The yearly BLS data allow us to estimate the approximate percentage of the workforce in each county that experienced a mass layoff from 1996 to 2012. Given that the mass layoffs data stop there, our numbers are conservative estimates. After all, mass layoffs did not come to a halt in 2012.

Unfortunately, BLS layoff data are organized by county rather than by individuals or precinct. So, for analytical purposes we must identify white working-class counties instead of individuals. (To be sure, no county is composed entirely of one particular class. But it is possible to differentiate counties that are likely to include more white working-class people.)

We define *white working-class counties* as those that were:

1. 90 percent or more white
2. Ranked in the bottom two-thirds of all the counties in the entire nation in terms of income (adjusted for differences in each state's income distribution)
3. Ranked among the two-thirds of all US counties that have the fewest residents with four-year college degrees

We define *managerial/professional counties* as those that ranked in the top one-third of all US counties in terms of income. (Included are all races, ethnicities, and educational levels within these higher-income counties, since that's where the managers are likely to live.)

Using these criteria there were 112 white working-class counties and 38 management counties in the Blue Wall states (out of a total 222 counties). Although there were many more working-class counties, the management counties were more populous—5.4 million total residents in the white working-class counties and 10.1 million in the management counties.

For example, in Pennsylvania the management counties were the wealthier suburban areas surrounding Philadelphia, Pittsburg, and Harrisburg (the state capital).

Not only is there an obvious urban–rural divide between white working-class and managerial counties, but the mass layoff rates and the change in the Democratic vote were shockingly different.

- On average, *one out of three* (33.3 percent) workers in white working-class Blue Wall counties suffered through mass layoffs between 1996 and 2012.
- The mass layoff rate in the management Blue Wall counties was only 14.6 percent—more than 50 percent lower than the white working-class counties.
- During that period, the average Democratic vote in the white working-class counties *declined* by 12.3 percent, while the Democratic vote in the managerial/professional counties *increased* by 8.1 percent.

We also can split the total 222 Blue Wall counties into four groups based on the race, income, and educational characteristics of the county. At one end of the spectrum are the white working-class counties in the bottom two-thirds in terms of income and education. At the other end are managerial/professional counties with a greater percentage of their populations with higher incomes. The groups in between have either one or two, but not all three of the working-class attributes.

Figure 2.2 shows a remarkable trend. As we go from managerial to white working class (WWC), the mass layoff rate increases step by step. And, as we

Figure 2.2. Blue Wall mass layoffs
Percent of workers laid off (1996–2020)

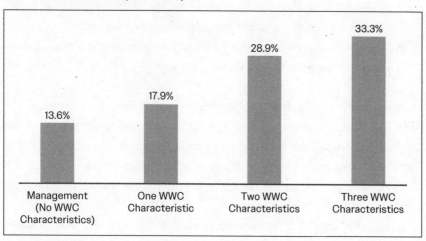

Blue Wall Democratic voters
Change in Democratic presidential vote (1996–2020)

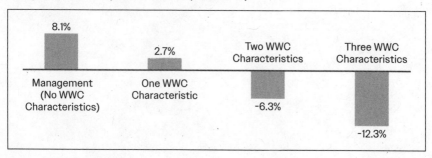

Source: The Labor Institute

go from counties that have none of the three white working-class character-istics to those that have all three, the Democratic vote goes down.

This relationship is confirmed by a county time-series panel regression for the three Blue Wall states using a fixed-effect variable. It shows that for every 1 percent increase in mass layoffs per capita, the Democratic vote in the Blue Wall states declines by 0.16 percent. The result is statistically significant to .0001.[29]

Schumer, Carville, Obama, Clinton, and now Biden certainly know where the Democratic votes are and aren't. The Democrats are losing the white working class, especially in rural areas, and gaining votes in metropolitan areas.

They may even accept what we have found in our study:

- White working-class rural counties have the highest mass layoff rates and the highest departures from the Democratic Party.
- Wealthier metropolitan areas have the lowest mass layoff rates and the greatest vote gains for the Democratic Party.

A word of caution: It is still possible to argue that these working-class folks increasingly compensate by "clinging to their guns or religion"—that they are becoming less liberal on key social issues, while the Democratic Party must take more liberal positions to attract metropolitan voters. If this is so, some might argue that Democrats winning significantly more white working-class votes is a lost cause.

But is that true? Or a rationalization? It's time to test this common assumption: Are white working-class voters becoming less liberal on key social issues?

CHAPTER 3

White Working Class Woke?

Increasing Liberalism on Divisive Social Issues

"The depression, the not knowing what was gonna happen or how you were gonna make it through, the anxiety. I started having horrible panic attacks. Even if I was just laying in bed at night, out of nowhere I would have the worst panic attacks of my life, like an elephant sitting on my chest. I can't breathe, you know, feeling like you're gonna throw up on yourself. Cried. Cried a lot . . . The depression sets in, where some days you just don't want to get out of bed. You don't wanna open the curtains, you don't wanna look outside, you don't want to help your children with their homework, you're just that emotionally drained. It was hard. It was very hard."   —Marsha Rae Douglas,

laid off at age 38, after 5 years of service

IT'S NOT A SECRET: THOSE WHO ARE WHITE AND WORKING CLASS have been leaving the Democratic Party for quite some time. They've got company, too. There are signs that Black and Hispanic voters are departing as well.[1] (See figure 3.1 on page 42 and figure 3.2 on page 43.)

Why? Are they sick and tired of woke Democrats? Are they increasingly resentful of minorities, angry at immigrants, turned off by people who identify as LGBTQ+?

Our research team has gathered compelling evidence on these questions by examining voter survey data. That data allow us to look at individuals, not just counties, matching their individual opinions, party registration, and voting with their demographics.

We define the white working class as those who call themselves white, are in the bottom two-thirds of the income distribution, and who do not have a four-year college degree. (And to double-check our work we tested this definition against an occupational definition of class as well. The comparative results

Figure 3.1. White working-class presidential vote percentages

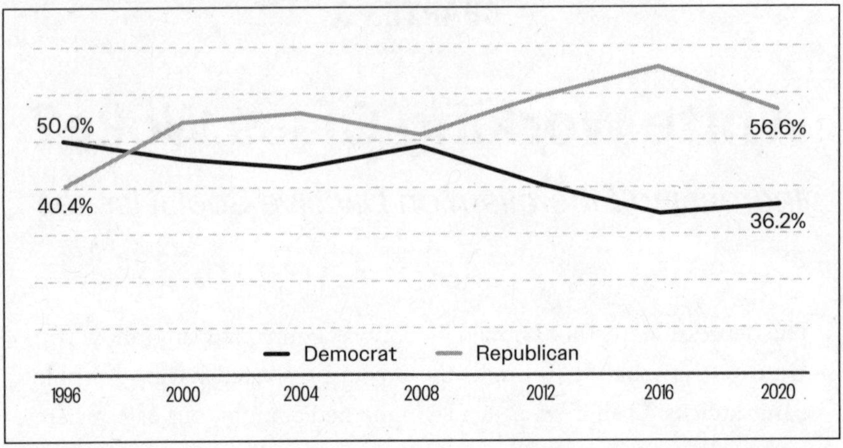

Source: ANES[2]

covering 12 social-issue questions were nearly identical.)* According to our definition, there are about 52.8 million workers in the white working class.†

We define the white managerial class simply as those in the top one-third of the income distribution who say they are white, regardless of educational attainment. (As I said in chapter 1, we believe that a person's class has mostly to do with their relation to the hiring, firing, and managing of working-class people, not necessarily with their educational attainment. Millions of well-paid managers and small business owners do not have four-year college degrees.)

When the Democratic white working-class vote started to crater after 1996, did that signal that the white working class was becoming less liberal—that their economic resentment was morphing into broader social resentment expressed at the polls?

Professor Justin Gest calls this theory the "moral narrative": "It juxta-poses the ostensible complacency, ignorance, and backwardness of white

* We used the occupational model created by Daniel Oesch as recoded by the Center for Working Class Politics.

† According to our definition, the Cooperative Election Study shows that 32.6 percent of all workers are in the white working class. The total US civilian labor force is about 162.8 million.

Figure 3.2. White working-class party registration percentages

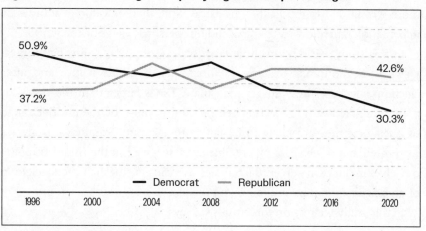

Source: ANES VCF0303[3]

working-class people with the industry, naiveté, and resourcefulness of immigrants, and minority groups, and the ingenuity and adaptation of metropolitan elites."[4]

But does the moral narrative's negative depiction of the white working class reflect reality? If it were true, we would expect to see two facts emerge from survey data: (1) there should be an increase in white working-class illiberalism over time; and (2) there should be stark differences between the opinions of the white working class and the white managerial class.

White working-class illiberalism should jump out at us from surveys. *But it doesn't.*

Before presenting our findings, we need to address what constitutes reliable evidence. All of us bring our own experiences to play when considering controversial sociological and political questions. We've talked to a diverse group of people. We've heard reports from others about white working-class attitudes. We've read and seen accounts in the media. We know a racist when we see one. But how sure are we that our personal experiences can be generalized across a country as large and varied as ours? And how can we settle a debate between opposing hunches, if we only can rely on our own experiences?

Well, there are pre-election polls. But the general public as well as many researchers have learned the hard way not to trust the polls that sprout like weeds before elections. Those polls seem to be less and less reliable, often more wrong than right, leading us astray. Still, there is value in sources of information that allow us to transcend our personal views of the world.

In this study, we rely on three large-scale voter surveys involving interviews with thousands or tens of thousands of adults before and after elections. Because these surveys are many times larger than the quick-hit polls conducted during election season, and because of their wider range of questions, they are likely to be far more accurate. Skepticism is always warranted, but if we write off credible evidence, we run the risk of trapping ourselves in our own perceptual bubbles. We can get stuck in a feedback loop of ad hoc observations and our own predilections.

In this study we rely on three mass surveys:

General Social Survey (GSS)	36,455 respondents (1996–2021)
American National Election Studies (ANES)	28,311 respondents (1996–2020)
Cooperative Election Study (CES)	524,713 respondents (2006–2021)

The General Social Survey (GSS) was started in 1972 by the National Opinion Research Center at the University of Chicago. It is funded by the National Science Foundation. Since 1994, survey questions have been asked every other year. Before that, it was conducted almost every year. The survey involves thousands of respondents (in recent years, about 2,500 per year). GSS data are intended to help social scientists and journalists investigate the relationship between demographic and economic factors and social and political beliefs, and to track trends related to these relationships. They also provide policymakers and students a valuable pool of information for research and rulemaking, and help them compare the US social scene with those in other countries.

The American National Election Studies (ANES) has interviewed thousands of US voters (in recent years about 5,000 per year) before and after every presidential election since 1977. ANES is based at the University of Michigan and has been run in partnership with Stanford University since 2005. The data generated from the surveys are intended to aid researchers, scholars, students, and journalists in evaluating how election results reflect broader ongoing social issues and vice versa.

The Cooperative Election Study (CES; originally titled the Cooperative Congressional Election Study) is a huge survey involving more than 50,000 respondents in presidential election seasons and about 15,000 in off years. The survey collects demographic, geographical, and electoral data along with survey responses pertaining to current political, economic, and social issues. It is run by the Institute of Quantitative Social Science at Harvard University, in conjunction with Tufts University.

White Working Class: Trending More Liberal or Reactionary?

From these extensive surveys, we've identified 23 social-issue questions that provide insight into the respondents' views on race, gender roles, sexual orientation, immigration, religious beliefs, and gun control.

- On 14 of the 23 social-issue questions, the white working class is trending more liberal over time.
- Only on three questions is the white working-class trend significantly less liberal over time: two questions on gun control (#22 and #23) and a question on increasing border patrols (#21). However, a majority of the white working class still support gun control.
- There are six questions with no statistically significant shifts over time.

A brief word about the meaning of *statistically significant*. Every poll attempts to understand what is actually going on in the population. In this analysis, we are trying to assess whether surveys about white working-class attitudes on divisive issues accurately reflect what's really happening in the country and whether those attitudes are much different from other groups. But of course, even the percentages captured by a rigorous survey never perfectly reflect reality. Rather, each number is an estimate that comes with a range called a "confidence interval"—the pluses and minuses we see in news reports.

The statistics found in this chapter and the next are evaluated using a 95 percent confidence interval and a 99 percent confidence interval. That means that according to the surveys, there's a 95 percent chance (at least) that responses to these questions actually reflect the distribution of viewpoints among the entire population. In the charts below, one asterisk (*) after a percentage signifies 95 percent confidence, and two asterisks (**) signifies 99 percent confidence.[5] Numbers with those asterisks are statistically significant—the real deal.

Table 3.1 reports on the white working-class responses to each of the 23 questions.

Column A is the starting year for the white working-class response.

Column B shows the latest year that we have comparable data for.

Column C shows the percentage change in a more liberal direction.

Table 3.1. White Working-Class Views on Social Issues

	A 1996	B Latest	C Liberal change
WOMEN'S RIGHTS			
1. Agree that "it should be possible for a pregnant woman to obtain a legal abortion if the woman wants it for any reason." (GSS abany, 1996–2021)	41.0%	54.9%	13.9*
2. Agree that "by law, a woman should always be able to obtain an abortion." (ANES VCF0838, 1996–2020)	33.5%	37.5%	4.0
3. Disagree strongly that "it is much better for everyone involved if the man is the achiever outside the home and the woman takes care of the home and family." (GSS fefam, 2021)	67.8%	78.8%	11.0
4. Agree strongly that "this country would have many fewer problems if there were more emphasis on traditional family ties." (ANES VCF0853, 2020)	51.7%	39.2%	12.5**
5. Strongly oppose "preferential hiring and promotion of women." (GSS fejobaff, 2021)	55.4%	39.5%	15.9*
RACIAL RESENTMENT			
6. Agree strongly that "Irish, Italians, Jewish and many other minorities overcame prejudice and worked their way up. Blacks should do the same without special favors." (GSS wrkwayup, 2021)	54.6%	28.6%	26.0**
7. Agree strongly that "Irish, Italians, Jewish and many other minorities overcame prejudice and worked their way up. Blacks should do the same without any special favors." (CES, 2010–2018)	53.4%	42.3%	11.1**

	A 1996	B Latest	C Liberal change
8. **Strongly oppose** "preferential hiring and promotion of Blacks." (GSS affrmact, 2021)	65.8%	54.1%	**11.7***
9. **Agree** that "the government should not be giving special treatment to [Blacks/African Americans]."† (GSS helpblk, 2021)	35.0%	32.5%	**2.5**
10. **Agree** that "most [Blacks/African Americans]† just don't have the motivation or willpower to pull themselves up out of poverty." (GSS racdif4, 2021)	56.8%	32.8%	**24.0****
11. **Agree strongly** that "if Blacks would only try harder they could be just as well off as whites." (ANES VCF9041, 2000–2016)	29.8%	23.7%	**6.1**
HOMOPHOBIA			
12. **Agree** that "sexual relations between two adults of the same sex" is "always wrong." (GSS homosex, 2021)	59.8%	29.3%	**30.5****
13. **Agree** that "gay or lesbian couples ... should be legally permitted to adopt children." (ANES VCF0878, 2000–2020)	38.2%	76.0%	**37.8****
14. **Agree** that "homosexuals should be allowed to serve in the United States Armed Forces." (ANES VCF0877, 2012)	64.9%	81.8%	**16.9****
15. **Favor** "laws to protect [homosexuals / gays and lesbians]† against job discrimination." (ANES VCF08076, 1996–2020)	60.5%	83.4%	**22.9****
RELIGION			
16. **Never** "attend religious services." (ANES VCF0130A, 1996–2020)	33.6%	53.8%	**20.2****
17. **Agree** that "the Bible is the actual word of God and is to be taken literally, word for word." (GSS bible, 2018)	31.6%	26.5%	**5.1**
18. **Agree** that their religion is "fundamentalist." (GSS fund, 1996–2021)	34.9%	13.7%	**21.2****

	A 1996	B Latest	C Liberal change
IMMIGRATION			
19. **Favor** decreasing a lot "the number of immigrants from foreign countries who are permitted to come to the United States." (ANES VCF0879A, 1996–2016)	35.5%	35.5%	**0.0**
20. **Favor** "grant[ing] legal status to all illegal immigrants who have held jobs and paid taxes for at least 3 years, and not been convicted of any felony crimes." (CES, 2010–2020)	32.1%	61.8%	**29.7****
21. **Favor** increasing "the number of border patrols on the U.S.-Mexican border." (CES, 2010–2020)	67.8%	72.6%	**-4.8***
GUNS			
22. **Favor** "a law which would require a person to obtain a police permit before he or she could buy a gun." (GSS gunlaw, 2021)	79.6%	57.4%	**-22.2***
23. **Favor** "ban[ning] assault rifles." (CES, 2013–2018)	59.6%	52.6%	**-7.0****

*   95% confidence interval
** 99% confidence interval
†   Language in brackets changed over time.

Sources: ANES, GSS, CES[6]

What Are the Strongest Progressive Trends Among Workers?

Figure 3.3 lists the five questions with the largest progressive trends among the white working-class survey data. Clearly, there have been major liberal advances on questions related to homophobia, xenophobia, and racial resentment.

Workers or Managers: Who Is More Liberal?

The white managerial/professional class is about 7 percent more liberal on each of these questions. However, on 12 of the 23 questions there is no statistically significant gap between the white working class and the managerial class.

From the perspective of the Democratic Party, the question is all about "persuadables"—those white working-class voters who might be enticed to support

Figure 3.3. Top five increases in white working-class liberal responses

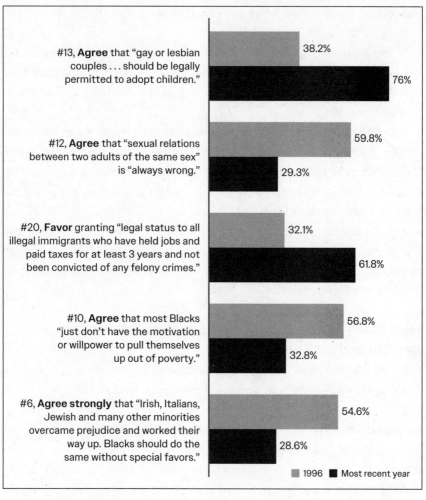

#13, **Agree** that "gay or lesbian couples . . . should be legally permitted to adopt children."
38.2%
76%

#12, **Agree** that "sexual relations between two adults of the same sex" is "always wrong."
59.8%
29.3%

#20, **Favor** granting "legal status to all illegal immigrants who have held jobs and paid taxes for at least 3 years and not been convicted of any felony crimes."
32.1%
61.8%

#10, **Agree** that most Blacks "just don't have the motivation or willpower to pull themselves up out of poverty."
56.8%
32.8%

#6, **Agree strongly** that "Irish, Italians, Jewish and many other minorities overcame prejudice and worked their way up. Blacks should do the same without special favors."
54.6%
28.6%

■ 1996 ■ Most recent year

Sources: ANES, GSS, CES

the Democrats. If the vast majority of white working-class liberals are already Democrats, then there's really nothing more the Democrats need to do. They already have all the white-working-class folks that they are likely to attract.

But, if there are large numbers of white working-class folks who are liberal on social issues and who are *not* voting for the Democrats, then the Democrats should be hard at work trying to reach this basketful of persuadables. (The flux in working-class votes can be seen in the change in support for Obama and Trump. In 2008, Obama received 43.3 percent of the white working-class vote. That dropped to 41.9 percent in 2012. In 2016, Trump captured an astonishing 67.3 percent of the white working-class vote, though it slipped to 64.8 percent in 2020.[7])

To figure out who these persuadables are and what they believe in, we need to dig deeper into the party affiliations of white working-class folks who have taken liberal positions on social issues. Are they Democrats or non-Democrats?

The CES survey asks each respondent to identify with one of seven categories ranging from strong Democrat to strong Republican. We define Democrats as all those who say they are strong Democrats, not very strong Democrats, and leaning to the Democrats. In the non-Democrat group are Independents, leaning to the Republicans, not very strong Republicans, and strong Republicans. Overall, 64 percent of the white working class are non-Democrats, 32 percent are Democrats, and 4 percent are not sure, according to the CES. That translates into about 33 million white working-class people who are non-Democrats.

How Many White Working-Class Non-Democrats Are Liberal on Social Issues?

On several social issue questions, we calculated what percentage of white working-class non-Democrats provided the most liberal answer.

Immigration: Over 40 percent of the white working-class non-Democrats took the liberal position on these immigration questions.

Support Grant legal status to all illegal immigrants who have held jobs and paid taxes for at least three years, and not been convicted of any felony crimes. (2020) — **62.4%**

Oppose Increase spending on border security by $25 billion, including building a wall between the US and Mexico. (2020) — **43.9%**

Support Provide permanent resident status to children of immigrants who were brought to the United States by their parents (also known as Dreamers). Provide these immigrants a pathway to citizenship if they meet the citizenship requirements and commit no crimes. (2020) — **56.4%**

Oppose Reduce legal immigration by 50 percent over the next 10 years by eliminating the visa lottery and ending family-based migration. (2020) **47.8%**

Oppose Withhold federal funds from any local police department that does not report to the federal government anyone they identify as an illegal immigrant. (2020) **44.9%**

Oppose Send to prison any person who has been deported from the United States and reenters the United States. (2018) **40.6%**

Racial Issues: The percentage of non-Democrats taking the most liberal position on these racially charged questions drops to about 20 percent. However, instead of just two choices—support or oppose—these questions provide five choices ranging from strongly agree to strongly disagree. The responses below only record the strongest liberal position.

Strongly disagree Irish, Italians, Jewish, and many other minorities overcame prejudice and worked their way up. Blacks should do the same without any special favors. (2018) **15.2%**

Strongly agree Generations of slavery and discrimination have created conditions that make it difficult for Blacks to work their way out of the lower class. (2018) **22.1%**

Strongly agree Over the past few years, Blacks have gotten less than they deserve. (2018) **21.8%**

Strongly disagree It's really a matter of some people not trying hard enough; if Blacks would only try harder, they could be just as well off as whites. (2018) **21.5%**

Strongly agree White people in the US have certain advantages because of the color of their skin. (2018) **21.4%**

Abortion and Women's Rights: Approximately 30 to 45 percent of the non-Democrats take the most liberal positions on abortion rights and attitudes towards women.

Support Always allow a woman to obtain an abortion as a matter of choice. (2020) **45.7%**

Oppose Prohibit the expenditure of funds authorized or appro-   **43.8%**
priated by federal law for any abortion. (2020)

Strongly disagree When women lose to men in a fair competi-   **29.4%**
tion, they typically complain about being discriminated
against. (2018)

Strongly agree Feminists are making entirely reasonable   **29.6%**
demands of men. (2018)

LBGTQ+ Rights: Clearly there is significant support among white working-class non-Democrats for LBGTQ+ rights.

Support Legalization of gay marriage. (2016)   **50.5%**

Oppose Ban on transgender people in the military. (2018)   **45.2%**

Support Amend federal laws to prohibit discrimination on the   **57.3%**
basis of gender identity and sexual orientation. (2020)

Gun Control: And here's a shocker. About one half of all white working-class non-Democrats show support for this set of gun control policies.

Oppose Make it easier for people to obtain a concealed-carry   **50.1%**
gun permit. (2020)

Support Background checks for all firearm sales, including at   **61.2%**
gun shows and over the Internet. (2018)

Support Ban assault rifles. (2020)   **49.2%**

What Do These Results Mean for the Democratic Party?

The Democrats currently are leaving behind somewhere between 20 and 50 percent of white working-class non-Democrats who are moderately to very liberal on the most divisive social issues. That translates into approximately 10 to 25 million socially liberal white working-class people who are non-Democrats. Given how close elections currently are, neglecting these workers should be considered political malpractice.

But why aren't millions of these socially liberal workers already in the Democratic fold? If it's not social issues, what really is moving them away from the Democrats? Maybe they are turned off by the personalities of Democratic candidates. Or maybe they have pet peeves—like critical race theory—that the Republicans are able to exploit. (It certainly is not because of religiosity: biblical literalism, fundamentalism, and church attendance within the white working class are in decline.) The working hypothesis of this book, therefore, is that one key issue, perhaps *the* key issue, is job insecurity.

Unfortunately, the data to test this hypothesis are limited. There are very few CES questions, for example, that deal with mass layoffs or job insecurity. But the trade-issue questions listed in table 3.2 are telling. They show *wide gaps* between white working-class Democrats and white working-class non-Democrats.

What accounts for these gaps on trade policies? The answer, we believe, is straightforward: Trade polices, like the North American Free Trade Agreement (NAFTA), and China's permission from the US to enter the World Trade Organization led to devastating job losses, especially in manufacturing. The Clintons, Barack Obama, and Joe Biden strongly supported these policies. The Obama administration tried to add yet another trade treaty—the Trans-Pacific Partnership (TPP) agreement. The CES survey shows that white working-class non-Democrats view the TPP very unfavorably, especially in comparison to white working-class Democrats.

Results in 2020 on one additional CES question also show a profound distinction between those who *oppose* strengthening the EPA enforcement

Table 3.2. Trade Agreements and Tariffs, CES Survey Responses from WWC

	Dem	Non-Dem
Support $200 billion worth of tariffs on goods imported from China. (2020)	20.2%	75.8%
Support 25% tariffs on imported steel and 10% on imported aluminum, *except* from Canada, Europe, and Mexico. (2020)	23.8%	72.3%
Support Increased tariffs on European aircraft and agricultural products. (2020)	18.1%	77.5%
Support Withdraw the United States from the Trans-Pacific Partnership trade agreement, a free-trade agreement that includes the United States, Japan, Australia, Vietnam, Canada, Chile, and others. (2018)	16.9%	64.9%

Source: CES[8]

of the Clean Air Act and Clean Water Act even if it costs US jobs. Of white working-class non-Democrats, 85.7 percent oppose strengthening EPA regulations that might cost jobs, compared to only 9.6 percent of white working-class Democrats. Why such large differences on this environmental question? We suspect that the white working-class non-Democrats fear that the jobs lost could be their own.

What does all this data suggest?

- Working-class people are trending more liberal on most social issues.
- The differences between the white working class and the white managerial/professional class on many divisive social issues are statistically insignificant—although overall, managers are somewhat more progressive.
- From 20 to 50 percent of all white working-class non-Democrats are liberal on social issues, amounting to 10 to 25 million persuadable people.
- White working-class non-Democrats are extremely worried about foreign competition and job loss due to environmental regulations.

Given these findings, we see no reason for Democratic Party leaders—or political pundits—to write off the white working class. We also see no reason for the Democratic Party to moderate its views on social issues to cater to working-class voters.

Nevertheless, the Democrats have a real problem. How can the party of Clinton and Obama and Biden convince working-class non-Democrats that it is serious about tackling job insecurity, given the party's leadership on job-destructive trade deals? Do the Democrats have the wherewithal or even the desire to disentangle themselves from the corporate forces that thrive on these trade deals and shed jobs by the thousands?

In our opinion, to win back working people, the Democratic Party needs to make mass layoffs a cornerstone issue. Standing in the way is (in addition to the Democratic Party's deep addiction to corporate cash) a deep fear of reactionary populism. For even if the overall trend is more liberal among the white working class as a whole, it is still possible that there are millions upon millions of white working-class populists who are racist, sexist, homophobic, xenophobic, and the like. The Democrats want nothing to do with that mob.

But does this populist mob really exist?

CHAPTER 4

Are You a Reactionary Populist?

*How Social Attitudes of the White Working Class
Are Similar to Those of Other Classes
and Ethnic Groups*

"It was because of the way that we were disposed of that I didn't want
to look for a new job. Because, I mean, getting a job is like joining
a family. And when your family just throws you out, it's damaging.
It takes some soul-searching and reflection to figure out how you
ended up the way you did. It felt like you were just a used piece of
toilet paper."
                                    —Eugene McCormick, age 38
                                    laid off after 9 years of service

WE'VE BEEN POUNDED WITH NEGATIVE IMAGES OF WHITE WORKING-
class people for decades—from 1963, when throngs of adoring fans cheered
Alabama Governor George Wallace's call for "Segregation now! Segregation
tomorrow! Segregation forever!," to 2021, when the white rabble attacking
the Capitol waved Confederate flags, hurled racial epithets, and defecated in
the rotunda.

The words *populist* and *populism* are often used to characterize the white
working class as a massive nativist horde that is fueling illiberalism all across
the country and around the world. But is that image based on fact or fiction?

We need a reality check on two common assumptions people make about
white working-class populism:

1. It is assumed that right-wing populists generally hold the full spectrum of reactionary positions on divisive social issues—they are racist *and* sexist *and* homophobic, and so forth.
2. It is assumed that white working-class people have many more racial resentments than other classes and ethnicities.

Are these assumptions accurate?

This chapter (and the previous one) takes a deep dive into voter surveys covering many years and many questions. To prevent the main points from getting lost in a blur of numbers, here is the summary of our findings:

1. The white working class is leaving the Democratic Party, especially in rural areas that have suffered the most per-capita mass layoffs.
2. There is little evidence that white working-class people are moving strongly to the right on divisive social issues. On only three of twenty-three questions do we see an illiberal trend since 1996 (on gun control and on increasing guards on the Mexican border).
3. The white working class is less liberal than the white managerial class, but the differences tend to be modest.
4. Some 10 to 25 million white working-class people are liberal on social issues but don't identify as Democrats.
5. These non-Democrats are extremely worried about trade deals and imports, which likely reflects their concerns about job loss and job insecurity.
6. While there is a cadre of people who take illiberal positions on a set of five basic issues, they are a very small minority of the population as a whole.
7. White working-class people are more likely than other groups to have racial resentments. But the gap between the white working class and the white managerial class is relatively small, especially when it comes to attitudes about immigrants.

The bottom line: The case is not strong for writing off white working-class people because of their attitudes on key social issues. The idea that there is a massive reactionary working-class populist base in America is a fiction.

In this chapter, we examine data from two major demographic surveys:

General Social Survey (GSS)   36,455 respondents (1996–2021)
American National Election Studies (ANES) 28,311 respondents (1996–2020)

From each, we've chosen five survey questions that we expect would elicit an emphatic reaction from right-wing populists. Below are the questions for each survey as well as what constitutes an illiberal response.

REACTIONARY POSITION ON GSS QUESTIONS

Oppose "It should be possible for a pregnant woman to obtain a legal abortion if the woman wants it for any reason."

Strongly oppose "Preferential hiring and promotion of Blacks because of past discrimination."

Agree "On average Black people have worse jobs, income, and housing than white people because most Blacks just don't have the motivation or willpower to pull themselves up out of poverty."

Agree "Sexual relations between two adults of the same sex are always wrong."

Disapprove United States Supreme Court ruling "that no state or local government may require the reading of the Lord's Prayer or Bible verses in public schools."

How many people provided illiberal responses to all five GSS questions? 440 out of 15,803 respondents (2.78 percent).

REACTIONARY POSITION ON ANES QUESTIONS

Agree strongly "It's really a matter of some people not trying hard enough. If Blacks would only try harder, they could be just as well off as whites."

No "Do you think gay or lesbian couples, in other words, homosexual couples, should be legally permitted to adopt children?"

Oppose strongly "Laws to protect homosexuals / gays and lesbians against job discrimination."

Agree "By law, abortion should never be permitted."

Agree "The number of immigrants from foreign countries should be decreased a lot."

How many people provided illiberal responses to all five ANES questions? 67 out of 8,280 respondents (0.81 percent).

If we project each of these percentages to the US population of approximately 264 million adults,[1] we get the following estimates for the number of people in the United States who hold illiberal positions on these five divisive social issue questions:

GSS   7.3 million

ANES   2.1 million

While those numbers shouldn't be dismissed as irrelevant, they make up but a very small proportion of the US population. At most, three out of every 100 adults consistently answer illiberally.

The Dark Side of Populism

Racism! That's the charge most often used to indict the white working class. People's views on gay and lesbian rights and sexism might have become more liberal, many argue, but racial resentment is growing, and it's steering the white working class into the arms of authoritarians. In other words, white working-class racist populists are the problem.

To see if these concerns are accurate, let's examine responses to three unambiguous questions that measure racial resentment, from a survey taken by the Cooperative Election Study in 2018, a year after Trump took office. We all should be able to agree that the answers listed below would indicate significant *racial resentment*—the polite phrase for racism used by social scientists. (The CES survey collected about 50,000 responses to these questions.)

Strongly disagree "White people in the US have certain advantages because of the color of their skin."

Strongly agree "Irish, Italians, Jewish, and many other minorities overcame prejudice and worked their way up. Blacks should do the same without any special favors."

Strongly agree "It's really a matter of some people not trying hard enough. If Blacks would only try harder, they could be just as well off as whites."

How Many Resentment Responses Does It Take to Make a Racist?

Does just one strong racial resentment response signify that you are a racist? Maybe you've been hiding your resentment on the other questions, but it finally slipped out? If that's the case, does the white working class have a higher percentage of members who provided one or more strong racial resentment responses?

Figure 4.1 shows that about half of all white and Hispanic respondents provided at least one answer reflecting strong racial resentments. White workers had the highest percentage (54.4 percent) followed by Hispanic workers (48.2 percent). Clearly the largest gap is between white and Hispanic workers and managers compared to Black workers and managers.

Figure 4.1. Percent by class showing racial resentment on one or more race question

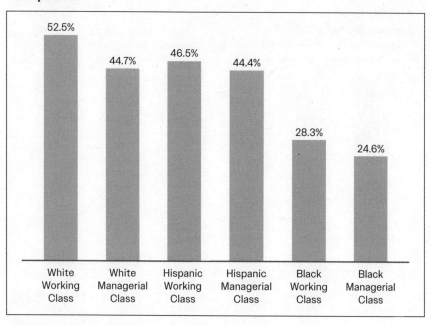

Source: CES²

DOES WHITE SKIN GIVE AN ADVANTAGE?

About one in four white workers and managers strongly disagree that whiteness provides advantages (see figure 4.2). Black and Hispanic respondents show significantly lower percentages, suggesting they believe white skin does indeed provide certain advantages.

SHOULD BLACKS BE ABLE TO WORK THEIR WAY UP WITHOUT ANY SPECIAL FAVORS?

On this question, as you can see in figure 4.3, once again, the white working class shows the most racial resentment, with 42.3 percent agreeing with this statement. But an astonishingly high percentage of Black working-class respondents (28.1 percent) and Hispanic managers (26 percent) also strongly agree with the pick-yourself-up-by-your-bootstraps statement.

ARE BLACK PEOPLE NOT TRYING HARD ENOUGH?

And yet again, the white working class show somewhat more racial resentment. The largest gap is between white and Hispanic workers and managers on one hand, and Black workers and managers on the other (see figure 4.4).

Figure 4.2. Strongly DISAGREE
White people in the US have certain advantages because of the color of their skin.

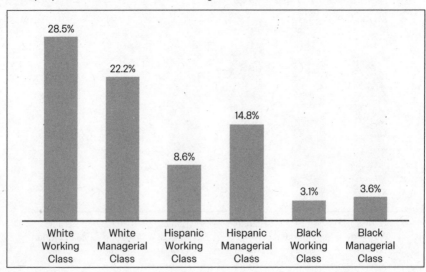

Source: CES³

Figure 4.3. Strongly AGREE

Irish, Italians, Jewish, and many other minorities overcame prejudice and worked their way up. Blacks should do the same without any special favors.

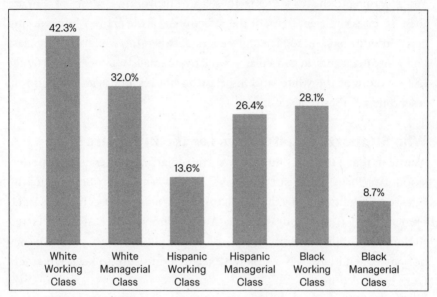

Source: CES[4]

Figure 4.4. Strongly AGREE

It's really a matter of some people not trying hard enough.
If Blacks would only try harder, they could be just as well off as whites.

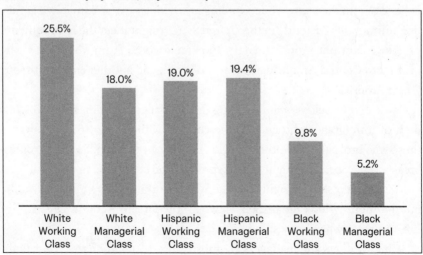

Source: CES[5]

OVERALL, DOES THE WHITE WORKING CLASS SHOW MORE RACIAL RESENTMENT?

Yes, according to the responses to these three provocative questions. But are the responses sufficient to merit the indictment of the entire white working class? In our opinion, no. The differences between the white working class and white managers, in particular, are relatively small. And most importantly, half or more of the white working class do not respond with strong racial resentment to these questions.

Who Supports Legal Status for the Dreamers?

The fear that Hispanic immigrants are replacing whites is also understood as a form of racism. The level of this fear might be revealed by how respondents react to the legislation known as the Dream Act (Development, Relief, and Education for Alien Minors) and DACA (Deferred Action for Childhood Arrivals). As of January 2024, the Dream Act has not passed, and DACA is a stopgap executive measure to keep Dreamers from being deported.

These programs are designed to provide a path to citizenship for "Dreamers," the children of immigrants who were born and educated in the United States and who have known no other homeland than the United States. The programs would provide current, former, and future undocumented high-school graduates and GED recipients a chance for citizenship if they go to college or join the army while avoiding any felonies. Approximately 1.8 million immigrants currently in the United States might meet the requirements of the Dream Act. Approximately 70 percent come from Mexico, 14 percent from Central America and the Caribbean, and another 6 percent from South America.[6]

Some people believe that providing this special path to citizenship for children of immigrants who entered the country without legal papers rewards those who broke the law. Others see this as a way for these children, who didn't break a law by being brought here, to prosper and contribute to our society.

We can gain some insight into the white working class's attitudes about immigration by looking at their views on the Dream Act and DACA. Figure 4.5 shows where they stand.

White workers and managers are mostly in agreement on this issue: Only about 30 percent of the white working class oppose the Dream Act.

Figure 4.5. OPPOSE

Provide legal status to children of immigrants who are already in the United States and were brought to the United States by their parents. Provide these children the option of citizenship in 10 years if they meet citizenship requirements.

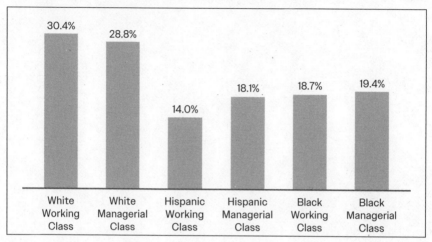

Source: CES[7]

It's worth repeating our bottom line finding: *The case is not strong for writing off white working-class people because of their attitudes on key social issues. The idea that there is a massive reactionary working-class populist base in America is a fiction.*

As the next chapter will show, the entire idea of reactionary populism is a conceptual disaster that undermines our ability to understand the needs and interests of working-class people.

CHAPTER 5

The Use and Abuse of Populism

The Mischaracterization of White Working-Class Politics

"The people have to have more of a voice. The workers have to have more of a voice." —Michele, age 52, laid off after 7 years of service

DOES THE WHITE WORKING CLASS FORM THE HARDCORE ACTIVIST base of the Republican Party, driving it further and further to the right as it dominates primary elections?

The populist base of the Republican Party, supposedly, is enthralled with the culture warriors, the conspiracy theorists, and the white supremacists. These working people, we are told, believe that their former way of life is being destroyed by woke Democrats, immigrants, and minorities, and they subscribe to the replacement theory—the idea that there is an active plot to replace white people. This rabid white working-class populism, we are warned, is polarizing the nation and threatening democracy.

Our data suggest this conventional wisdom is incorrect. Using our definition of class, a higher percentage of white managers (30.4 percent) than of white workers (25.1 percent) say they voted in the Republican congressional primaries.[1] Hispanic managers are the next largest group of Republican primary voters (15.5 percent).

The 2018 Primaries Project at the Brookings Institution provides more detailed profiles on these Republican primary voters:[2]

They are disproportionately white: 86.4 percent.

They are better educated: 46.8 percent of Republican primary voters had either a college degree or postgraduate study. Another 26.8 percent had some college or an associate degree. Only 15 percent of these voters had only finished high school or dropped out before graduating high school (compared to 34.2 percent of the general population in districts where the primaries took place).

They are richer: Republican primary voters are considerably richer than the rest of the population in their primary districts. For example, 26.9 percent of Republican primary voters (and 21.5 percent of the Democratic primary voters) have household incomes above $150,000 per year, compared to only 15.4 percent of the general population in the average district.

They attract fewer lower-income voters: On the other end of the income spectrum, only 20.9 percent of Republican primary voters (and 27.5 percent of the Democratic primary voters) have household incomes under $50,000, compared to 39.6 percent of the general population.

They are older than the general population.

Clearly, the Republican base is not dominated by the white working class. Then why call the Republican base populist?

The Massive Misunderstanding of White Working-Class Populism

Many of the most astute liberal journalists are certain that the white working class is driven more by racial resentment than by economic insecurity. Economist Paul Krugman, for example, writes, "And does anyone doubt that resentment on the part of those who felt disrespected was central to the rise of Donald Trump? Are there any pundits left who still believe that it was largely about 'economic anxiety'?"[3]

Our research strongly suggests, however, that economic concerns predominate for working-class people and should be taken very seriously. Studies from around the globe show, and have shown, that job insecurity, not racism, causes a decline in trust in government, support for right-wing political formations, and a loss of faith in democracy.

- In Britain, researchers confirmed that an increase in political populism "is associated with a rise in workers worrying about job loss as well as an increase in individuals holding politicians and politics in disrepute. . . . [J]ob insecurity was indeed indirectly related to feelings of political cynicism via the experience of distributive injustice."[4]

- In Australia, an academic study reported that "[m]oving beyond the usual anti-statism and racism attitudinal explanatory foci . . . popular support for these parties is associated with the job insecurity that populist party leaders have attributed to deepening international economic integration, or economic globalization."[5]

- In Europe, researchers found that "[e]conomic insecurity shocks have a significant impact on the populist vote share, directly as demand for [trade] protection, and indirectly through [declining] trust [in established political parties]."[6]

- A study by researcher Andrew Wroe examined 18 European countries and found that "job insecurity generates lower levels of trust in politicians, political parties and political institutions and lower levels of satisfaction with democratic performance."[7]

- Looking at the United States, Wroe also found that "Americans who think that their job is at risk, who fear losing their healthcare, who worry about paying the rent and putting food on the table, and who are alarmed about paying for their children's education and getting into debt are significantly more likely to distrust the federal government than Americans who feel more economically secure."[8]

- In examining the impact of trade liberalization with China, researchers found that US "voters in areas subject to higher import competition shifted votes toward the party more likely to restrict trade."[9]

- Job insecurity is also linked with votes that were drawn away from the two major parties. Researchers found that "the political effects of job insecurity are distinctive. In a [statistical] model of electoral choice in the 1996 US presidential election, job insecurity is associated with support for the third-party candidate, Ross Perot."[10]

Echoing the themes of our book, Democratic Party pollster Mike Lux recently reported that economics, not racism, is driving rural voters in Rust Belt states. He writes:

[C]ontrary to many pundits' assumptions, economic issues are driving the problems of Democrats in non-metro working-class counties far more than the culture war. . . . [T]hese voters wouldn't care all that much about the cultural difference and the woke thing if they thought Democrats gave more of a damn about the economic challenges they face deeply and daily. . . .

[T]he voters we need to win in these counties are not inherently right wing on social issues.[italics added][11]

Giving a damn about the economic challenges means doing something about job insecurity. The Democrats are hoping that the infrastructure bills will speak to the needs of these people. The jury is out. These working-class people do know, however, that Bill Clinton, Hillary Clinton, Barack Obama, and Joe Biden have worked tirelessly to expand global trade, which clearly *increased* job insecurity for millions of Americans. International climate accords also provoke fears that more jobs will be destroyed. Clearly, Trump's anti–free trade / climate accord positions contributed to the collapse of the Democratic Blue Wall in 2016.

Arguing that expanded trade creates more jobs than are lost provides no solace for those suffering mass layoffs. Labeling workers who oppose trade deals as xenophobic populists is a poor excuse for inaction. Working people want job stability. That's a human right, not a moral flaw. Drifting toward authoritarianism, as these studies show, is what happens when the political system refuses to address mass layoffs.

Disparaging the white working class as reactionary populists is suicidal for the Democrats and dangerous for our democracy. It also is an affront to the rich history of American populism, which seems to have been studiously ignored or forgotten by those who so carelessly use that label.

Populism: America's Progressive Tradition

The American populist movement of the 1880s and '90s was America's homegrown political rebellion against rising autocratic financial and corporate power. In this short section we can't do justice to the rich and complex evolution of what was called the Populist movement, which emerged when the National Farmers' Alliance and Industrial Union grew into the People's Party. However, we all need to know something about it, since today the word *populism* is used so often, and so loosely.

After the Civil War, farmers in the South and Midwest suffered mightily from exploitation by banks, local merchants, grain elevator and stockyard operators, and the mighty railroad barons. To free themselves from virtual bondage, small farmers and laborers fought back by building a massive movement based around cooperatives and alternatives to a financial system that was entirely owned and controlled by private banks, led by the titans of Wall Street.

As one of the movement's national leaders, L. L. Polk of North Carolina, put it, "You will see arrayed on the one side the great magnates of the country, and Wall Street brokers, and the plutocratic power; and on the other you will see the people . . . there will be no Mason and Dixon line on the Alliance maps of the future." Then, Polk seems to time travel and speak directly to us: "I believe both parties are afraid of Wall Street. They are not afraid of the people."[12]

The Populists developed the idea that the producing classes—farmers and industrial workers—needed to create a new system to free themselves from the giant corporations that had begun to rule the country after the Civil War. At the time, there were no government regulations to speak of.

The Populist view of the world was in stark contrast to the prevailing theories based on social Darwinism—the survival of the fittest—that were often deployed to justify the social and economic hierarchy. Many elites believed that those with wealth deserved it all, and neither the government nor the lower classes should stand in their way. Doing so, they argued, would be a fundamental violation of nature because the fittest had to be free to exercise their god-given talents as they battled their way up the economic ladder.

The Populists, however, used their own prodigious talents to create state and county chapters, along with journals and national conventions. They formed hundreds of state and local cooperatives to sell their goods and purchase what they needed to farm and survive. They fielded 6,000 lecturers across the country to provide grassroots education, spread the word of their movement, and bring local insights back to state and national leaders.[13] Through these efforts, and many more, they built a national organization that numbered in the millions.

As a movement striving to ally with Black farmers as well as white, many of the Populists resisted the efforts of Southern elites to disenfranchise working people of all races. The struggle, at times, was fierce. Ballot box stuffing became routine as the white supremacists tried to beat back the populist uprising. In a reign of terror, "night riders" destroyed Populist offices and lynched Black Populist activists. In Wilmington, North Carolina, for example, a coalition government that included the Populists was violently overthrown by white supremacists in 1898. The insurrection led to the death of scores of Black citizens.

Ultimately, the Populist movement was defeated in its attempt to establish an independent national political party. But it did achieve many state and local electoral victories. It also placed the idea of curbing corporate power on the national agenda. This laid the groundwork for activists to push for—and win—many of the reforms of the 20th century: restricting child labor, busting trusts and monopolies, regulating corporations, protecting workers' rights, and creating public banks like the Bank of North Dakota.

Those who today use the word *populist* so indiscriminately should think of these brave men and women who tried to build a new system based both on private property and cooperatives. As historian Lawrence Goodwyn writes, "It was a campaign never to be waged again."[14] (Yet.)

Populism Transforms into a Negative Epithet

For white supremacists, corporations, and banks, *populism* had always had a negative connotation. The media controlled by these elites mercilessly pictured the populists as destructive, wild-eyed radicals.[15] During the first half of the 20th century in the upper Midwest, however, populism endured, leading to the rise of reformist progressive governments on both local and state levels.

By the mid-20th century, the idea of populist progressivism was challenged by sociologists and political scientists, who called themselves pluralists. They believed mass movements encouraged and enabled the rise of totalitarian regimes led by Hitler, Mussolini, Stalin, and Mao.

The pluralist scholars also worried about the growing power of a home-grown totalitarian: Wisconsin Senator Joseph McCarthy. They watched with increasing horror as McCarthy trampled the civil liberties and livelihoods of anyone he and his minions chose to label as "communists" or "communist sympathizers." *McCarthyism*—anti-communism run wild—became a new and soon-to-be widely used term in American culture.

While McCarthy was eventually discredited and defeated, the paranoia about mass movements remained. One widely accepted explanation for the frightening phenomenon of McCarthyism came from sociologist Seymour Martin Lipset in his highly influential 1959 article in the *American Sociological Review*, "Democracy and Working-Class Authoritarianism."[16]

Lipset argued that while mass organizations like trade unions and rural farmers' alliances might hold progressive economic positions, they also were likely to hold reactionary social positions. He claimed that surveys from several countries showed that "ethnic prejudices flow more naturally from the situation of the lower classes than from that of the middle and upper classes in modern industrial society." The same held true, he claimed, for democratic values: Working-class people tended to dislike "civil liberties for unpopular political groups, civil rights for ethnic minorities, legitimacy of opposition and proper limits on the power of national political leaders."

In short, the masses of working people, while liberal on economic issues, had a weakness for anti-democratic demagogues like Senator Joseph McCarthy. The solution Lipset and other pluralist scholars suggested was to buffer direct democracy by encouraging negotiations among interest group leaders: that is, pluralism.

In a pluralist society, ideology would be secondary for the leaders of trade unions, business associations, civic organizations, farmers' alliances, political parties, and governmental bodies. Instead, these leaders would focus on negotiating among themselves to get things done. Stakeholder elites making pragmatic and reasoned agreements would constrain the masses and make polarizing assaults on our democracy, like Joseph McCarthy's, less likely.

For evidence of the masses-run-wild theory, the pluralists pointed to what they believed to be an obvious fact: Joseph McCarthy was elected to the Senate from Wisconsin, and Wisconsin was a populist state—that is, the Populist movement and populist values in the 1950s still shaped much of the state's political culture.

Before the rise of McCarthy, Wisconsin voters had elected many progressive congressmembers, senators, and governors who supported Populist economic programs. Progressive Robert La Follette was elected to all three of those positions. But these same voters, it was argued, also sent McCarthy to the Senate. For the pluralists, this was strong evidence that Populist workers and farmers, progressive on economic issues, also harbored authoritarian impulses that attracted them to McCarthy's assault on democratic norms.

What the pluralists considered rock-solid facts, however, were called into question by Michael P. Rogin in his book *The Intellectuals and McCarthy* (1967). After carefully analyzing where McCarthy received his support in Wisconsin, Rogin found that "progressive counties tended to oppose McCarthy more than other counties in the state."[17] Further, Rogin argued that "what the pluralists see as populist-authoritarianism is found with conservative rather than left-wing attitudes."[18] Rogin demonstrated that McCarthy's core support in Wisconsin came largely from local Republican elites—small-town bankers, attorneys, real estate operators, and small business owners.

Most importantly, Rogin faulted the enabling actions and passivity of national Republican officials, who tolerated McCarthy and allowed him to violate countless democratic norms. National Republican Party leaders saw great political advantage in the turmoil created by McCarthy's ruthless anti-communist campaign—a campaign that most liberals also supported in its less virulent forms.

The working-class masses did not create the federal loyalty oaths instituted by President Truman's Democratic administration. And those masses did not create the blacklists that harmed the careers of so many in government, education, and Hollywood. For Rogin, McCarthyism was primarily an elite phenomenon, not a mass phenomenon.

The Continued Mischaracterization of Populism

We can see a similar pluralist critique of the masses emerge again in accounts of the Tea Party, the right-wing movement that took off in 2009. These accounts often assume that the Tea Party was driven by disgruntled white working-class reactionaries who fundamentally resented intellectuals and the media, immigrants, LGBTQ+ people, and minorities. But a comprehensive study by Theda Skocpol and Vanessa Williamson, *The Tea Party and the Remaking of Republican Conservatism* (2012), provides an entirely different view of the socioeconomic status of Tea Party members: "Tea Party supporters and activists are better-off economically and better educated than most Americans. . . . Most are not truly wealthy, however. Comfortable middle-class might be the best way to describe grassroots Tea Partiers."[19]

White? Yes, almost entirely so. Working class? Decidedly not, as defined by income, education, or occupation.

The January 6, 2021, insurrection is similarly mischaracterized. The Chicago Project on Security and Threats at the University of Chicago published demographic information on 656 of the 861 insurrectionists who had been charged, as of July 22, 2022, with illegally entering the Capitol or Capitol grounds. The study found the following:

- 93 percent of the insurrectionists were white.
- 54 percent were white-collar or business owners.
- Only 22 percent were blue-collar (non–business owners, no college degree).
- And 25 percent had a college degree.[20]

The study does not have information on those insurrectionists with graduate degrees, but we do know that the founder and leader of the Oath Keepers, Stewart Rhodes (sentenced to 18 years in prison for sedition and other charges from his January 6 activities) is a graduate of the ultra-elite Yale Law School.

January 6, 2021, was not a white working-class riot.

When authoritarians who violate democratic norms emerge, be it a McCarthy or a Trump, the "masses-run-wild" theory provides a convenient, but inaccurate, explanation. As of this writing, thousands of highly educated professionals and executives still cling to the lie that the 2020 presidential election was stolen. As with Joseph McCarthy, Republican politicians have actively enabled the continuing violation of democratic norms.

It doesn't have to be this way. When McCarthy attacked the Army, President Eisenhower finally pushed back hard, and in a matter of months McCarthy was ruined—a drunken, irrelevant politician. One wonders what would have happened to Trump if the Republicans had turned on him after he so clearly tried to overturn an election and provoke a violent insurrection?

For Democrats and the media to blame the white working class for this dereliction of duty by Republican elites is to make the same mistake that the pluralists made with McCarthyism. The white working class does not have the franchise on authoritarianism, racism, sexism, xenophobia, homophobia, religious intolerance, or violence. Authoritarianism can only irreparably damage society if political leaders refuse to hold the authoritarians to account.

Liberals, too, can become unwitting enablers by blaming the white working class for the sins of these elites.

Nevertheless, white working-class alienation is real and growing. Their abandonment of the Democrats started two decades before the rise of Trump. Our analysis strongly suggests that these working-class people may be losing faith in the Democrats and democracy not because of social issues, but rather because their livelihoods are continually threatened by mass lay-offs. The alienation increases as the victims are scapegoated for the illiberal beliefs that, in reality, they do not hold disproportionately.

The Democrats are unlikely to reconnect with these working-class people until they actively challenge Wall Street, which has been systematically trashing working-class people and their jobs for more than 40 years. This is the story we will examine next.

CHAPTER 6

Before Greed Was Good

The Unwinding of Post–World War II Working-Class Prosperity

"I have a lot of friends there still and . . . I think [the college is] going to screw them, too. I think they're just trying to do away with the unions because they don't want to pay nobody health benefits, they don't wanna pay a proper wage. They want transient employees in there [so] that they can keep the wages low. They don't have to give them anything for longevity—no health benefits, no retirement. When you work for somebody a long time, you would hope they cared enough about you that they'd want you to be able to live a decent life when you retire. Not just work you to death and not give you nothing in return. But that's what they're doing."　　　　　　　　　　**—Jack Kubicki, age 59,**
laid off after 12 years of service

OUR ECONOMY, OUR POLITICS, AND EVEN HOW WE THINK ABOUT ourselves, have changed dramatically since 1980. This transformation was so profound that today it is difficult to recall that the exclusive focus on *economic efficiency* (the polite term for runaway greed) was not always our most important economic value. Hopefully, the next two chapters will remind us that specific policies created by humans changed our world, and that these policies can be changed again. Here are a few of the transformations before and after 1980:

Before: Wall Street was tightly regulated and controlled.
After: Wall Street has broken free of these constraints.

Before: Government and public officials were held in high esteem.
After: They are scorned.

Before: More than 1 in 5 business-sector workers were members of labor unions.
After: Only 1 in 15 are members of unions.

Before: Corporations believed it was their duty to serve multiple stakeholders, including workers, local communities, consumers, stockholders, and the country.
After: Only shareholders matter, dominated by Wall Street banks, private equity companies, and hedge fund activists.

Before: Wages, on average after inflation, rose year by year in line with productivity gains.
After: Wages have stalled and productivity gains are flowing upward, resulting in massive wealth increases for the rich.

Before: The gap between top CEOs and their average workers was 30 to 1.
After: The gap has reached 800 to 1.

Before: Mass layoffs were rare.
After: Mass layoffs now are everywhere.

This is not to say that *before* was the golden age for working people. Work was dangerous. Toxic substances were spewed about with virtually no controls. (OSHA and EPA regulations weren't enacted until 1970.) Work-related illnesses and deaths were endemic to mining and manufacturing. But there was steady employment, a rising standard of living for many, and a sense of self-worth that employment and well-functioning communities provide.

For Black workers the transformation to "after" was discouraging and painful. During the 1960s and 1970s, many had moved into semiskilled and skilled, unionized blue-collar jobs, which gave them access to union bargaining, cost-of-living increases, seniority rights for promotions and layoffs, defined pension plans, and company-funded health care. When plant closings swept through during the 1980s, many Black workers—who were last hired—became the first fired.

Before switched to *after* around 1980. Learning what changed and how it changed will help us better understand why we now live in an era marked by layoffs of mass destruction and their devastating aftermath.

Before

In the United States, corporations of all kinds—large and small, for-profit and nonprofit, barring some constraints in some union contracts—have always had the right to terminate workers at will. But until the late 1970s, during nonrecessionary periods, the number of industrial jobs was increasing. (See figure 6.1 on page 78.) Some cyclical industries, like automobile manufacturing, would shut down facilities when supply outstripped demand or when it was necessary to retool the assembly lines for new products. The workers involved, however, knew they would be reemployed after the furlough. To be sure, a significant number of corporations did flee to locations in the South, where unions were rare and labor costs were lower, taking advantage of the 1947 Taft–Hartley Act that made it harder to organize unions. Still others moved from cities to the suburbs to escape heavily unionized urban areas. For the most part, however, mass layoffs happened only in periods of economic stress, like deep recessions.

Take a look at the rise and decline of manufacturing jobs since WWII in figure 6.1.

Something did indeed change around 1980. What happened?

The Standard Account

The widely accepted account of what happened in the US economy after WWII is compelling but flawed. And it helps explain the widespread fatalism about mass layoffs that afflicts us today. It goes like this:

American industry came out of the war unchallenged globally. It produced the best and most critical products needed to rebuild war-torn Europe and Japan. But that superiority could not last. It was inevitable that other countries with highly skilled productive capacities would rebuild and reemerge as competitors. In fact, the United States, as leader of the free world, had a geopolitical interest in ensuring that these economies recovered fully and partnered with us in favorable trade deals.

Figure 6.1. US manufacturing employees, 1946–2022

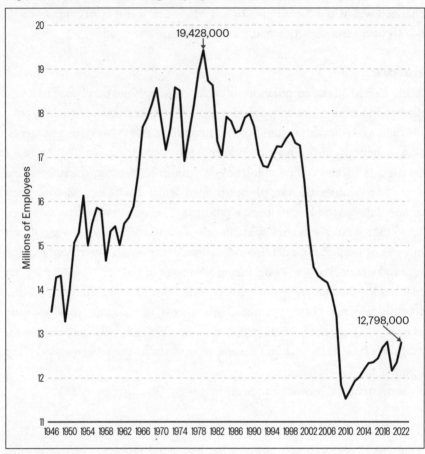

Source: Federal Reserve Bank of St. Louis[1]

By the late 1960s, it was clear that Europe and Japan were competing successfully in key product areas, such as electronics, steel, and automobile manufacturing. That competition pressured US industries to find new efficiencies—ways to profit even though, to stay competitive, they had to keep their prices low. This made mass layoffs a necessary corporate strategy.

Production became more automated as new technologies ripped through the economy. This was further accelerated by the rise of the digital revolution, altering the workplace dramatically. New technologies also made it possible for corporations to coordinate global supply chains and to ship jobs abroad, even as robots replaced workers at home. Meanwhile, a digital divide emerged between those trained and equipped to engage in the "knowledge economy" and those without college degrees, who could not compete for these jobs. The latter found themselves in direct competition with lower-paid workers all over the world, a competition that American workers would have difficulty winning.

By 2000 or so, all of these technological forces merged to create mammoth global corporations operating in a vast global marketplace. It became routine to export jobs, manage international supply chains, and chase the lowest labor costs around the world.

Mass layoffs became the price we had to pay to fully participate in this complex, highly technical, vast global economic system.

This account seems plausible. The modern digital revolution certainly seems to have upended job security in many sectors. But the story also raises vexing questions. For example: Why have mass layoffs racked the United States but not Japan and Germany? Those technologically advanced countries are far more dependent on global trade than the United States is, yet the number, size, and impact of mass layoffs there are nothing like what we have endured.

Why here and not there?

My Account: Cold War Capitalism

We need an account for why mass layoffs became a key strategy for corporate America in particular. While much more research is needed to nail down this complex story, here is my synopsis:

After WWII, the emergent United States led a global anti-communist struggle built upon the premise that capitalism improved the lives of working people far better than communist economies ever could.[2]

Corporations felt cultural and political pressure to engage in an unwritten social compact with government and organized labor to (1) fight global communism, (2) deliver a higher standard of living to working people, and (3) extend civil rights to minorities. American leaders understood that it wouldn't look good to the rest of the world if US capitalism destroyed its trade unions and attacked the livelihoods of working people. Yes, there were significant labor struggles during this period, many more than today. However, even the many strikes conveyed a Cold War message—that labor under capitalism was free to wage these fights. (Nevertheless, stopping the spread of unions through the 1947 Taft–Hartley Act and undermining shop-floor power always were and remain corporate goals.)

That changed radically when Ronald Reagan declared open season on unions. By this point, global communism was no longer a serious competitor to capitalism (although that's not how his administration acted). In short order, the unwritten compact that had entwined organized labor within the corporate order collapsed. As the restraints on corporations loosened, mass layoffs became an increasingly common and highly profitable corporate tool.

The historical arc of union power in the United States mirrors the arc of the Cold War. In 1955, more than one in three business-sector workers were union members, and corporations strove to prevent the large economic disruptions that union strikes could cause. Union power was greatest in key industries like oil, automobiles, steel, rubber, and electronics, where union density (the percentage of workers in unions) was as high as 80 percent or more. Employers in those sectors thought twice about initiating mass layoffs, because they needed the cooperation of these powerful worker organizations.

But as union density declined—today unions represent only 6 percent of the business-sector workforce—their ability to fight mass layoffs declined as well.

The Cold War also eroded union power from within. The bulk of the US trade union movement after WWII took up the fight against domestic and international communism. In 1948, key communist-leaning unions were purged from the most aggressive labor federation—the Congress of Industrial Organizations (CIO). Thereafter, many of the most talented and committed left-wing organizers were driven from unions. Unions bled from the loss of these highly motivated unionists, who excelled at recruiting new workers and at resisting new corporate attacks. When the CIO merged with the more conservative American Federation of Labor to form the AFL-CIO in 1955, its leadership, including Federation president George Meany, became even more involved in US anti-communist foreign policy. The AFL-CIO top brass worked hand-in-glove with the State Department and the CIA to promote anti-communist unions, especially in developing nations. The Federation also threw its weight behind the war in Vietnam, billed as a struggle against global communism.

Organized labor, however, paid a price for its interventionism. Many of its young men died or were seriously wounded in combat. And across the country, a new generation of young workers, opposed to the war, were alienated from these leaders and their unions.

Nevertheless, with organized labor at its peak during the 1950s and '60s, corporations saw that the surest path to profitability was to invest in the productive capacity of their workers, rather than finding ways to get rid of them. This corresponded with the significant rise of manufacturing jobs during this period. (See figure 6.1 on page 78.)

A corporate cultural norm probably helped maintain this balance of power as well. A mass layoff was seen as a sign that corporate executives had failed. Only struggling, mismanaged companies had to resort to such drastic actions. Successful corporations provided job security, good wages, and benefits, with the goal of keeping workers attached to the company throughout their work lives.

The 1983 *New York Times* article, "Lifetime Employment, US Style" is a historical artifact from the period when the worker-oriented business model was rapidly being replaced by mass-layoff capitalism.

> High unemployment has put greater importance on job security, and the handful of large companies—including Eli Lilly, I.B.M. and Hewlett-Packard—that shun layoffs has drawn some of the attention that usually goes to Japan for its "lifetime employment" policies. In fact, because major Japanese companies only guarantee jobs for men, and workers may be forced to retire in their 50's, some American companies provide greater job security. American plans protect all employees and permit later retirement.[3]

The article also notes that "most no-layoff programs have been in place for decades and are part of a program aimed at using workers as efficiently as possible."

In the article, Sheldon Weinig, chairman of Materials Research Corporation, claimed that lifetime employment was a major part of his business model, along with heavy investment in research and development.

But clearly the pressure was mounting to weaken such long-term commitments to workers. "Mr. Weinig faced constant criticism," the *New York Times* reported. "Stockholders lectured him on his responsibilities to maximize profits."

A cover story in *BusinessWeek* a few years later, "The End of Corporate Loyalty?" (1986), captures the accelerating mass-layoff trends, especially the impacts on salaried workers. "What's new is the growing willingness of some of the most successful corporations to slash jobs. In troubled industries these staff reductions are often needed to survive. But plenty of healthy companies are paring away, too."[4]

The connection to the rising power of Wall Street is clearly noted: "Nearly every time a company announces cutbacks, its stock price ticks up a dollar or two."[5]

This article also provides evidence that the pre–"greed is good" culture still lingered among America's largest corporations. Many of them, like DuPont, avoided forced layoffs. Instead, they provided generous buyout packages so that tens of thousands of mid-level managers, mostly in their 50s, would leave voluntarily. Non-compulsory mass layoffs are long gone in America.

Economist William Lazonick refers to this strategy of a bygone era as "retain and reinvest." The idea was to use profits to upgrade worker skills and develop robust research and development programs to create competitive high-quality products and services, as well as lower prices. But by the 1980s, "retain and reinvest" was being replaced by what Lazonick calls "downsize and distribute,"[6] which is a polite way of saying, "Let's slash our workforce, take the money, and run."*

This shift from "retain and reinvest" to "downsize and distribute" is the key to understanding the rise of layoffs of mass destruction. It's a story of transformation from a relatively equitable economy to one driven by

---

* More recently Lazonick added a further category, "dominate and distribute," which is how Apple, Facebook, Google, and Microsoft operate. They use their size and market control to buy up fledgling competitors and new technologies while siphoning hundreds of billions of dollars into stock buybacks and slashing tens of thousands of workers.

runaway inequality. It's a story of how the economic problems of the 1970s, fueled by the Vietnam War and the global Cold War, helped to unleash a "greed is good" corporate ethos that normalized layoffs of mass destruction. It's a story, first and foremost, of how Wall Street financially strip-mined the economy on behalf of the few.

The Rise of the Greedy Economy

My colleagues at the Labor Institute and I regularly conduct economic work-shops for union members in which we ask working people why they think the economy changed so radically around 1980.[7]

Most often, they say "greed." At first, that answer made no sense to us. Did someone, all of a sudden, turn on the greedy switch in human nature? After hearing that response again and again, we realized that the greedy switch indeed had been flipped—not in human nature but in policy.

To be sure, the world was changing rapidly because of globalization, competitive pressures, and new technologies. But key policies also changed—including a corporate response to those economic shifts that led us to the current era of mass layoffs.

The 1970s were a decade of inflation and unemployment, two phenomena that Keynesian economic theory claimed could not happen simultaneously. The conflicting pressures created by these economic trends opened up space for alternative theories and new policies aimed at solving these daunting challenges. The new theory that took hold was really an old theory from the 19th century that claimed government interference with the business of capitalism undermined profits, stunted job creation, and threatened freedom as well. The magic bullet was deregulation—getting the government out of the economy. As this theory was put into practice, the fundamental moderating rules and norms of post–WWII capitalism were undermined entirely.

Until the mid-1970s, more than 11.5 percent of the US economy was tightly regulated by government. Many of these rules were intended to fix identified problems that had led to market failures. In the late 19th century, new giant corporations conquered many core industries, leading to monopoly power and crippling inequality. The problems that ensued inspired the rise of mass popular movements defending workers and their families. Under pressure from these movements, the government instituted new regulations to break up the big trusts, like Standard Oil, and break the stranglehold other monopolistic

Table 6.1. Regulated Industries in the United States, 1975 versus 2006

Sector or industry	Regulated in 1975	Regulated in 2006
Oil and gas extraction (deregulated in 1980)	Yes	No
Railroads (1976, 1980)	Yes	No
Airlines (1978)	Yes	No
Trucking (1980)	Yes	No
Pipelines (1978, 1985)	Yes	Yes
Electricity (1992)	Yes	Yes
Telecom (1984, 1996)	Yes	Partially
Radio/TV (1985, 1987)	Yes	Partially
Finance (1978, 1980, 1982, 1987, 1989, 1994, 1996, 1998, 2001, 2003)	Yes	No
Insurance	Yes	Yes
TOTALS		

Source: The Brookings Institution[8]

companies had over key industries like railroads, utilities, and communications. These new regulations were intended to promote and maintain stability.

The reforms were moderately successful for a time, but when the free-market economy crashed entirely in 1929—due in large part to Wall Street malfeasance—Congress passed strict regulatory requirements that reined in the financial sector. For the next 25 years there were no major financial crises. During the years of the New Deal and WWII, regulatory controls were placed on other industries as well. First, the government stepped in to create jobs and limit cutthroat price competition. Then, during the buildup for war, government leaders enacted other controls designed to maximize military production, including wage and price controls. Labor unions were legalized by federal statute under a complex web of rules that entwined corporate and labor relations with the force of law.

By the 1950s, although American free enterprise was constrained considerably, the United States had become more productive and prosperous than any other country in world history.

Homer Robinson, an old-school Republican entrepreneur who helped found Alaska Airlines, put it this way: "Regulations were good for us. We

Percent of economy regulated in 1975	Percent of economy regulated in 2006	Percent decline in regulations
0.89%	0%	100%
0.25%	0%	100%
1.02%	0%	100%
1.25%	0%	100%
0.07%	0.07%	0%
1.19%	1.19%	0%
2.10%	0.70%	67%
0.70%	0.23%	67%
3.28%	0%	100%
0.77%	0.77%	0%
11.52%	**2.96%**	**74%**

earned a solid, stable profit, but not too much. And unions took the competition out of the cost of labor. We all knew what we had to pay. That gave us stability. We did well."*

When US corporate prosperity came under stress during the 1970s, a new generation of corporate leaders and economists (strongly connected to the University of Chicago) took aim at the entire regulatory edifice. They tapped into a growing sense that government rules and regulations were rigid and confining—that they held back innovation and saddled our productive forces with crippling constraints. The deregulation advocates claimed that a new, more powerful economy was straining to break free of its government shackles. As table 6.1 shows, those arguments carried the day, and the deregulatory movement succeeded. Between 1975 and 2006,

---

* Homer Robinson, the father of my good friend Ted Robinson, would take us to dinner in the late 1970s and entertain us with stories about his life as an entrepreneur. Having picked up that I was interested in labor issues, he would share his views on regulations.

there was a 74 percent reduction in regulations in significantly regulated industries. How did that come about?

The 1970s Breakthrough for Corporate America

From WWII until the mid-1970s, the real wages of the average worker rose year after year along with gains in productivity. Even those groups that endured institutionalized discrimination, like Black workers, for the most part saw a rise in their standard of living. In fact, as figure 6.2 shows, the earnings gap between white and Black males closed considerably between 1940 and 1980: Black men's median incomes being about 38 percent of white men's and peaking at 60 percent.[9]

During the 1970s, economic pressure on US industry grew on a number of fronts. Europe and Japan rebounded fully from the lingering effects of war and were again capable of competing with core US industries. It took more intensive research and development, more worker skill enhancement, and more precise production methods to produce competitive, high-quality products. The era of US companies thoroughly dominating the global economy came to an end.

The costs of conducting the Cold War created significant burdens for the US economy. It cost dearly to support more than 700 military bases around the world while attempting to contain global communism.[10] Taking over the war in Vietnam from the French, who had fought in vain to maintain its anachronistic colony, was also very costly—tragically so to the several million Vietnamese and 50,000 Americans who died. The Vietnam War was disruptive to the US economy as well: $1 trillion (in 2022 dollars) was spent on war expenditures.[11] Postcolonial nationalism was the order of the day, and the United States suffered for trying to turn back the clock.

At about the same time, there were growing demands by civil rights groups for a significant increase in government social spending to end poverty. It was time, they argued, to share American prosperity with those who had been shut out and left behind. But all this military spending made it more difficult to federally fund job-creation programs for low-income urban minorities and rural, predominately white populations in places like Appalachia.

With the economy running at full capacity, a classic "guns versus butter" dilemma forced a real choice on policymakers: Either continue massive military spending or provide economic support for the poor. The Vietnam War budget won out over the War on Poverty, and cities all over the country

Figure 6.2. Black men's median earnings as a percentage of white men's

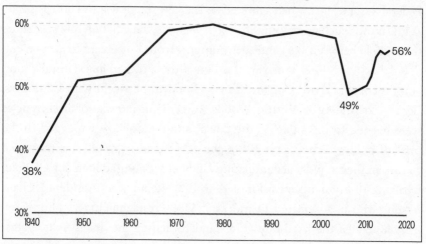

Source: New York Times[12]

suffered. In Detroit and Newark, rioting made it look like the Vietnam War had come home, with the National Guard occupying Black neighborhoods and gunning down dozens of residents in the process.

These were very dark days. Martin Luther King Jr. and Robert Kennedy were assassinated in 1968. With antiwar sentiment rising, President Lyndon Johnson, who had won a historic landslide in 1964, dropped out of the race for a second term. The 1968 Democratic Convention in Chicago to choose a new presidential candidate turned into a police riot captured live on prime-time television. In the late 1960s, radical groups were bombing dozens of Bank of America branches. George Wallace, the avid segregationist, was running for president as a third-party candidate, and winning the South and about 10 percent of Northern states. The country was split down the middle on the Vietnam War and fractured over civil rights as well.

And yet, the economy was humming like never before. In 1969, unemployment was reduced to what was at that time a post-WWII low of 3.5 percent. Americans were, on average, getting wealthier. But, in fact, the economy was overheating. According to Keynesian economic theory, sizable tax increases, large budget cuts, or higher interest rates from the Federal Reserve were required to prevent inflation. But President Johnson definitely did not want to broadcast to the public what the war in Vietnam really cost, and he didn't want the Fed to slam on the brakes before the 1968 election. To placate the Federal Reserve, he pushed a limited tax increase, but it was too little too late. With far too much money chasing too few goods, the inflation rate rose more than sixfold between 1964 and 1969, jumping from 1.0 percent to 6.2 percent.

At the same time, the war, the hundreds of US military installations, and US corporate overseas investments flooded the world with US dollars. Because of the 1944 Bretton Woods Agreement, international currencies were pegged to the value of the dollar, and the dollar was pegged to the price of gold, which was set at $36 per troy ounce. As other countries tried to cash in their rapidly accumulating (and depreciating) dollars for US gold, a balance-of-payments crisis loomed. In 1971, Republican President Richard Nixon (who had defeated Democratic Vice President Hubert Humphrey in 1968) ended the fixed-rate gold standard, letting the dollar float against other currencies—a policy change economists had been suggesting for years. While the move was almost certainly the right one, it also led to an increase in the price of imports, further fueling the inflationary surge.

Though Nixon had railed against price controls during WWII, he instituted them in 1971 to beat back the spiraling inflation. The inflation rate fell to a more reasonable 3.4 percent in 1972, but history teaches that inflationary periods make economies vulnerable to unforeseen shocks. One such shock hit with a fury during the 1973 Arab–Israeli War. When the United States provided critical weaponry to the Israelis, OPEC (the Organization of the Petroleum Exporting Countries; the cartel of Arab oil-producing states) initiated an oil embargo, which more than quadrupled the price of oil and led to shortages and long lines at gas stations across the US. Because the massive US economy had evolved during an era of very cheap oil, the oil shock caused further price increases throughout the economy. Unions, still relatively strong at this point, had negotiated many contracts with cost-of-living clauses, so wages rose along with inflation, which led to even more price increases.

The United States then experienced a phenomenon that was theoretically impossible, according to Keynesian economics: *stagflation*, a combination of both rising inflation and rising unemployment. In 1974, unemployment hit 7.2 percent while inflation soared to 12.3 percent, both post-WWII highs. This created a painful policy dilemma. Lowering unemployment by cutting taxes or spending money to create new jobs would push up prices. But lowering inflation by cutting government spending, raising taxes, or increasing interest rates would slow the economy down, sending unemployment skyward.

Enter Milton Friedman and Trickle-Down Economics

Milton Friedman, the star of the conservative economists, had a ready answer, one that he and others at the University of Chicago had been developing for years: If the goal is freedom and prosperity, the corporate drive for profits is all that counts!

In a widely read column in the *New York Times*, written in 1970, Friedman argued it was time for corporations to stop pretending to have a social conscience. The purpose of business, he argued, is not about "providing employment, eliminating discrimination, avoiding pollution and whatever else may be the catchwords of the contemporary crop of reformers. . . . Businessmen who talk this way are unwitting puppets of the intellectual forces that have been undermining the basis of a free society these past decades."[13] Instead, Friedman claimed that in a free society "there is one and only one social responsibility of business—to use its resources and engage in activities designed to increase its profits."

Friedman was driven to write this piece because Campaign GM, an effort by a group of young consumer-advocate lawyers, put forth resolutions at General Motors (GM) shareholder meetings demanding that the company add three new members to the board to represent the public interest—René Dubos, a biologist on President Nixon's Citizens' Advisory Committee on Environmental Quality; Reverend Channing Phillips, a Black civil rights leader; and Betty Furness, consumer adviser to President Johnson. The goal was to encourage more public accountability from GM concerning safety, pollution, and minority employment.[14] The proposal was rejected, but GM did set up an ad-hoc public interest committee.[15]

In effect, the Chicago School of Economics put forth what labor economist Ken Peres called the Better Business Climate model: cut taxes, cut regulations, and cut social welfare programs, then privatize as many government services as possible (see figure 6.3 on page 90). The theory was (and still is) that less government will lead to more incentive to work, more investment, more profits, and more jobs, all without inflation and high unemployment.

Members of both political parties flocked to this model. Deregulation seemed like an inexpensive and politically pain-free policy to adopt. What

Figure 6.3. The Better Business Climate model (neoliberalism)

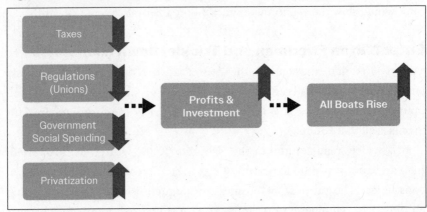

Source: The Labor Institute

resistance there once was to deregulation collapsed, in part because Americans' trust in government and labor unions had plummeted. This lack of trust happened for a number of reasons:

- The government's lies about the Vietnam War undermined its trustworthy image. Faith in government crashed from 75 percent in 1965 to 54 percent in 1970.[16] Much of the 1960s generation felt betrayed after being asked to serve in a bloody war that had been justified by a nonstop series of fabrications. The widespread prosecution of recreational drug use only added to alienation from government. The youth rebellion of the 1960s was also, for many, a libertarian revolt against not only big government but big corporations, big labor, and big everything (except big rock concerts). The freedom to live as you wished seemed antithetical to government controls.
- Then came Watergate, the constellation of crimes perpetrated by President Nixon to secure his reelection in 1972. Within two years he became the first president to resign from office, with his own tape recordings revealing the extent of his crimes. His vice president, Gerald Ford, took office and soon pardoned Nixon, which further lowered trust in government. After Jimmy Carter was elected in 1976 and failed to revive the economy during his only term, trust in government fell to a new low. In 1980 it stood at only 25 percent.

- The congressional hearings led by Senator Frank Church in 1975 further eroded faith in government. Those hearings revealed scores of political dirty tricks conducted by US government agencies, including assassination attempts on foreign leaders and the illegal monitoring of American citizens in the United States. Among the targets were Supreme Court justices, reporters, government officials, and political activists. Also revealed was the FBI wiretapping of Martin Luther King Jr.[17] This was not a government to be proud of.

- Government support for the civil rights movement alienated millions who harbored racial resentments, especially among white Southern Democrats, who had switched en masse to the Republican Party during the Nixon years. By enforcing antidiscrimination laws like school integration and calling in National Guard troops for enforcement, the federal government became their enemy. Even state governments north of the Mason–Dixon line faced backlash in response to fair-housing rules, busing to desegregate schools, and affirmative action policies that benefited those who had been systematically excluded.

- Large labor unions also faced a crisis of legitimacy among their members. Rank and file caucuses sprang up, often led by younger activists rebelling against the leadership's support for the Vietnam War and efforts to suppress internal union democracy. Some of the biggest unions, notably the Teamsters and the United Mine Workers of America, were riddled with corruption and nepotism, further alienating their own members and the public.

The Powell Memo

Attitudes about corporate responsibility started to change in earnest when significant amounts of corporate money start to flow to the Heritage Foundation, founded in 1973, and the reconstructed American Enterprise Institute. The goal of these think tanks was to wage ideological battle within the academic and policy communities, grooming a new generation of free-market ideologues. They played a long game.

The intellectual foundation for these institutions grew in large part out of a highly influential memo written in 1971 by Lewis F. Powell Jr. for the US Chamber of Commerce.

Ironically, Powell wasn't worried about government controls on Wall Street or the proliferation of social welfare programs like Medicare and Social Security. He wasn't concerned about civil rights legislation, unlike the Republicans aligned with Senator Barry Goldwater.

Instead, Powell was concerned that the entire system was under attack by a combination of radical students, professors, and journalists. And the biggest threat of all, he believed, came from Ralph Nader: "Perhaps the single most effective antagonist of American business is Ralph Nader who—thanks largely to the media—has become a legend in his own time and an idol of millions of Americans."[18]

Powell quoted from a *Fortune* article, describing the devil incarnate, and fretted that Nader would bring class war to America:

> The passion that rules in him—and he is a passionate man—is aimed at smashing utterly the target of his hatred, which is corporate power. He thinks, and says quite bluntly, that a great many corporate executives belong in prison. . . . This setting of "the rich" against the poor, of business against the people, is the cheapest and most dangerous kind of politics.

Powell claimed that business had responded to this calamity "by appeasement, ineptitude and ignoring the problem." Although they knew how to run their businesses, he said, "they have shown little stomach for the hardnosed contest with their critics, and little skill in effective intellectual and philosophical debate."

At stake for Powell was nothing short of the "survival of what we call the free enterprise system, and all that this means for the strength and prosperity of America and the freedom of our people."

To halt this assault, he argued, required business to exert its influence by developing stronger and more sophisticated public relations. This, he said, would bring more free-market professors into universities, lead to equal time for non-leftist speakers, and create more "balanced" textbooks. But he cautioned, "The objective always must be to inform and enlighten, and not merely to propagandize." Powell wanted to bring new conservative voices to the media, scholarly journals, books, paperbacks, and pamphlets, as well as in paid advertisements.

Powell lamented that business was so weak in the political arena. The "Marxist doctrine that the 'capitalist' countries are controlled by big business" was just not true, he said. If only! He implored big business to combat the forces of consumer protection and environmentalism, which he said were relentlessly attacking free enterprise. He saw great potential in mobilizing 20 million American stockholders as voters to promote "a genuine understanding of our system or in exercising political influence."

Learning from the left, Powell wanted business interests to influence the courts the way the American Civil Liberties Union did. Surely they could foster a new generation of jurists who supported business and free enterprise. Couldn't they?

All in all, Powell was calling for a massive intellectual and political mobilization to protect business from the likes of Ralph Nader and his minions. Corporations needed to invest more money in politics and conservative think tanks—and learn to become aggressive. He wrote:

> There should be no hesitation to attack the Naders, the Marcuses* and others who openly seek destruction of the system. There should be not the slightest hesitation to press vigorously in all political arenas for support of the enterprise system. Nor should there be reluctance to penalize politically those who oppose it.

The fight was fundamental—regulation for the public interest versus reliance on the creativity of free markets. The battleground was the public domain—winning the hearts and minds of the people. The corporate mobilization that Powell inspired would focus like a laser on getting the government out of the economy.

(Shortly after writing this memo, Louis F. Powell Jr. was appointed to the Supreme Court by Richard Nixon. In 1973, he unexpectedly voted to legalize abortion in *Roe v. Wade*.)

---

* Herbert Marcuse, a neo-Marxist scholar from the Frankfurt School of Critical Theory, was very popular with the New Left during this period.

Deregulatory Foreplay

With deregulation becoming attractive to politicians of all stripes, in the mid-1970s, President Ford went after trucking regulations (something that Nixon had refused to do for fear of alienating the industry and the Teamsters Union, which supported him politically).

Until this point, US trucking rates and routes were regulated by a combination of federal rules and Teamsters contracts. As a result, unionized truck drivers did very well, earning about 20 percent more than unionized autoworkers. Following Ford's deregulation, thousands of new trucking businesses flooded the market, and workers' wages collapsed. Shipping costs radically declined, too, eventually facilitating the rise of big box stores and companies like Amazon.[19]

Trucking deregulation also ushered in a new phenomenon—contingent labor. Instead of working for a single company, contingent laborers worked for contracting firms that supplied labor for multiple employers in a particular industry. As trucking became more competitive, many drivers decided they would have more control over their lives if they bought their own trucks and contracted themselves out to employers. This was ideal from the corporate point of view since these independent truckers took on responsibility for their equipment and their own benefits. Ultimately, this led to a terrible downward spiral. Wages for independent truckers today can be so low that many barely earn minimum wage.

As deregulation and mass layoffs spread through the economy, more and more economic space was created for subcontractors and contingent labor. In all kinds of industries, contingent workers are forced to compete for work, driving down wages and benefits alike.

Jimmy Carter, who defeated Ford for the presidency in 1976, further pressed the deregulatory agenda. Joined by Ted Kennedy, one of the Senate's most liberal Democrats, he pushed hard for the deregulation of the airlines, arguing that increased competition would lower prices and expand airline travel.

By the end of the decade, deregulation had become the new mantra, the new cure-all and new antidote to lowering inflation. It was claimed that deregulation would increase competition and efficiency, tame big unions, and then break the back of inflation while also making US industry more competitive globally.

President Carter did not get the opportunity to see his deregulatory vision play out. He lost the 1980 election to Ronald Reagan, in part because of another oil price shock out of the Middle East. After decades of US support for the autocratic Shah of Iran, Mohammad Reza Pahlavi, an Islamic revolution ousted him and held hostage 52 US embassy personnel in Tehran for 444 days. During this turmoil, the price of crude oil rose yet again, accelerating inflation in the United States. Prices shot up by 13.3 percent in 1979 and another 12.5 percent in 1980, even as unemployment jumped to 8.5 percent.

Deregulation meant something very personal for many who fought to get the government off their backs. Deregulation created golden opportunities for financial elites to make more and more money. Their rebellion against regulations was also a rebellion against equality. Economist Claudia Goldin refers to the period between WWII and 1980 as the "Great Compression." Income and wealth between the top and the bottom were more evenly distributed than ever before. To be sure, there still were millions of wealthy people who lived on large estates, sent their kids to exclusive private schools, flew in private planes, had multiple homes, and could afford the most expensive of creature comforts. But the gap was modest by today's standards, as figure 6.4 shows.

Figure 6.4. Average income of top 1 percent versus bottom 90 percent
(in 2021 dollars, adjusted for inflation)

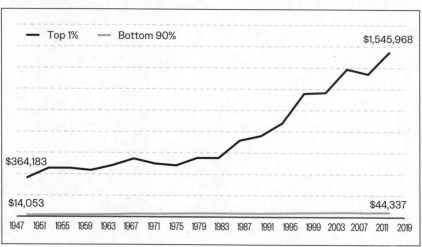

Source: World Inequality Database[20]

The Deregulation Agenda

Michael Jensen, a highly influential conservative economist during the 1980s, was a fierce advocate for financial deregulation and maximizing shareholder value. He believed that "populist laws and regulations approved in the wake of the Great Depression" prevented corporate raiding, and such raiding, he believed, would be good for the economy.[21]

Jensen made it clear precisely which laws and regulations had to go, or at least be greatly relaxed: "the Glass-Steagall Banking Act of 1933, the Securities Act of 1933, the Securities Exchange Act of 1934, the Chandler Bankruptcy Revision Act of 1938, and the Investment Company Act of 1940." He believed these laws and regulations "created an intricate web of restrictions on company 'insiders' (corporate officers, directors, or investors with more than a 10% ownership interest), restrictions on bank involvement in corporate reorganizations, court precedents, and business practices that raised the cost of being an active investor." As each of these regulations was weakened or removed, "insiders" would cash in, extracting more and more wealth for themselves.

Figure 6.5. CEO-to-worker pay gap soars
How much a top-100 CEO got in compensation for every $1 earned by the average worker

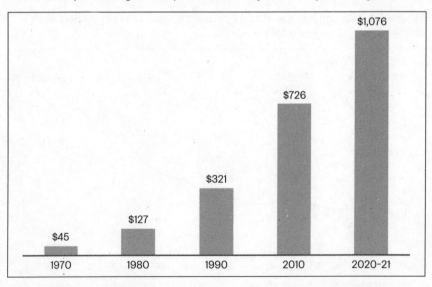

Sources: Forbes, Equilar/New York Times, Equilar/AP, Bureau of Labor Statistics[22]

The new agenda of deregulation opened the door to the unconstrained pursuit of more and more riches. Friedman, Jensen, and others provided the intellectual justification for increasing inequality. They made the case that the pursuit of profits and wealth was an absolute good, not only for the individual but for the entire society. That pursuit, they argued, created an incentive to take risks and innovate, thereby creating more jobs and income for everyone. Corporate managers, they believed, should focus on enhancing short-term shareholder value above everything else, since the shareholders are the owners and allegedly the true risk-takers.

What they probably also understood but refrained from saying in public was that the deregulatory movement justified out-and-out greed. The more money you could make, the better. You might even consider it your patriotic duty. President Kennedy's call, "Ask not what your country can do for you, ask what you can do for your country," was turned inside out. It became "Ask not what you can do for your country other than to make as much money as possible for yourself!"

As we shall see, this new era of greed enabled the few to make vast fortunes by destroying the livelihoods of the many through mass layoffs.

CHAPTER 7

After Greed Was Good

How Wall Street Looting Normalized Mass Layoffs

"It is terrifying to be that age and be literally out on the street. What did I have? Mostly custodial skills, a little bit of maintenance skills. I had worked at McDonald's years ago and it's like, what am I going to do?"
—Diane, age 61, laid off after 17 years of service

FROM 1980 TO 1988, PRESIDENT RONALD REAGAN INJECTED THE deregulatory agenda with steroids. He became the first president in memory to explicitly run against the entire idea of government with a special emphasis on eliminating government regulations. He famously said, "The nine most terrifying words in the English language are: I'm from the government, and I'm here to help."

Reagan had no use for interference in the economy from the government or from the biggest interferer of them all—labor unions.

After spending years as a highly paid spokesperson for General Electric (now GE), a notoriously anti-union company, Reagan understood that labor unions are a major regulatory force that constrains corporate power.[1] Union contracts bring enforceable rules into the workplace. Government regulations on pollution and safety might lead to periodic inspections, but from the perspective of a corporation like GE, unions are there 24/7, undermining management control. How were American corporations going to win the global competition, the argument went, with unions clogging up the works?

Nevertheless, until 1980 or so, most managers viewed unions as a fact of life. You had to bargain with them. You wanted to avoid strikes. And even if you didn't have a union at your company, you needed to match union wages and benefits to attract and hold your employees and to delay (if not prevent) unionization. Even the notoriously pro-business Powell memo did not attack labor unions.

Of course, a significant number of employers resented unions and tried to undermine them. For example, major corporations in the construction industry were eager to break the back of the powerful unionized construction trades, which represented nearly 40 percent of their workforce. Union density was particularly high in metropolitan areas, where large corporations often located their factories and offices. In the late 1960s, a handful of CEOs of large corporations organized a well-funded union-busting coalition, eventually called the Business Roundtable, with the express purpose of replacing as many of their unionized workers as possible with nonunion labor. The Roundtable also wanted to undermine labor's ability to picket construction sites and enforce union contracts. By 1982, Charles Brown, former CEO of DuPont and a Roundtable leader, could boast about the group's successes: "The construction industry was monopolized by the union segment with no apparent alternative in sight. Fortunately for all of us, the capitalistic system worked again. 'Free market' forces prevailed."[2]

Reagan took the Business Roundtable message and amplified it so that every corporation in every industry heard it loud and clear. In 1981, he fired and then permanently replaced around 12,000 air traffic controllers who, in defiance of federal law banning public employee strikes, walked off the job after failed contract negotiations.* The controllers' union, the Professional Air Traffic Controllers Organization (PATCO), along with the rest of the labor movement, was stunned. It had long been customary, when strikes violated the law, for an eventual settlement to lead to some fines on the union for illegally striking. No one at that time could recall replacing the entire bargaining unit with nonunion workers, especially in the government sector.

Labor reacted. More than 400,000 supporters attended a demonstration on September 19, 1981, at the National Mall in Washington called Solidarity Day—a reference to the anti-communist Solidarity labor movement in Poland that gained worldwide popularity in the early 1980s. Many expected and hoped that the crowd, urged by national labor leaders, would march to

---

* In striking, the union violated 5 USC (Supp. III 1956) 118p (now 5 USC § 7311), which prohibits strikes by federal government employees.

National Airport, shutting it down until Reagan agreed to bargain in good faith and rehire the PATCO workers.

That kind of labor militancy made the staid AFL-CIO president Lane Kirkland very uncomfortable. As a player within the highest levels of the Democratic Party establishment, he tried to rally the crowd with, "The next Solidarity Day is Election Day!" If workers could just get Democrats elected, he argued, the PATCO members would be rehired. That never happened.

A year later, a socially conservative Catholic construction worker in Milwaukee shared his thoughts with me about the destruction of PATCO: "We should have laid down our tools nationwide when Reagan did that."

Corporate America certainly got the new message. Although it had been legal since the 1930s to replace striking workers with nonunion workers, the tactic was rarely used for fear of making the strike even more disruptive and possibly getting labor-friendly government regulators and the courts involved.

Now Reagan declared open season on striking workers, providing a template for corporate managers nationwide on how to topple unions. The message from Reagan was clear: You no longer need to put up with unions. You want to crush them? Go ahead. The government will not interfere.

Wall Street, Liberated!

While Reagan overtly attacked the regulatory power of unions, a quieter and subtler but no less devastating campaign to free Wall Street from as many regulations as possible was also underway. Financial elites wanted to unshackle themselves from the myriad of 1930s regulations and agencies put in place to combat the Great Depression and prevent another one. Wall Street envisioned a new way of doing business that would extract wealth as quickly as possible.

By the 1980s, a half century after the Depression, proponents of deregulation argued that those old rules and protections were now antiquated and unnecessary. Their step-by-step removal of regulations was the start of a long period of worker wage stagnation. Deregulation greatly accelerated mass layoffs which, in turn, contributed mightily to growing inequality. This steady eradication of rules regulating corporations also marked the beginning of the end of the Democratic Party's longstanding support of the working class. After all, the Democrats also jumped on the deregulatory bandwagon and even helped to vote in the Reagan tax cuts that benefited the rich. After the election of President Clinton in 1996, Democrats led the charge to implement new corporate-friendly trade deals and further regulatory relief for Wall Street.

The deregulation of the finance industry happened across two decades and three presidents (Reagan, Bush, and Clinton, 1980–2000). They delivered for Wall Street primarily in two ways: by gutting antitrust enforcement and by legalizing stock manipulation. Both moves radically changed the face of our economy and led to a nationwide scourge of mass layoffs. Between 1996 and 2012 alone, 20,186,640 workers suffered mass layoffs, according to the Bureau of Labor Statistics.[3]

Wall Street Playing Monopoly

First came the gutting of antitrust enforcement. As these guardrails were removed, corporate mergers and acquisitions became a booming business. Corporations gained more power and became ever bolder as the SEC and the Antitrust Division of the Justice Department refused to step in to limit highly leveraged mergers and consolidations.

Proponents of this hands-off stance argued that banks and corporations needed to grow larger to compete globally. If consolidation didn't overtly harm the consumer (usually measured by higher prices), then the merger would be approved by the Antitrust Division. In this global economy, monopolies didn't really exist, the argument went. There was always competition coming from other countries that would keep markets competitive.

Financial deregulation meant that banks were allowed to buy other banks almost at will. During the Clinton years, the Glass–Steagall Act, which separated commercial banking from riskier investment banking, was repealed. Insurance companies and banks also began to merge after Citigroup and Travelers Insurance led the charge.

Some corporations, like GE, led by Jack Welch, turned acquiring companies from many different sectors into a compulsion. "Neutron Jack" couldn't get enough of it. Buying other companies, however, nearly always led rapidly to the slashing of payrolls. Welch believed that the bottom 10 percent of all operations should be cut every year, and any division that wasn't first or second in its field should be dropped. Such practices could make a lot of money, but the cost was actually borne by workers and the communities where these companies were located. While swashbuckling capitalists like Welch set the tone, the practice could only happen if government turned a blind eye.

This was especially true when it came to financial power. To buy up companies required money—usually borrowed money, and lots of it. It became commonplace for companies to finance their acquisitions with debt and then place the debt on the books of the acquired company.

Was this permitted by law? The Celler–Kefauver Act (1950) and the Williams Act (1968) could have been used to prevent hostile takeovers but were ignored. The Reagan administration had no desire to limit this activity. Deregulation was the order of the day. The SEC could have used existing laws to intervene if it found that the behavior was threatening to the economy, but it didn't. Instead, the SEC allowed Michael Milken, on behalf of the Wall Street firm Drexel Burnham Lambert, to create what turned out to be a very shady "junk bond" market to finance mergers and acquisitions. By the end of 1990, Milken was in jail and Drexel Burnham Lambert had collapsed, the first Wall Street firm to go bankrupt since the Great Depression.[4] Thousands of savings and loan banks, many of which had gobbled up the junk bonds as they fished for high yields, went belly-up, costing taxpayers an estimated $124 billion.[5]

Before this 1980s "greed is good" zeitgeist, corporations were not often loaded up with debt—junk or otherwise. Perhaps they feared that the regulatory arms of the government would intrude. Or perhaps they didn't like the stigma and the potential risk of carrying so much debt. Whatever the underlying motivation, corporate debt was practically unheard of before the new era of deregulation began. If a company wanted to buy a different business— which was not uncommon during the 1960s conglomerate era—it used its own profits, not debt, to close the deal. Clearly that changed with a vengeance.

As figure 7.1 (see page 104) clearly shows, corporate debt ballooned beginning in the late 1970s and accelerated as the deregulatory policies of the Reagan/Bush/Clinton years kicked it into high gear.

Once a company is purchased via massive debt financing, the pressure mounts to reorganize and downsize the workforce. Do you really need two HR departments or two accounting staffs? Why so many bank branches? Surely you can combine divisions and cut down headcounts here, there, and everywhere. In this way, debt financing and boosting profits went hand in hand with mass layoffs. And they still do.

Figure 7.1. Corporate debt (annual, seasonally adjusted), 1946–2022

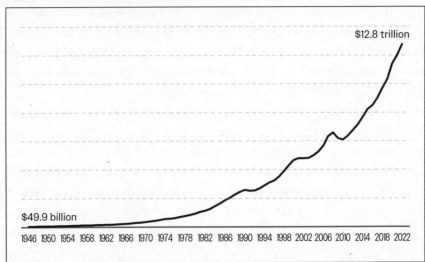

Source: Federal Reserve Bank of St. Louis[6]

Over time, the debt burden put on the purchased corporations threatened their viability, leading to bankruptcies and more mass layoffs. Reagan's own SEC chair, John Shad, a former officer of the Wall Street firm EF Hutton, identified this problem in 1984: "The more leveraged takeovers and buyouts now, the more bankruptcies tomorrow."[7] But after getting pushback from the Reaganites, he did nothing about it.[8]

Legalized Stock Manipulation

The second way that government delivered for Wall Street during the 1980s and 1990s was by facilitating stock manipulation via stock buybacks. Our economy has never been the same since.

Before 1982, stock buybacks, if done in large quantities, were considered a form of stock manipulation. And stock manipulation of any kind is a big no-no in finance and one of the suspected causes of the Great Depression. In market theory, no single buyer or seller should have sufficient market power to manipulate the price. This was forbidden by the Securities Exchange Act of 1934. Until the1980s, corporations avoided stock buybacks.

But SEC chair John Shad had the agency adopt a new rule (10b-18) that in effect enabled a corporation to pour its profits into its own stock without fear of getting nailed for stock manipulation.[9] It was assumed that this must be the best use of its capital. If it *wasn't* the best use of its capital, then supposedly the company would suffer and lose out to other more capital-efficient companies—the law of the capitalist jungle and the key to our prosperity. Or so the theory goes. Shad posited that whatever was good for the shareholder would be good for the economy. More money circulating through financial markets would lead to more money available for capital formation—the facilitation of investments that help us produce more.

It's highly doubtful that Shad, who died in 1994, had any idea what he had unleashed. He was from old school Wall Street, and his free-market theories were relics of a bygone era. He believed your word was your bond, your handshake was as good as a written contract, and you just didn't cheat your Ivy League corporate buddies. Shad even endowed the Harvard Business School's Business Leadership and Ethics program. But he never realized that in the unfolding "greed is good" world, it was all about finding the quickest way to get rich, with nary a thought for the impact on working people and their communities or even other Wall Streeters.

Shad's former firm, EF Hutton, certainly was deep into the greed game: In 1985, it got charged and fined for "2,000 counts of wire and mail fraud for using a scheme similar to 'check kiting' to fraudulently obtain as much as $250 million in interest-free funds a day from 400 banks across the country," according to the *Los Angeles Times*.[10]

In the early 1980s, corporate raiders (today called private equity and hedge fund managers) set about buying up company after company using borrowed money. To profit from these investments, the raiders needed to have CEOs fully committed to driving up the price of the stock, at which point the raiders could cash out and make a killing. But how do you, a corporate raider, get the CEO and top officers to do what needs to be done?

Left on their own, some business leaders might have decided to invest in the skills and safety of their employees, or to expand research and development, or to just give themselves more perks. For corporate raiders, however, that would not do. Their goal was to get the CEO to focus on the stock price and only the stock price. And the best way to do that, it turned out, was to make sure nearly all CEO compensation came in the form of stock grants and options, not in salaries and bonuses. That way, the CEO's interests would be tightly aligned with the raiders' greed. If the CEOs drove up the price of the stock, the major stock owners and top officers would prosper.

So, what's the best way to jack up the share price if you're the CEO? Skill-up your workforce? No. Create successful new products? No again. Develop new markets? Takes too long. A much surer and quicker path is to squeeze the company for every bit of cash you can find, and then use that money to buy back the company's own shares. During a buyback, the price of the stock goes up, which immediately benefits you and makes your major shareholders very happy. The sooner you can do this, the better.

Inevitably, the need to locate the cash for buybacks creates pressure for . . . mass layoffs. Send the plant to Mexico. Reduce the research staff. Get rid of all those workers who do preventive maintenance. Cut the environmental control staff. Cut, cut, and cut again. And then take that money and buy back more stock. Down the road, if the cycle of cuts and buybacks harms the company to the point it can't survive, so be it. If all goes well, you will have cashed out your stock long before the doors are shuttered.

Is this for real or is it just some crazed anticorporate conspiracy theory? Well, take a look at the data. Figure 7.2 shows the proportion of CEO pay from salary and bonuses as compared to stock incentives. Figure 7.3, which inevitably follows from figure 7.2, shows the incredible rise in the percent of all profits going into stock buybacks.

Take a close look again at figure 7.3. It shows that, as of 2018, nearly 70 percent of all corporate profits were going to stock buybacks! Not to research and development, not to normal dividends, certainly not to worker raises and improved benefits. After the early 1980s, corporations have increasingly decided that a big part of their businesses, maybe the major part, is to buy back their own stock.[11]

What should a CEO do when the company runs out of profits to fund stock buybacks with? That's simple: Put more debt on the company and use the borrowed money for *more* stock buybacks. Hundreds and hundreds of companies are doing that right now. In fact, JPMorgan Chase reports that in 2016 and 2017, up to 30 percent of stock buybacks were funded by corporate debt.[12] To pay the interest on all that debt, of course, creates more pressure for mass layoffs.

How many corporations really do this? The Academic-Industry Research Network calculated the profits going to stock buybacks from 2012 to 2021

Figure 7.2. How the top 500 executives are paid (2018)

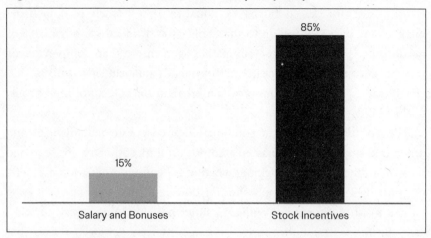

Source: Matt Hopkins[13]

Figure 7.3 Stock buybacks as a percent of all profits

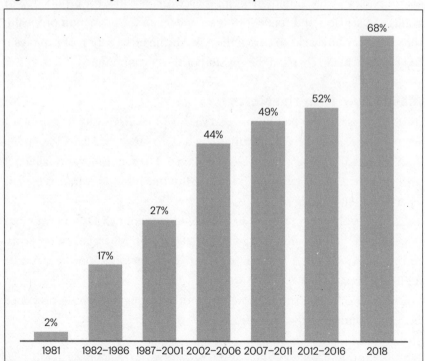

Source: S&P Compustat[14]

for 474 Fortune 500 corporations. Those businesses "funneled $5.7 trillion into the stock market as buybacks, equal to 55% of their combined net income, and paid $4.2 trillion to shareholders as dividends, another 41% of net income."[15] Sixty of these companies spent more than 100 percent of their profits on stock buybacks. And if dividends are included, then 38.4 percent of these 474 corporations moved more than 100 percent of their profits to shareholders.[16]

There's little doubt that the combination of corporate debt financing and unfettered stock buybacks has created powerful incentives to go "lean and mean"—to send workers packing, whether by shifting production overseas, outsourcing at home, or simply shutting down entire operations.

The work of economist William Lazonick highlighting stock buybacks (see "Profits Without Prosperity," *Harvard Business Review*[17]) shows that modern business is undergoing a profound paradigm shift. It was once generally believed that the goal of capitalist enterprises was to create high-quality goods and services, and to make a reasonable profit doing so, while also providing stable employment for their workers. Now, the production of goods and services and stable jobs is secondary to the extraction of wealth through stock buybacks to enrich the few. The financialization of capitalism has fundamentally changed the mission of the corporation.

Mass Layoffs in the News

By 1996, mass layoffs had become so massive that *Newsweek*, then one of the nation's leading news magazines, ran a cover story by Allan Sloan titled "Corporate Killers," in 50-point blood-red type. The subhead was smaller but no less telling: "Wall Street Loves Layoffs. But the Public Is Scared as Hell. Is There a Better Way?"[18]

The cover also features mugshot-like photos of four CEOs with captions that read: "Robert B. Palmer, Digital, Cut 20,000 jobs; Albert J. Dunlop, Scott, Cut 11,000 jobs; Robert E. Allen, AT&T, Cut 40,000 jobs; Louis V. Gerstner Jr., IBM, Cut 60,000 jobs."

The interior layout shows more mugshots that might be better described as trophy pictures of the number of kills:

- Walter Shipley, CEO, Chemical/Chase Manhattan, 12,000 layoffs
- Charles Lee, CEO, GTE Corp., 17,000 layoffs

- John McDonnell, Chairman, McDonnell Douglas, 17,000 layoffs
- Robert Stempel, former CEO, General Motors, 74,000 layoffs
- Edward Brennan, former CEO, Sears and Roebuck, 50,000 layoffs
- Michael Mills, former CEO, Phillip Morris, 14,000 layoffs
- Frank Shrontz, CEO, Boeing, 28,000 layoffs
- William Ferguson, former CEO, NYNEX, 16,800 layoffs

Although the piece makes no pretense of providing economic analysis, it does have some zingers:

> Indeed, one reason that chief executives are meaner and greedier than they used to be is the 1980s: no company was safe from raiders if its stock price was depressed. If you didn't unload your losers and fire "surplus" workers, a takeover troll would buy your company and fire everybody. . . .
>
> Al Dunlap has become the poster boy for the folks who say CEOs have gone too far. The 58-year-old CEO of Scott Paper, known to detractors as "Chainsaw Al," cut 11,000 jobs in 1994. After merging the company with Kimberly-Clark, he walked away with about $100 million in salary and stock profits and other perks. Dunlap previously downsized seven other companies.

Newsweek played to the worries of its audience by conjuring up a parade of negative phrases to describe mass layoffs: "discarded"; "fired"; "downsized"; "littered with bodies"; "mass firings"; "job cutting"; "keeping payrolls lean"; "Wall Street spitting on the victims' bodies"; "zapping workers to cut down costs"; "slaughtered *en masse*"; "thousands of little people were fired to save money"; and "he loved downsizing in the early 1990s." And our personal favorite, "offer up employees as human sacrifices to Mammon, God of Wall Street."

Despite this searing account of job destruction, Sloan's proposed solution was hopelessly trapped within his own libertarian ideology: "The federal government can't save us. . . . And we can't go back to the days of the 1950s and '60s when big companies offered lifetime employment. . . . You solve this problem one company at a time with innovative programs."

Since this 1996 *Newsweek* piece, at least another 30 million workers have succumbed to mass layoffs, "one company at a time."

Contingent Labor

Some AT&T workers quoted in the *Newsweek* story said that their boss, Robert Allen, "will soon fire everyone but himself, and AT&T will stand for 'Allen & Two Temps.'" This gallows humor reflects the devilish connection between mass layoffs and contingent labor. Theoretically, as one goes up, so will the other. And that's exactly what has happened.

Once mass layoffs were normalized, it became clear to corporate America and Wall Street profiteers that companies were no longer obliged to provide stable employment or even to offer traditional forms of employment within the corporation. Much more money could be made for CEOs and wealthy shareholders if the company shed workers and used cheaper contingent labor to fulfill many of their functions.

While many congressional Democrats sided with Reagan on tax cuts and financial deregulation that increased inequality, many also worried about the rise of contingent labor—the early stages of the gig economy. In 1986, they passed legislation, signed by Reagan, that was meant to shut down the worker-leasing business, as it was then called. The legislation, however, did not eliminate worker leasing. A Bureau of Labor Statistics report released in 1996 revealed that up to 6 million workers still could be considered contingent. From there it grew and grew.[19]

Even without knowing the exact number of contingent workers in the United States, we all can see that the gig economy is everywhere. And it's not just Uber, Lyft, DoorDash, and Amazon. For most companies in America, temporary workers are a vast corporate money-saver and money-maker. In a report to Congress in 2015, the Government Accountability Office found that contingent laborers made up more than 40 percent of the labor force in 2010 (see figure 7.4). Staffing Industry Analysts reported that 52.0 million workers (35 percent of the workforce) were contingent workers in 2021.[20]

In 2022, MBO Partners, a management consulting firm, released a report that said, "nearly one in three workers at large enterprises are already contingent. The number is growing and growing even faster if you already use contingent labor."

They went on to raise their champagne glasses in praise: "Contingent labor is the gift that keeps giving. . . . Once it is a corporate imperative, benefits are seen, it is used strategically, and firms use even more contingent labor."[21]

Figure 7.4. The explosive rise of contingent labor
Contingent workers as a percent of total workforce

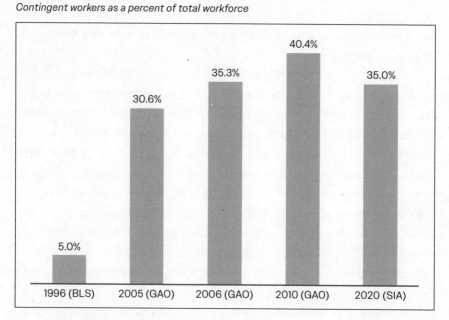

Source: *BLS, GAO, SIA*[22]

We appear to be headed to a brave new atomized world where no one, except a few elites, has steady employment. Management replaces laid-off workers with contingent workers. Laid-off workers become contingent workers. We're all on our own, jumping from gig to gig, taking care of our own wages, benefits, and expenses . . . until we drop.

While this may not be problematic for a few highly skilled and paid STEM workers, it breeds high levels of insecurity for the rest of us. Not long ago, mass layoffs were justified by the excuse that they were necessary in order to save even more jobs. Now those jobs turn out to be contingent gigs. That's capitalism, and don't you dare stand in its way.

Prison Labor

As traditional employment collapses under the weight of mass layoffs and the growth of contingent labor, it is perhaps inevitable that new contraband markets form and thrive. The War on Drugs, initiated by Nixon, ramped up by Reagan, and then turbocharged during the Clinton administration, helped to develop a highly profitable illicit drug market.

We can refer to the drug dealers who furnish the country with an array of pleasure-inducing highs as drug entrepreneurs. They have set up illegal small businesses (and several massive ones as well) to serve the public—and of course earn profits.

Every new effort in the War on Drugs creates more profit opportunities for illegal drug entrepreneurs. The more government agencies enforce drug laws and try to halt the shipment of drugs from abroad or from domestic labs, the higher the street price goes. And the higher the prices, the more profits enjoyed by, yes, good old capitalistic risk-taking criminal entrepreneurs. Drug enforcement, as opposed to legalization, is a classic price-support system, no different in effect than tariffs. The money spent on the entire drug enforcement apparatus,[23] from the federal Drug Enforcement Administration to the local police, makes illicit drugs more valuable, pushing up their sale price from wholesale importers to street peddlers. And the more drug entrepreneurs who are apprehended, the higher the profits for the drug entrepreneurs who have *not* been apprehended.

The demand for feel-good drugs is as old as humankind. It is virtually insatiable. We know that the prohibition of alcohol in the 1920s did not work. And we know that the high demand for illicit drugs means that the supply will be produced no matter how draconian the laws and enforcement. The collateral damage, inevitably, will be an ever-increasing prison population, 45 percent of whom are there because of drug convictions.[24]

Government can pour billions of dollars into drug interdiction, but that won't quell demand, or the cravings of human nature. It also won't quell the demand for the good-paying jobs that drug dealing provides.

Free-market economics teaches us that more enforcement leads to more people in prison, leads to more profit for those in the trade, leads to more dealers entering the trade . . . leading to more crime and more prisoners. So, rather than taking on Wall Street's insatiable greed and creating stable employment for all, we now manufacture more prisoners than any country in the world. It all comes together in a tragic confluence of trends—more drug-related deaths (figure 7.5), more prisoners (figure 7.6), and more money for CEOs (figure 7.7 on page 114).

Note that all these trends kicked into high gear around 1980, just when Wall Street was unleashed.

Figure 7.5. Rise in drug-related deaths (per 100,000)

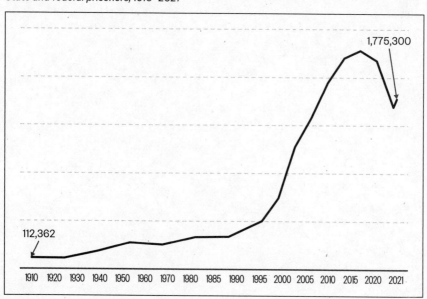

Sources: New York Times; National Center for Health Statistics; CDC/NCHS[25]

Figure 7.6. Rise of the prison population
State and federal prisoners, 1910–2021

Source: US Bureau of Justice Statistics[26]

Figure 7.7. Rise in CEO-to-worker pay gap

How much the CEO gets for every $1 earned by the average worker

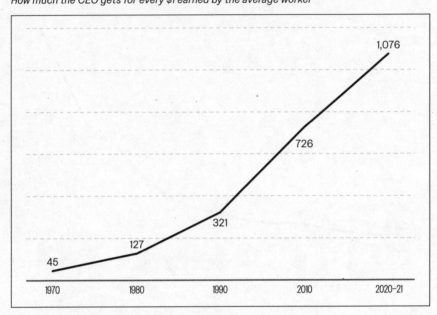

Sources: *Forbes, New York Times/Equilar, Bureau of Labor Statistics*[27]

CHAPTER 8

Halting Mass Layoffs

A Bridge Too Far for the Democrats?
How Joe Biden, Chuck Schumer, and
Bernie Sanders Refused to Intervene

"Having a family, being a single dad, it was very tough to be able to manage. . . . I just started cutting lawns and stuff on my own to try to make
ends meet. And I ended up losing my house in Grafton. . . . I mean, I
lost everything. . . . For a while there, I just, I wasn't eating. So then the
V.A. started supplying food for me to help me out food-wise, because
every penny I had, every penny I made went towards my children."

—"Jonathan Barton," age 38, laid off after 10 years of service

IN THE 1980S, COMMUNITY ORGANIZATIONS AND UNIONS ACROSS THE
country, especially in the Midwest, fought valiantly against factory closings.
Countless times, they struggled to organize worker buyouts of plants that
were about to close. Millions of dollars were spent on these efforts. And yet,
they mostly failed. It seemed that unless top political leaders were willing
to intervene and change the rules, worker buyouts were next to impossible.

Neither Reagan, nor Bush I, nor Clinton, nor Bush II, nor Obama intervened to prevent mass layoffs. The prevailing position in both political parties
was that these factory and office closures were bound up with the unstoppable forces of trade and technology. Trying to halt them would be like
standing in front of an economic tsunami.

Mostly these political leaders were able to get away with the job carnage—
especially if, as during the Clinton years, employment numbers eventually
rose. That the new jobs paid much less than the old, unionized jobs, and that
few jobs made their way into rural areas, didn't seem to matter to Democratic
or Republican party elites. Good times were rolling, and so were the votes.

By early in his first term, Clinton, ever astute, realized that the Democratic Party had bought the corporate logic that long characterized the party's Republican rivals. He reportedly said during an Oval Office meeting with key staff: "Where are all the Democrats? I hope you're all aware we're all Eisenhower Republicans. We're Eisenhower Republicans here. . . . We stand for lower deficits and free trade and the bond market. Isn't that great?"[1]

Clinton saw where the forces he faced were coming from and where they were headed, and he made the decision to go along with them. He, and later Obama, chose not to use their unique political gifts to fight for the imperiled manufacturing facilities that dotted the countryside. Neither would go to rural Pennsylvania, for example, to demand vehemently that a corporation stay open or else. Clinton and Obama failed to use the bully pulpit and the power of their office to interfere with corporate layoff decisions.

Donald Trump enjoyed playing the bully.

Trump's intervention happened at Carrier. The air-conditioner maker, the most profitable division of United Technologies (UT), had been highly successful for decades. Nevertheless, UT announced in February 2016 that it would eliminate 1,400 jobs at two Carrier facilities in and near Indianapolis and move them to Mexico over the course of three years. The reason, they said, was that they had to keep up with their competitors who also were moving to northern Mexico.

As is so often the case, there was a stock buyback lurking behind this story. Here's a March 2016 report from analysts at Stone Fox Capital:

> United Technologies is making good on the promise to return $22 billion to shareholders via dividends and stock buybacks from 2015 through 2017. The plan got off to a fast start with a $6 billion accelerated stock buyback to end 2015. In total, the industrial company spent $12 billion on capital returns last year alone. With a market cap of only $83 billion, United Technologies is returning a large portion of the market cap to shareholders.[2]

Who are these shareholders receiving a big chunk of what the company was worth? Here's a headline from the financial news website *Seeking Alpha* in June 2015: "Hedge Funds Piling into United Technologies." *Forbes* reported in July 2015 that 14 hedge funds had bought up significant amounts of UT shares.[3] By the end of 2018, there were 64 hedge funds with positions in the company.[4]

Why were hedge funds "piling into" UT? Because they saw an opportunity to pressure the company's management to undertake massive stock buybacks that would raise the share price, yielding fat profits for share sellers. Those buybacks required UT to squeeze various parts of the company to come up with more cash. The Carrier division could make its contribution by moving to Mexico, which would save the company more than $65 million per year.[5] The union representing the workers, United Steelworkers, offered up to one-third of that amount in worker wage and benefit concessions to keep the US plants from closing, but to no avail.

The Democrats would likely have benefited if they'd put out more statements like the one by Indiana Senator Joe Donnelly: "This is about Carrier chasing wages at $3 an hour. They put together a $16 billion stock buyback and just went wherever they could to try to pick up a few extra pennies."[6]

Trump jumped on this case during his 2016 presidential campaign. Rather than exposing the egregious stock buybacks, he wanted to show he was tough enough to stop the move to Mexico. This was his chance to be seen taking a stand against job carnage:

"These companies aren't going to be leaving anymore," he said. "They're not going to be taking people's hearts out."[7]

Trump made a point of saying he supported workers.

"This is the way it's going to be," Trump said in an interview with the *New York Times*. "Corporate America is going to have to understand that we have to take care of our workers also."[8]

Of course, neither Trump nor corporate America believed a word of it, but Trump was pressed by workers to deliver on these promises. A Carrier employee named TJ Bray, who voted for Trump, dared the new president to "do what you said you were going to do. We're going to hold you accountable." According to *Bloomberg News*, "The president-elect happened to see the report. Trump would later tell Carrier workers that he didn't think he'd actually promised to save their jobs. But shortly after seeing Bray on TV, he arranged for a call to [United Technologies CEO Gregory] Hayes."[9]

Hayes understood immediately that given UT's role as a major defense contractor, it might be a serious error to cross Trump. As *Bloomberg* reported, "Trump didn't mention UT's billions of dollars in defense contracts, but he didn't have to. 'I was born at night, but not last night,' Hayes told CNBC. . . . And that was weeks before Trump proposed to boost military spending by $54 billion."

After previously blasting Trump's campaign attacks on free trade and the Carrier move, Hayes, with his tail between his legs, agreed to keep the plant open, giving Trump a quick political victory.

Vice President–elect Mike Pence, still governor of Indiana during the transition, came up with $7 million in grants and tax breaks to sweeten the deal for United Technologies.

For Trump, sticking to the facts was a nonstarter, so instead of bragging about the 700 to 800 jobs saved at Carrier, Trump claimed it was 1,100. He was taken to task by the local union president, Chuck Jones, who correctly, if not artfully, said that Trump had "lied his ass off." Trump responded as he always does to critics, slamming Jones on Twitter, knowing full well that Trump fanatics would respond by making Jones's life hell. Trump tweeted: "Chuck Jones, who is President of United Steelworkers 1999, has done a terrible job representing workers. No wonder companies flee country!" And a few minutes later he added, "If United Steelworkers 1999 was any good, they would have kept those jobs in Indiana. Spend more time working—less time talking. Reduce dues."[10]

Trump drew fire from the right and the left for his Carrier move. Corporate-oriented people said that the government had no business picking "winners and losers"—even though the government does that every day with its trillion-dollar national security and defense budgets. The left correctly argued that it was outrageous to throw bribe money at a highly profitable corporation.

In truth, the practice of handing public money to corporations to keep jobs from fleeing—what critics call corporate welfare—is ubiquitous. We're talking big money: 65 corporations have each received $1 billion or more since 1976, with Boeing alone receiving more than $15 billion.[11]

The "bribe" for Carrier was barely a rounding error in the tens of billions of dollars in public money and tax breaks lavished upon corporations by Republicans and Democrats alike. Profits depend on the well-honed corporate art of playing states and countries against each other in order to feast at the public trough. The conservatives' beloved free-enterprise system has never been free of corporate bribes and jobs blackmail.

A telling example comes from US Senator Chuck Schumer and the state of New York. In 2015, Alcoa was scheduled to eliminate 600 jobs at its aluminum facility in Massena, New York, through 500 layoffs and another 100 open positions that would not be filled. Lo and behold, Democratic Governor Andrew Cuomo and Senator Schumer came to the rescue with $38.8 million in capital and operating expenses from the state's economic development arm and another $30 million in energy-cost assistance. Alcoa promised to keep the jobs in New York for at least three years. The public cost per saved job was seven times higher at Alcoa than Carrier. "I heard last night: Alcoa said they were going to keep the plant open. That was the best birthday present I could have received," said Schumer, who had turned 65 a day earlier.[12]

(As of June 2022, the Alcoa smelter in Messina, New York, still employed approximately 450 workers.)[13]

In addition to the size of their bribes, there was another notable difference between Trump's approach and Schumer's. Trump used the office of president and an implied threat to end the company's federal contracts (plus a little cash from Governor Pence) to bring UT to heel. By contrast, Schumer was on his knees begging. Bribing corporations to move in or stay put is commonplace, but few politicians are willing to axe contracts to keep jobs in the United States. That would challenge the assumption that corporations have an absolute right to eliminate jobs. Having corporate job-killers blasted publicly and threatened by the president of the United States was something new.

To be clear, Trump's Carrier intervention was a one-off event. He failed as miserably as every other president since 1980 to stop mass layoffs. It was the perfect moment to put Trump to the test by bringing workers from hundreds of mass layoffs to Washington with placards saying "What about us?" Unfortunately, the progressive movement let him off the hook.

Nevertheless, Trump did show that using the bully pulpit—and other powers—of the presidency can, at least in some cases, slow, reduce, or even reverse some layoffs. Ultimately, putting a dent in the epidemic of mass layoffs will likely require a major overhaul of our financial system, with the active support of the American people and their elected representatives. But overt interventions by top political leaders certainly could prove helpful—and send an important signal to working people.

So, what did the Democrats learn from Trump's Carrier intervention?

It Ain't Gonna Happen!

Two years after Trump's Carrier intervention, Senator Bernie Sanders, running for president for the second time in 2019, gave the following talk to a group of imperiled employees at the Siemens facility in Iowa. (The talk was quickly turned into a slick campaign video.)[14]

> Tell your friends at Siemens that a new day is coming when Bernie's in the White House.
>
> Tell them if they think that they're going to get $725 million dollars in federal contracts after shutting down a plant in this country and moving abroad, they got another thing coming.
>
> It ain't gonna happen!
>
> Right now, in general, what we say is, "Okay, the federal government will purchase products from those companies who come in with the lowest prices." Ain't good enough.
>
> We want to make sure that the price is right, but we also want to make sure that they treat their workers with respect and dignity. And that does not mean shutting down plants and moving in this case to India. That's wrong.

At the time, Siemens, a massive German-based industrial corporation, had approximately 400,000 employees worldwide, providing products and services in energy, health care, industrial automation, AI, and infrastructure. To gain a large footprint in the American energy sector in 2015, Siemens bought the fossil-fuel-extraction equipment manufacturer Dresser-Rand. The acquisition gave Siemens the ability to sell compressors, turbines, high-speed engines, and modular power stations for the hydraulic "fracking" of oil and gas. But in 2018, the fracking and oil market became saturated and collapsed. Siemens cut its losses by announcing it was pulling out of this business and eliminating 7,800 jobs globally, with 1,400 US layoffs scheduled for 2020.

At the end of 2018, Siemens announced the shutdown of its Burlington, Iowa, facility, eliminating 125 jobs in a town of 25,000 people. The plant had been in operation since 1870. They also began shutting down the Siemens plant in Fort Madison, Iowa (population, 10,174), 20 minutes down the road from Burlington, which would cost workers another 200 jobs. On his watch,

Trump had done nothing to keep these plants open. These were the facilities Sanders referred to on his campaign visit to Iowa.

Then, a year later, in the middle of the pandemic, Siemens announced plans to close its Olean, New York, plant. (Like Oberlin College, Siemens showed a disregard for the health and well-being of its small-town employees, who would be left to fend for themselves in trying conditions.) Corporations had been making equipment in Olean for more than 100 years. Now, to add to the gloom in the deindustrialized Southern Tier of New York, Siemens's 530 decent-paying union jobs would disappear.

Corporations (and colleges) always have a rational explanation for the job carnage. In this case, Siemens said they wanted to get out of the fossil fuel business and focus more on renewable energy, a story that would play well with environmentally minded politicians. But as with nearly every corporate job-killing move, a stock buyback was on the horizon. From September 28, 2020, to March 18, 2021, Siemens Energy bought back 394 million euros worth of its own stock.[15]

Why would a corporation facing economic difficulties loot its own treasury? Well, that's the business model of choice: Use as much corporate money as possible to buy back stock, boost the stock price, and enrich top corporate officers and the large share sellers, including the largest stockowner of them all—Siemens AG, the German company itself.

By this time, Bernie Sanders, having lost his second bid to become president, was chair of the Senate Budget Committee with the Democrats controlling the House, the Senate, and the Presidency. But did Sanders threaten to pull the federal contracts awarded to Siemens? Did he move "to make sure they treat their workers with respect and dignity. And that does not mean shutting down plants"? Would Schumer use the levers of his powerful Senate position to prevent Siemens Energy from abandoning these workers in rural New York State, which he represented? No, no, and no, it turns out.

To be fair, Sanders undoubtedly has done more to put working-class issues on the political map than any other politician since the New Deal. Unlike Trump, who revels in spurring race, gender, and immigration divisiveness, Sanders truly believes in solidarity among *all* working people. He deserves much credit for helping to rekindle a politics of hope among a new generation of labor justice advocates. Nevertheless, one wishes he had used his position of power to intervene in plant closings. Had he taken up those fights, he might have led the Democrats back to the working class.

Schumer, however, did get angry at Siemens Energy for not giving him adequate notice. According to the *Olean Times Herald*, he said: "I'm upset not just about the hundreds of jobs lost and families impacted in the midst of a pandemic, but their complete unwillingness to work with me, my office, or any government entity in advance of this decision."[16]

Schumer also worked to lure another corporation to occupy the facility. As of this writing, Cimolai-HY LLC, a joint venture startup company, is renovating the Olean facility to fabricate structural steel. It will have a $2 million loan forgiven by the county if the company creates 200 jobs.[17] While we don't have access to any behind-the-scenes conversations, Sanders voiced no public criticism of the Olean shutdown. None at all.

And what did President Biden do? He invited Siemens USA CEO, Barbara Humpton, to the White House signing of the 2021 infrastructure bill. Said Humpton on her blog post, "This is a historic moment in America—one that sets the stage for decarbonizing the economy, boosting US manufacturing, creating jobs, and increasing equity. And we extend our congratulations to the Biden-Harris Administration and applaud the bipartisan process in Congress that brought this bill to life."[18]

And there she is in the signing photo, in the front row, along with Senator Schumer.

The Defense Production Act to the Rescue?

At a moment when the economy was cratering, the pandemic offered elected political leaders a powerful tool for fighting mass layoffs: The Defense Production Act (DPA). The DPA allows the president to expedite and expand the supply of materials needed for national defense. It also bolsters the government's capacity to increase emergency preparedness, restore critical infrastructure, and support a range of other activities to stop and respond to terrorism. Both Trump and Biden used the DPA to strengthen the federal response to the pandemic, including to produce protective equipment, ventilators, tests, and vaccines.[19]

The president can use the DPA to compel a company to stay open in order to provide vital products and services for the country. In 2022, the federal government used the act three times to deal with a pandemic-driven shortage of baby formula.

But would it be used to stop a mass layoff? In the middle of the pandemic, Viatris (formerly Mylan) decided to lay off 1,500 workers in Morgantown, West Virginia. On average these workers earned about $70,000 per year, making them among the highest blue-collar earners in this perpetually economically depressed state.

Viatris makes generic drugs. And if there is one lesson to be learned from the pandemic, it's that we should keep production of critical goods like pharmaceuticals close to home. But the company decided to move production from its Morgantown plant to India and Australia. You would think keeping the West Virginia facility open, at least temporarily, would have been a powerful and popular use of the DPA.

But it was not used to save these 1,500 jobs in 2020.

The background to this story takes us again into the world of corporate mergers and mega CEO pay packages. In 1996, Mylan was the world's second-largest generic-drugs company. One of its products was lorazepam, the generic version of Valium. Like many other drug companies, Mylan used its market power and corporate deals to force up the price of its drug. In the case of lorazepam, the price went up tenfold. In 1998, the Federal Trade Commission stepped in and forced Mylan to pay a $100 million fine for price fixing.[20] In 2009, it had to cough up another $118 million to settle a false claims suit. By this point Mylan also was the maker of the EpiPen, an injection device.

Heather Bresch, who also happens to be the daughter of West Virginia Senator Joe Manchin, became Mylan's CEO in 2012. She was the first woman to run a Fortune 500 pharmaceutical company and ranked #22 on *Fortune*'s "Most Powerful Women" list that year. Bresch, with no prior pharmaceutical experience, got into the company via an interview set up by her father. She claimed an MBA from West Virginia University that she didn't earn:

> The *Pittsburgh Post-Gazette* reports that Bresch did not actually have enough credits for an MBA from West Virginia University, even though the news release announcing her new, high-profile job said she had earned one. The school, through its own investigation, found Bresch had been given grades "pulled from thin air" because of her "high profile." The university later withdrew her MBA.[21]

Exercising her power, she initiated a campaign to let the world know about the use of EpiPens to counter anaphylaxis for people with severe allergies. Mylan had 85 percent of the market share, and Bresch did what any monopolist would do—she raised the price of the life-saving pens again and again and again, from $100 for two pens in 2009, to $609 by May 2016. The estimated cost of manufacturing a two-pack was $10.

In 2017, mid-level Mylan executives told the *New York Times* that these price increases were unethical. But Bresch pressed ahead. The price gouging eventually cost Mylan $465 million in Justice Department fines for ripping off Medicare and Medicaid. Shortly thereafter the chairman of Mylan's board, Robert Courey, hauled in a $98 million pay package. Between 2012 and 2019, Heather Bresch took in more than $113 million in pay and realized gains from awards and options.[22] With more coming.

After helping to engineer a merger with Pfizer's Upjohn division in 2020, Bresch retired with a $42.5 million golden parachute.[23] A new corporation, Viatris, was born, led by company president Rajiv Malik and CEO Michael Goettler.

Let's go back a few years to see how this Mylan saga unfolded from the workers' point of view. After many years of stability in the company, workers were hit hard by job cuts in 2018. Bill Hawkins, a United Steelworkers union local president, told us that at the time there were 1,342 members in his Mylan bargaining unit—and 400 of those jobs were slated to be cut.[24] The union negotiated a deal with the company that would save one job for every person near retirement who would voluntarily accept the company buyout. Fifty-one left voluntarily, so 51 jobs of the 400 were saved. For a time.

Malik made it clear to the workers that they had better face up to the competition in India. *Vanity Fair* reported that in October 2018, Malik ordered the union to fall in line, agree to 12-hour shifts, and allow workers to be moved anywhere in the plant that management chose. Otherwise, he threatened, according to three meeting attendees, "I will bury Morgantown. It will all go to India and my people will get the benefits."

Viatris denied this account.

> Bill Hawkins, the union vice president, came away from the meeting with a clear message from Malik: *I can pay my people over there $400 a year, or I can pay you people $70,000 a year, so you do what I want.*[25]

Hawkins made clear that he certainly understood the economics:

> If you could profit $2 billion here, you take your stuff overseas where they're paying a factory worker in India $400 a year to make these drugs. They don't have to follow the American FDA and all these regulations over there. And you can make $7 billion instead of $2 billion. That's why they moved over there. And there were no repercussions for it.

In November 2020, Mylan officially merged with Upjohn, and the new corporation was called Viatris. In nearly every merger, job cuts follow, and in this case it didn't take long. In December 2020, Viatris announced that the entire Morgantown facility would be closed, and approximately 1,500 jobs would be moved to Australia and India.

In nearly every plant closure, politicians scramble to find a new buyer rather than pressuring the company to stay put. As Hawkins recalled, someone from the economic development office said, "There's a buyer. I can't tell you who, there's a confidentiality agreement. But just hang in there. We'll be OK." And, as in most cases, a buyer was never found.

The feisty union local held rallies, built coalitions, pressured Manchin, and put the heat on Biden. They did everything they could think of except take over the facility to prevent it from closing. They even asked the governor to have the state purchase the plant and continue to operate it as a public utility.

It is doubtful we'll ever find out why nothing was done, in spite of the combined clout of Manchin, Biden, Sanders, and Schumer, all holding powerful positions in the Senate. In particular, there is controversy over what Manchin said, did, and didn't do. One would think it would be a no-brainer for Manchin to save 1,500 of the best-paying blue-collar jobs in all of West Virginia. Manchin claimed that, "For months, I have engaged in conversations with Viatris, Monongalia County, the Morgantown Area Partnership, and local and state leaders to find a solution that protects every single job," according to *Vanity Fair*. Union officials saw it differently:

> [W]hen officials with the United Steelworkers Local 8-957 managed to get roughly two minutes of his time, over a video call he took from the US Senate floor, there was no fight at all. "Sorry about your

luck," he told them, according to a union official and confirmed by five others who participated in the March 10 call. "It sounds like they've reached a corporate decision. There is very little I can do."

Hawkins is still bitter about the lack of vision shown by Manchin and so many others. How could they not see that this was the perfect opportunity for the government to step in and do something really good for these workers and for society? Hawkins told us, "Manchin could have gone to Joe Biden and get the government to buy that facility and we will produce enough prescription medicines for your veterans, for anybody that works for a government agency, for prisoners, for those on government assistance, social security, disability. We could supply all those people."

Hawkins then repeated many of the political themes of this book:

> The President. Vice President. Senator. In my opinion, they all have their own personal agenda. . . . I don't care about the Democrat/Republican thing—to me both of them are so screwed up. When I was growing up—I'm 48 years old now—your Democrat Party was your working-class party. The Republican Party was for your white-collar workers, the Democrats for blue-collar workers. Well, now it seems like everything's flip-flopped and changed around. Yeah, I don't think any of them know what the hell's going on in the world. Everybody's got to quit worrying about what party they are in and get the country straight, or there's going to be a lot more of this going on.

There's little doubt that Bernie Sanders and President Biden heard the pleas from these desperate workers. Our Revolution, a national progressive organization set up originally by the Sanders forces, joined with the workers and dozens of other organizations in a last-ditch effort to save the plant before it closed in the summer of 2021. They asked President Biden to use the Defense Production Act to prevent the dismantling of our infrastructure. In a letter to the Biden administration, they wrote:

> In the absence of a national industrial strategy for US pharmaceutical manufacturing, we have every reason to expect privately

held corporations like Viatris will continue outsourcing American jobs and dismantling our manufacturing capacity. Only long-term strategies, like taking the pharmaceutical sector into public ownership, can successfully block key industries and jobs from being outsourced by corporate interests.[26]

Did Sanders actually get the message? Yes, but he had bigger fish to fry according to Our Revolution director Joseph Geevarghese: "[It's] on Bernie's radar, but as Budget Committee chairman, most of Sanders's attention is on the infrastructure legislation and other money matters at the moment. Also, the ball falls more properly in Manchin's court, since the plant is in his home state, and he holds a pivotal position in the Senate."

Perhaps Sanders or Biden made the political calculation that 1,500 excellent union jobs would have to be sacrificed to keep Manchin in the fold for an infrastructure bill that would supposedly create hundreds of thousands of jobs. Interfering in West Virginia without Manchin's full blessing would have been problematic. (Although you have to wonder why Manchin would be upset about efforts to save 1,500 good-paying West Virginia jobs.)

A similar logic may have been at play with Siemens. The Biden administration wanted corporate support for the infrastructure bill, which did indeed become law. Why alienate the Siemens leadership by pressuring them to keep the plant open to save 500 union jobs? More jobs will be created by the infrastructure bill, so let's invite the job-killing CEO to the signing.

It's macro versus micro, future jobs for somebody else versus the job you are losing right now. Their logic is clear: the infrastructure bill supposedly will both create new jobs and make many other jobs more secure. That hopeful calculus, used repeatedly when Democrats are in power, overlooks the underlying corporate imperative to turn a profit by any means necessary, including through stock buybacks. So even as the infrastructure bill spurs new domestic production, merger-related job cuts will continue.

It's possible that for every new battery plant that might be opened through infrastructure subsidies, we're likely to see dozens of downsizing efforts in other industries. As long as there are no enforceable brakes placed on stock buybacks and unnecessary mergers and acquisitions, mass layoffs will proceed unabated.

The macro perspective also ignores one critical fact: Rarely, if ever, do the new jobs created by macro policies go to the victims of mass layoffs. There is a time/space/quality problem: The new jobs usually aren't located where the old ones were lost. Even when they are within geographic reach, the timing is wrong: The new jobs aren't created in time to help those who suffered mass layoffs. Further, the new jobs that laid-off workers eventually might find usually pay less and have fewer benefits, leading to a decline in their standard of living over the course of their careers.[27]

The Morgantown and Olean workers were sacrificed. Like others left behind in hard-hit regions, they are not likely to reward the Democrats for jobs they will never see.

Can we really do something concrete about mass layoffs, beyond trying to address the problems they leave behind? Can we do anything other than bribing corporations to move into these depressed areas or providing a stronger safety net for the victims? There must be a better approach than what ProPublica's Alec MacGillis described in the *New York Times* in 2022:

> For years, too many leading Democrats stood by as the wrenching transformation of the economy devastated communities, while accruing benefits to a small set of highly prosperous cities, mostly on the coasts, that became the party's gravitational center. It was so easy to disregard far-off desolation—or to take only passing note of it, counting the Dollar Stores as one happened to traverse areas of decline—until Mr. Trump's victory brought it to the fore.[28]

When we first began researching this book, it seemed that the only viable systemic approach to mass layoffs would be for the government to serve as the employer of last resort for struggling areas, and to strengthen the safety net for the victims of mass layoffs. Direct interference with corporate mass layoff decisions looked to be impossible in any national context.

Then we heard about what happened at Siemens in Germany.

CHAPTER 9

There Is Another Way

How a Major Capitalist Democracy Avoids Mass Layoffs

"Everybody's afraid of losing their job. Everybody's mad, everybody's unhappy. I mean, that's not a good environment, man. You know, the environment shouldn't have to be that way, you know? And it didn't used to be like that." —"Curtis Thompson," age 59, laid off after 19 years of service

IS IT REALLY POSSIBLE TO STOP MASS LAYOFFS IN A HIGHLY ADVANCED economy operating in the modern global marketplace?

Apparently so, because workers and their unions managed it at Siemens Energy in Germany, the world's fourth-largest economy. Their win happened because of a corporate decision-making model called *codetermination*, which places workers and their representatives deep inside the corporate decision-making structure, even onto the boards of directors. That model is based on a very different notion of the value of labor than what we're familiar with in this country.

In the United States, the post-1980s corporation is designed to maximize shareholder value. You buy a stock, you are a part-owner, and you get a claim on the corporation's assets and profits. And because you are an owner risking money, your claim is the most important of all. Everyone who actually works for the corporation has only a contractual relationship. The workers go to work, get paid, and go home. Extra value goes only to shareholders.

Historically, workers and their collective organizations (unions, guilds) are a direct challenge to the idea that shareholders have the most skin in the game. It is workers, not shareholders, who put their lives in danger, spend large amounts of time away from home and family, and worry about job security. Their employment commits them to producing—whether they're manufacturing products, providing a service, or building a skyscraper.

By contrast, shareholders can and do diversify their portfolios to minimize risk. And they can rapidly sell their shares through stock exchanges if the risks mount. Capital is flexible. Workers, are not. If they lose one job, they usually don't have another one to fall back on.

In reality, most stockholders aren't even individuals. Major activist shareholders today are large hedge funds, private equity concerns, investment banks, and asset management firms. These proxy executives and owners face little or no personal risk. They also face no personal risk when providing investments for university endowments and pension funds, which are liable for the losses.

Shareholder primacy often becomes an argument for corporate authoritarianism. Interference from the workers below, it is claimed, threatens shareholder value and must be quashed.

Labor unions and codetermination challenge the idea of shareholder primacy, pitting workers' safety, security, and remuneration against the preeminence of profits. Where the balance is struck reflects the legal and ethical values we collectively claim.

It's always a battle about power, not just efficiency. In the United States, from the late 19th century until the New Deal, corporations did all they could to criminalize the very idea of labor unions. They hired thugs to beat up labor organizers, secured court injunctions to outlaw strikes, and used government injunctions—and government troops—to crush those who would not surrender. Unions had to fight their way to the table.

The story in Germany is very different. There, a much broader deal was struck and reaffirmed over time to include workers in real decision-making, not just through collective bargaining over wages and working conditions. German unions gained significant input into corporate planning. But this didn't come easily. It was a long and very rocky road to bring a modicum of democracy into large German corporations.

The first stirrings of codetermination came in Frankfurt during the revolutionary upheavals against the aristocracy that spread across Europe in 1848. Germany's short-lived parliament drafted a bill, pushed by a single progressive factory owner and backed by workers and their nascent unions, that required "councils in every German business district to be composed of representatives chosen by factory committees, one-third elected by workers and two-thirds by the employer." The German aristocracy crushed this fledging bourgeois government, and this first attempt at worker empowerment collapsed. The setback slowed future unionization, because afterward the government outlawed worker organizing unless it had the permission of the police.[1]

The effort to increase worker input into corporate governance was slowed but not stopped. By the late 19th century, German trade unions had become so massive and so powerful that Chancellor Otto von Bismarck tried to outlaw any union that called for overthrowing the state and instituting some kind of socialist democracy. In an attempt to co-opt the growing worker movement (3.7 million out of a workforce of approximately 7 million in 1912, of which 2.5 million were affiliated with the socialist unions),[2] Bismarck instituted national health insurance in 1883, with an interesting twist: It required that "the managers of new company health schemes, in firms of over 50 staff . . . be elected by a general meeting where the workforce held two-thirds of the votes and the employer up to one third."[3] According to Ewan McGaughey's book, *The Codetermination Bargains*, this might be the modern world's first instance of statutory codetermination.

Kaiser Wilhelm II, who forced Bismarck to resign in 1890, was more sympathetic to worker rights and argued that "factory orders should no longer be issued unilaterally by enterprises, rather than be agreed with representatives of the workforce."[4] Wilhelm and the country's elites, however, were worried about the rapid rise of the workers' Social Democratic Party, which was becoming a major force in German society. To preempt the Social Democrats, in 1890 the Kaiser's government drew up an optional works council plan for employers. And the next year, he offered the Worker Protection Act of 1891, by which "employers had the legal duty to issue workplace rules on four main issues: working times and breaks, the type and time of wage payment, notice periods and reasons for dismissals, and workplace punishments." The union-backed Social Democratic Party opposed it as "a sham constitutional fig leaf, trying to conceal factory feudalism."[5]

Nevertheless, the voluntary works council system gained some traction, and by 1905 about 10 percent of German companies with more than 20 employees had works councils. Firms in Germany adopted this codetermination precursor without pressure from union agreements or government laws because they thought it would improve morale, productivity, and profits. The employers believed that too much autocracy was, in fact, bad for business. And they no doubt understood that such reforms might temper socialism among these workers.

The German trade union movement and the Social Democratic Party (a socialist political formation that by the eve of World War I [WWI] was the largest political party in Germany)[6] soon saw that such councils, if endowed with real power, could be an important step forward. German miners in 1905, for example, called for compulsory councils as part of their strike demands. When the brutal bloodshed during WWI forced the government to seek cooperation from the Social Democrats, it instituted a new regulation that challenged an employer's right to unilaterally manage. As a result, disputes over certain work rules and reprimands would not only be heard but could be subject to compulsory arbitration.

As Germany collapsed into revolutionary chaos at the end of WWI, the economy lay in tatters. Trade unions and employers signed the Stinnes–Legien Agreement, which said there would be "common resolution of all economic and social questions in German industry and trade."[7] Furthermore, employers agreed to allow freedom of association, end sham company unions,* and accept work councils in companies with 50 or more employees. This was an economy-wide collective bargaining agreement and a negotiated contract, not a statute. When the new liberal government (often called the Weimar Republic) and constitution were created in 1919, Article 165 gave workers "legal representation in workers' councils."

The hardships forced by draconian WWI reparation payments imposed by the Allies crippled German industry and sent trade union membership and unity tumbling. Nevertheless, the Weimar government implemented code-termination and mandated for the first time the election of one or two worker representatives on supervisory councils (boards of directors) with three directors or more. Unfortunately, the courts did not enforce the law, and employers soon found a myriad of ways to water down worker power despite the law.

The combination of high unemployment following the 1929 Wall Street crash and the rise of Nazism in the following years doomed the

---

* To prevent unionization, some corporations set up their own internal organizations that looked like unions but had no power.

works councils, trade unions, and the entire idea of political democracy in Germany. After ascending to the chancellorship in 1933, Adolph Hitler demolished independent trade unions, arrested and imprisoned their leaders, sent Communist Party members to concentration camps, and issued decrees that outlawed all organized resistance. Instead, workers were required to join the one and only union organized by the Nazis, in which no dissent was tolerated. Even the hint of codetermination was formally abolished in 1934. At every firm, the new Nazi ideology claimed, the leader is always right. Business owners became absolute bosses over their workers, subject only to the decrees of the absolute leader of the state—the Fuhrer!

Germany lay in ruins yet again after WWII, and so did the reputation of its mighty corporate establishments, which had supported and supplied Hitler's ambitions. The American occupiers learned quickly that union-oriented German workers were less likely to be Nazi sympathizers and could become a vital collective force to keep fascism from reemerging. In the American occupation zone,[8] works councils formed and spread, giving workers formal power so that they could act as a check on the autocratic tendencies of corporate leaders.

Having experienced the Nazi nationalization of nearly every aspect of society, German trade unions stepped back from their traditional socialistic interest in nationalizing industries. They focused instead on direct participation and power within existing corporate structures. By 1947, labor and management in the German steel industry had agreed to a board of directors with five members chosen by shareholders and five chosen by the unions, with the board chair chosen by the government.

To prevent a large coal strike in 1951, the Christian Democratic Union government of Konrad Adenauer passed the Mining Codetermination Act, which applied to workplaces of 1,000 or more. Codetermination spread quickly to railroads, engineering firms, and the chemical sector, pushed by collective bargaining. In 1952, a federal law was passed that gave workers throughout the economy the right to one-third of board seats. The unions, however, wanted more.

The Social Democratic Party government, led by Willy Brandt, was elected in 1964. In 1970, it produced a report that recommended "more employee representatives on the supervisory board . . . with the proviso that shareholder representatives retain a slight majority."[9] The 1976 Codetermination

Act was approved by all of the major political parties. Brandt remained in office until 1987.

Nearly a half century later, codetermination is still functioning throughout Germany—and within Siemens.

A Tale of Two Countries

Today, if you work for Siemens Energy in the United States, you might as well be on a different planet from the employees of Siemens Energy in Germany.

The major German union representing workers at Siemens Energy (and its parent company Siemens AG) is IG Metall, which has more than 2.2 million members in electronics, steel, textiles, clothing, wood, plastics, and services. (There are approximately 8 million German union members in all, representing approximately 18 percent of Germany's workforce.)[10] The company and the union coexist within a complex set of rules and cultural norms that derive from Germany's 1976 Codetermination Act.

At Siemens in Germany there are approximately 100 local works councils, each with a chairperson and a number of members that depends on the size of the facility. In the larger facilities, there may be 30 or so members, many of whom work full time for the works council solving workplace issues. The number of full-time works council members is decided by the workers, not management. The company, by law, must cooperate with these works councils on issues like hours of work, work rules, working conditions, and even bonus allocations. Management not only has to discuss these issues with the works councils but also sign written agreements based on the outcomes of those talks. By law, works council members can leave their jobs in order to deal with these issues whenever they choose—without management interference.

In facilities across Germany, these councils and their leaders have more seniority and permanence than do plant managers, who come and go. As a result, the works councils are a vast repository of workplace knowledge vital for the success of the operations, valuable to management as well as workers.

Dirk Linder, the IG Metall coordinator for Siemens Global Union Network, said to us that a well-functioning works council develops significant informal powers as well. "If the works council acts cleverly," he said, "it may be able to get something [concessions] from the employer that the employer doesn't have to provide [by law or by labor agreement]."[11]

By law, at least four times per year, representatives from local works councils within a company convene as a central works council. At Siemens, the central works council meets five times per year. These delegates nominate six workers each year, three full-time national union officials, and one manager, to serve on the 20-person corporate supervisory board. Shareholders select the other 10 members. The final ratification of the central works council nominees is taken at a national assembly of more than 4,000 works council representatives.

Here's the shocker: The supervisory board is the highest official body of the corporation. That's right. This top-level board of six workers, three union officials, one manager, and ten shareholder representatives has a hell of a lot of power. To maintain a modicum of control, the management representative is the board's chairperson and has an additional vote in case of any ties.

Let's think about this for a moment. The chairperson of the top board of the corporation is a top manager chosen by the workers. As Linder points out, the workers are going to choose a manager who is more union-friendly and who has already cooperated with the works councils. Furthermore, there are three board members who are union officials. As Linder put it, "[T]hat union official on Monday could be calling for a strike and on Tuesday be attending a supervisory board meeting."

Let's be honest. As Americans, wouldn't we assume that this kind of German supervisory board—with all these workers and union officials—is a toothless body with no real powers? And if it *does* have real power, how in the world, you might wonder, can Germany possibly maintain its world-renowned automotive, mechanical engineering, chemical, and electrical industries, with all these empowered workers gumming up the works?

Our assumption about the board's impotence is wrong. The supervisory board has real power, including the hiring and firing of top corporate management. That's not solely a worker decision; it also requires the agreement of the shareholder representatives. But, as Linder explains, if the manager repeatedly sides against the unions and is a source of friction, the shareholders take notice: "If our side gives good reasons, then a manager we don't like has no future within the company. And usually, they don't want to take that risk of really offending us, because, of course, they want to keep their job."

So, while the Democrats and Republicans in our country have allowed "activist" hedge funds to invade boards of directors to push for more and more stock buybacks and financial strip-mining, the German worker "activists" are trying to protect employee jobs and livelihoods by making sure the corporation is well run for all its stakeholders.

For workers to truly protect their livelihoods, they need information. The supervisory board is where management in Germany must present and discuss the company's overall strategy. As Linder points out, the process provides the union with "very comprehensive flows of information." He also cautions us, however, not to get too giddy about these powers: "Nobody should overestimate our powers. It is not that we can force them to do something. But even if the union representatives cannot influence management, they can gain a very deep insight into how the company actually works. And they can take this knowledge back to the employees and then form a counterstrategy if needed."

Linder suggests that this multitiered process of codetermination, which engages so many workers and managers, builds a more cooperative culture. It's not like they become best buddies, but they do have to talk to each other about substantive issues on a regular basis. As Linder said, a kind of "common sense" of consensus-building is generated. Management wants to be seen as reasonable, so they try to convince the worker members of their strategy rather than forcing it down their throats.

Linder cautions us that even within a culture of cooperation, decisions about mass layoffs pose serious challenges. The supervisory board is the place where the overall corporate strategic direction is reviewed, but the discussion of mass layoffs takes place within the central works council on economic affairs. It is there that the company must make its case for layoffs. As long as this works council on economic affairs is seeking information and asking questions, it is unlawful for management to proceed with layoffs.

This is not a BS discussion group. The central works council members engage experts, present their findings, demand further detailed studies, and evaluate every aspect of management's layoff proposals. Inevitably, this slows down the mass layoff process, which for the workers is an important humanitarian victory. It gives more time for vulnerable workers to seek other employment opportunities and for older workers to move closer to retirement age.

By contrast, in the United States, the Siemens Energy union was presented with a done deal, with no discussion about the merits of the layoff decision or possible alternatives. The only dialogue was about what is called "effects bargaining"—severance benefits and the like. At Siemens Energy in Germany, the research and questioning process over layoffs took more than a year.

German management does have the power to stop a worker filibuster, Linder reports: "There can be a situation when management says, okay, we've had enough discussion. You are only asking questions to stall. This has to stop. If the workers say, 'No, we have more questions,' the issue can be taken to binding arbitration. But usually, there's some kind of compromise that is reached."

And the compromise at Siemens Energy in Germany was something that we Americans (and the former Siemens Energy employees in Olean, New York) can barely comprehend. Instead of the proposed mass layoff of 3,000 German workers and the shutdown of six facilities, this global corporation agreed to *no forced layoffs*! Not one person was forced out.

Management and workers agreed that the company would provide financial inducements for workers to leave voluntarily. Furthermore, it was agreed that all six threatened facilities would remain open, another key victory. Said Linder: "If the plant stays open, there is always hope that the work again will be expanded."

How is it possible for Siemens Energy to agree to this in Germany while in the United States the same company offered nothing other than severance payments as it shut down facility after facility?

Did the Siemens workers in Germany have enough power to stop the layoffs globally? Or did the German workers acquiesce to the Siemens American layoffs to save their own jobs? Linder believes that his union did not have the power to stop layoffs in other nations and that the only way for American workers to save their jobs would be to develop their own type of codetermination system.

So, why don't we have codetermination in this country? The issues become clearer if we pull back the lens.

First, we need to recognize that codetermination evolved from its historical German roots and was also pushed forward by the US occupiers after WWII. The Americans wanted German unions to be deeply involved in Germany's most powerful corporations to prevent them from again becoming handmaidens of fascism. At that time, US leaders understood that independent trade unions were a bulwark of freedom and democracy, something that we've almost forgotten today. Furthermore, by becoming deeply engaged within these corporate structures, German unions were drawn away from Soviet-style state socialism, an important consideration as the Cold War evolved after WWII.

Second, the German trade union movement is large and well-respected within German society, even more so than highly profitable corporations and financial institutions. Linder says that German attitudes about unions changed after the 2008 financial meltdown: "Before that we were the bad guys of Germany and everybody in politics hated us and tried to create laws to reduce the power of unions. But since the aftermath of the financial crisis in 2007–2008, we became the really good guys in Germany. We have helped companies survive. Management that once was anti-union now waves the union flag."

Dirk Linder and the German unions understand that the world has changed, and their hard-won standard of living is threatened: "We are not living like we did 50 years ago. I have to admit we have more precarious work—more part-time work and union density in Germany has declined. . . . So, we are in the middle of being happy, but also being angry at what we have not achieved. It's far from perfect, but not all bad."

The US victims of mass layoffs would certainly settle for that.

CHAPTER 10

TINA's Last Dance?

Facing the Fatalism of Mass-Layoff Capitalism

"The biggest part of working at Oberlin, I think, for anybody was just the students, dealing with the students, being around them, feeling like you're a part of something bigger, like Oberlin College. It was the first job I ever had where I felt like I was a part of something. . . . I really believed in the mission, you know what I mean? . . . Just being part of that community and being around the young minds that really do have the best interests of the future in their hearts. So that's what drew me there."
    —Eugene McCormick, age 38, laid off after 9 years of service

"THERE IS NO ALTERNATIVE" (TINA) IS AN EXPRESSION POPULAR-ized by former British Prime Minister Margaret Thatcher in the 1980s to justify her welfare cuts, deregulation, attacks on labor unions, and tax cuts for the wealthy. TINA became Thatcher's nickname—as well as a shorthand justification for all kinds of rightist policies.

As she battled to slash coal miners' jobs in 1983, Thatcher told the House of Commons, "It is an example of what happens to a protected industry. It's absolutely vital that it should return to viability."[1]

Mass layoffs? There is no alternative. It makes no economic sense, we are warned, to force corporations to keep redundant employees.

The same goes for political systems. There is no alternative to the triumph of democracy and capitalism around the globe, or so said Francis Fukuyama in his influential 1992 book, *The End of History and the Last Man*. Fukuyama argued that democratic capitalism would envelop the world, making irrelevant all other systems: "Liberal democracy as a system of government had emerged throughout the world over the past few years, as it conquered rival ideologies like hereditary monarchy, fascism, and most recently communism."[2]

The concept underlying TINA is powerful and straightforward: Government should leave free enterprise to its own devices, except for some transparent rules that ensure fair competition. State interference harms the markets, undermines freedom, and leads to autocracy. Letting markets be free will allow them to flourish, leading to prosperity and thriving democracies. As part of this bargain, we must accept what the influential Austrian economist Joseph Schumpeter in 1942 called "creative destruction," which he defined as the "process of industrial mutation that incessantly revolutionized the economic structure from within, incessantly destroying the old one, incessantly creating a new one."[3]

Such is TINA's siren song: If we truly cherish freedom and prosperity, we must accept the new overtaking the old, and part of that means accepting mass layoffs and all their pernicious impacts. That's the cost of doing business and there is no alternative. In fact, TINA says we should be thankful that we live in a wide-open free society in which mass layoffs are allowed to take place. Because freedom and democracy depend on a strong, global free-enterprise system that no government can control.

President Bill Clinton did more than his share to promote financial deregulation and globalization. In this he fit neatly into the economic lineage of Reagan, Thatcher, Blair, and Bush. He learned that his power as president was limited by the greater power of gigantic global capital markets—the largest markets in the world. Through these markets, the largest financial entities (bond vigilantes, they're called) buy and sell US government and corporate bonds. When those markets don't like a country's economic and social agenda, they can instantly move money out of that country, increasing interest rates and devaluing currencies.

Clinton displayed his understanding of the all-powerful bond markets in an interview with author Bob Woodward in 1993: "You mean to tell me that the success of the economic program and my re-election hinges on the Federal Reserve and a bunch of fucking bond traders?"[4]

Clinton's flamboyant advisor, James Carville, put it another way: "I used to think that if there was reincarnation, I wanted to come back as the President or the Pope or as a .400 baseball hitter. But now I would like to come back as the bond market. You can intimidate everybody."[5]

Conservatives can also run afoul of the all-powerful bond markets, as happened to Liz Truss, the short-termed British prime minister in 2022, who called for tax cuts for the rich while inflation was soaring. The bond vigilantes quickly dumped British bonds, which crashed the British pound and nearly melted down the British pension system. After only 45 days in office, Truss resigned. Actually, the bond market fired her.

And so, the myth asserts itself: TINA protects us all, disciplining misguided governments with its impartial free-market force. Markets limit what pernicious politicians can do to screw up the economy and curtail our freedoms. At the end of the day, that "bunch of fucking bond traders" are the real protectors of capitalist democracies—and of you. That is, if you make your living by investing, not by working.

Capitalism and Democracy?

While it is tempting to ridicule these libertarian fantasies, TINA is a formidable dictum that has traveled the globe. The power of large financial firms and their capital markets seems to preclude any real alternative to unfettered capitalism.

TINA's attraction also depends on two enduring assumptions that are now being questioned. The first is that capitalism inevitably leads to democracy. The second is that free markets, left to their own devices, produce more prosperity for everyone.

On the capitalism-leads-to-democracy claim, it turns out that modern capitalism has little trouble resting comfortably alongside authoritarianism. While China has embraced market capitalism, turning its economy into the second largest in the world, democracy has not followed. In fact, in recent years the opposite has happened. Bill Clinton was dead certain that more openness would flow as he pressed for China's entry into the tariff-free World Trade Organization. He put it this way in an address at Johns Hopkins in 2000: "In the new century, liberty will spread by cell phone and cable modem. . . . We know how much the Internet has changed America. . . . Imagine how much it could change China. . . . [The Beijing regime] has been trying to crack down on the Internet. Good luck! That's sort of like trying to nail Jell-O to the wall."[6]

But China did nail Jell-O to the wall, imposing the tightest social media controls in the world. In China the internet, and all its features, is monitored by the government. More than a billion Chinese residents have almost no uncensored access to global social media through which they might share their political concerns (although some controversial messages are able to get through on WeChat and Douyin). On controversial subjects, the government's message is often the *only* message, reinforced by an army of official influencers and monitors. Electronic surveillance is everywhere. Even *New York Times* columnist Thomas Friedman, a leading apostle of free trade, finally realized that globalization does not ensure freedom. He is horrified by China's "new tools of a surveillance state: drones, facial recognition, ubiquitous closed-circuit television cameras, cellphone tracking, and even tracking of restaurant patrons, who must present a QR code to be scanned and recorded."[7]

"Shock therapy" capitalism was also supposed to do wonders for the crumbling Soviet Union and emergent Russia as it weaned itself from state socialism. Smashing state-owned enterprises and rapidly turning over their functions to entrepreneurs was sold as a surefire way to usher in a Western liberal democracy. Instead, the Russian people got a capitalist system defined by appropriation and looting, run by a cabal of billionaire oligarchs and an expansionist dictator who has shut down all dissent. Clearly, the idea that capitalism foments and protects democracy just isn't true.

Actually, shock therapy in the name of democratic reform undermined democracy in Russia. Economic elites understood that the public would vote against many privatization measures and social service cuts, if given the chance. So, rapidly instituting these changes prevented the public from exercising their newly won democratic rights.

Overall, capitalism seems remarkably compatible with "oligarchs, tycoons, nepotists, profiteers, kleptocrats, inheritors, asset-strippers, mafiosi, hedgers, money launders, monopolists, loan sharks, fraudsters, arms dealers, racketeers, tax-dodgers, plutocrats, press barons, slave traders and cartelists," writes Jonathan Rée in the *London Review of Books*.[8]

Now let's move to the second TINA proposition: that capitalism, left to its own devices, creates prosperity for us all. That argument has one big chink in its armor: Wall Street! Once deregulated, Wall Street transformed corporate America into what economist William Lazonick has called a "predatory" enterprise that sucks the value out of formerly productive enterprises and puts it into the pocketbooks of the top 1 percent. "Since the mid-1980s, stock buybacks have become the prime mode for the legalized looting of the business corporation. I call this looting process 'predatory value extraction' and contend that it is the fundamental cause of the increasing concentration of income among the richest household units and the erosion of middle-class employment opportunities for most other Americans."[9]

None of the supremely confident founders of free-enterprise economics, including Schumpeter, Milton Friedman, or Friedrich Hayek, had any inkling of the looming perils of financialization or foresaw the coming of "predatory value extraction." As Wall Street and its corporate partners proceeded to turn productive enterprises into shells, the free marketeers kept selling the idea that market magic would cure all ills. Most didn't think Wall Street value extraction was problematic, because the drive for profit supposedly moves money to its best and highest uses. Instead, they believe:

- If corporations move vast sums into stock buybacks instead of investing in the productive capacities of the firm, it must mean that those corporations *should* do so.
- If Wall Street–engineered, leveraged buyouts and mergers lead to mass layoffs, then those mass layoffs must be good for the economy, moving workers from unneeded to needed employment.
- If the financial markets move money away from working people and toward a tiny elite, that must be a positive development because the markets know best. Any discomfort this causes is the price we pay for freedom and democracy.
- And if inequality grows and grows and grows, it just means that the best and brightest are the winners, and that is as it should be.

We have only to look around us to see how wrong the true believers are. Both their economic and their political claims are patently wrong.

Wall Street, left to its own devices, is not only greedily destroying millions of jobs, but time and again, its chaotic wealth extraction processes threaten our entire economic system. Wall Street's financial machinations melted down the entire economy in 2008, nearly sending us into another Great Depression. Were it not for government intervention that's where we'd be.

Unregulated markets, tellingly, have not produced a stronger democracy here at home. For the first time in our history, in 2020 a sitting US president refused to accept the election results. His supporters stormed the Capitol in January 2021 in an attempt to prevent Congress from certifying the newly elected president. Voting rights in many states are under attack. As our study of surveys suggests, the mass layoffs enabled by free-market fundamentalism have probably contributed to this dangerous situation.

The evidence is clear: Our Wall Street–dominated financialized economy, free from effective government controls, cannot lead us to a better life—unless we are one of the few at the top. Hiding behind TINA inevitably leads to a kind of "uncreative destruction" that robs many Americans of a pathway to prosperity and a good life. Their loss of hope and faith in the democratic process creates the raw material for authoritarianism.

TINA-Shaped Consciousness

If belief in the goodness and inevitability of our financialized economy was rooted only in the minds of free-market ideologues, the battle to curtail financial strip-mining would have rapidly gained strength—as it seemed to during Occupy Wall Street in 2011 and Bernie Sanders's first presidential campaign in 2016. Unfortunately, the TINA mindset has burrowed deep into our brains, obscuring root causes and potential solutions and limiting how we collectively view the world.

After 40 years of listening to the incessant free-market catechism, our "conventional wisdom" is so shaped by TINA that it becomes difficult to have a productive conversation about solutions to mass layoffs that goes beyond abject surrender to market forces. If you propose that the government create jobs in areas that have been left behind, the resistance is fierce. Isn't that communism? Isn't that what China does? Haven't socialist governments all over the world failed to serve as the employer of last resort? Why shouldn't people relocate to where the jobs are? And why should my taxes pay for the failures of others? Even those who might otherwise support such an idea are resigned: That will never happen.

Therefore, the first crucial step toward getting beyond TINA is acknowledging the degree to which our imaginations have been constrained by idealized visions of the free market and the sense of its inevitability. It is helpful to recall what political leaders thought possible in the 1960s, compared to today.

In the 1960s it was understood by influential civil rights and labor leaders that poverty was a structural problem—a function of significant job loss in areas like Appalachia and the inner city, a problem that affected white, Black, and brown working people. For example, Walter Reuther, then president of the United Auto Workers, and civil rights activist Bayard Rustin, who organized the 1963 March on Washington for Jobs and Freedom, called for big solutions, such as massive public job creation.

Today, poverty is seen as the failure of the poor to move themselves upward—a problem that only can be solved through taking personal responsibility, through personal investment in education, and through private investment (with tax subsidies) in poorer areas. Direct public job creation is off the table.

In the 1960s, the government sector was held in high esteem, as reflected in President Kennedy's efforts to inspire us to serve our country. Striving only for personal gain was secondary, and even subject to popular ridicule. In the 1967 movie *The Graduate*, the young graduate Benjamin (Dustin Hoffman) is seduced by his neighbor's wife, Mrs. Robinson (Anne Bancroft). Her husband approaches Hoffman for a heart-to-heart talk about how he should start his career and offers this sage advice, in all seriousness: "Plastics!" Movie audiences exploded with laughter in part because of a widely shared belief that a meaningful life was about more than making a ton of money in the lucrative but soul-crushing plastics industry.

Today, nonmilitary government service is held in low esteem. Government-sector workers are sometimes characterized as living off the taxpayer, working without market discipline, and just not good enough to make it in the business sector.[10] There is a constant pressure to eliminate or privatize government-sector jobs, or at least de-unionize them.

In the 1960s it was understood by national political leaders that crime was a function of economic hardship and the lack of decent job opportunities. A rising prison population signaled economic failure, and such a failure could not be tolerated because the United States, the leader of the free world, was competing against the evils of communism and its gulags. Our prison population then was one-twentieth the size of today's.

Today, the United States has the most prisoners in the world in both absolute numbers and per capita among developed nations (see figure 10.1 on page 146). Furthermore, we have grown accustomed to an economy that provides no viable employment and income for those left behind. Perhaps the most significant poverty program we have today, if not Medicaid, is jail. (As of 2018, 886,400 prisoners were white, 835,100 Black, and 439,100 Hispanic.)

Figure 10.1. International rates of incarceration per 100,000 population
(most recent year available for each)

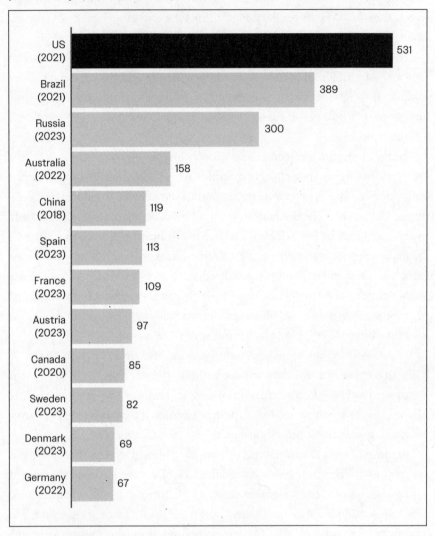

Source: Institute for Crime and Justice Policy Research[11]

Our TINA-shaped consciousness makes it extremely difficult to think beyond the received free-market ideology that defines our era. As we attempt to do so, we are likely to be heard as unrealistic, shrill, and even reckless.

But that's not how bold solutions to mass layoffs sound to those who have been left behind. People who have been laid off and those who are struggling to make it in a world structured by runaway inequality are looking for answers. To challenge Wall Street's hegemony and prerogatives, we must develop proposals that place everyday working people, of all shades and creeds, at the center of our reforms.

The place to start is by challenging the fundamental pillars of modern economic thought.

The purpose of any economic system should be the creation of stable, fulfilling jobs at livable wages for us all, not just to enrich the few. As Franklin Roosevelt said in 1944 in his call for a second Bill of Rights, "We have come to a clear realization of the fact that true individual freedom cannot exist without economic security and independence. Necessitous men are not free men. People who are hungry and out of a job are the stuff of which dictatorships are made."[12]

Shareholders are not the only stakeholders who matter. Workers and their communities should also help shape productive corporate enterprises. We need to reimagine what *ownership* means, especially when it comes to financial institutions that we, the American people, bail out incessantly. Worker-owned business also should be spread and supported.

Mass layoffs, especially those created by stock buybacks and leveraged buyouts, are not inevitable. They can and should be prevented or delayed as much as possible. And if they must occur, they should be accompanied by a fair and just transition program.

There *are* alternatives.

CHAPTER 11

Isn't Automation *the* Problem?

"The best thing to do to prevent [mass layoffs] in the future is to organize, to build bonds and make friends. [Build] these strong friendships and just fight. That's all you can do." —Geoff, age 35, 3 years of service

No MATTER THE ARGUMENTS AND DATA PRESENTED, IT IS NEARLY impossible to free our minds from technological determinism—the idea that machines inevitably will kill jobs and harm our society. Even as we decry Wall Street greed, somewhere in the back of our minds a little voice tells us that automation is the big culprit and there's not a damn thing we can do about it. That's not an accident. As the media becomes concentrated in fewer and fewer corporate hands, the information oligarchs would much rather raise fears about automation than report on how corporate looting, including their own, is causing mass layoffs.

Nevertheless, this book claims that automation, even AI, are insignificant job killers in comparison to legalized corporate looting.

It's understandable that the awesome power of technological change spurs our imaginations. The Industrial Revolution turned the world upside down and is still doing so. Each new technological achievement has a negative effect on employment, or at least it feels that way. Modern practices have eliminated nearly all our farmers while also producing high yields that feed the growing population. Horse and buggy drivers are no more (except in New York's Central Park and Amish country). Automated elevators, a marvel in themselves, don't need operators. Offices run without secretaries. Robots build cars. And now AI can write books, perhaps just like this one!

Writers, too, have fueled our imaginations about the godlike power of machines. The first novel about AI may have been *A Mexican Mystery* (1888) by Reginald Colebrooke Reade.[1] The short story "I, Robot" (1939), by Earl and Otto Binder, was perhaps the first that gave robots names and personalities.[2] And ever since, science fiction books and movies by the hundreds have featured thinking machines that take their revenge on us.

> "Open the pod bay door, HAL."
> "I'm sorry, Dave. I'm afraid I can't do that."
> (*2001: A Space Odyssey*, 1968)

Kurt Vonnegut's first novel, *Player Piano* (1952), connected automation to mass layoffs. Sensing the huge increase in productive power growing out of the WWII war effort, Vonnegut depicted a world in which nearly all working people are replaced, rendered obsolete by machines.

Given the saturation of popular culture with tales of machines taking revenge or replacing us, it is little wonder that each time a new technology comes onto the scene (computers, the internet, robotics, AI), a phalanx of prognosticators sound the alarm, and we are predisposed to believe them, again and again.

If automation is an unstoppable job killer, then TINA—there is no alternative—would win, hands down. Due to these inevitable technological advancements, the naysayers say, we'd better get used to never-ending and continuously growing waves of job destruction. That is the essence of technological determinism.

More to the point, if you buy into the demon-automation memes that are peddled after each technological lurch forward, you are likely to reject most of this book's claims.

Andrew Yang, the technologist who unsuccessfully ran for president in 2020 and for mayor of New York in 2021, would most definitely wonder why this book isn't focusing on the obvious threat of automation. Coming to politics from a career in the high-tech sector, Yang sees Vonnegut-style automation and destruction everywhere. During the October 2019 Democratic presidential debate, he said:

> They see what's happening around them. Their Main Street stores
> are closing. They see a self-serve kiosk in every McDonalds, every

grocery store, every CVS. Driving a truck is the most common job in 29 states. . . . [There are] 3.5 million truck drivers in this country. And my friends in California are piloting self-driving trucks. What is that going to mean for the 3.5 million truckers or the 7 million Americans who work in truck stops, motels, and diners that rely upon the truckers getting out and having a meal?[3]

In a follow-up *New York Times* op-ed, Yang proudly pointed to a study (uncovered by Associated Press debate fact-checkers) that he said supported his claims.[4] Unfortunately, the AP and the self-proclaimed "numbers guy" misread the study, which describes the effects of productivity growth, not automation, on job loss. According to this research, "Almost 88 percent of job losses in manufacturing in recent years can be attributable to productivity growth, and the long-term changes to manufacturing employment are mostly linked to the productivity of American factories."[5] But this claim is highly questionable as well.

Productivity Does Not Mean Job Loss

Productivity, the measure of output per worker-hour, has been rising in the United States since the dawn of the nation. To be sure, productivity depends on technological development. But it also depends at least as much on many other factors, including worker effort, skills, and loyalty, as well as public investments in education, physical infrastructure, research, and health care.

Successful high-performance corporations deploy new technologies along with investing in workers to achieve increases in productivity. These investments, when done right, lead to higher-quality products at lower prices, which in turn mean more sales and greater market share.

Economist William Lazonick, a leading expert of high-performance companies, walks us through how this process works.[6] In corporations that "retain profits and reinvest in the productive capabilities of the labor force, more and better jobs can result, even though the introduction of productivity-enhancing technologies might eliminate some existing jobs." He cites three reasons why this occurs:

1. Since automation is not usually deployed in all of a company's facilities at the same time, corporate growth may require hiring more

workers, including some who do tasks that automation is eliminating in other facilities.

2. Because the company has retained, rather than distributed, its financial resources, it can invest in upgrading the skills of workers whose former jobs are eliminated.

3. Automation provides a platform for the company to offer new types of products to customers (typically in the form of enhanced "services" as distinct from "goods") that can create not only more jobs but better jobs.

Lazonick, however, cautions us that these investments in working people do not fall from the sky. They were the result of two decades of intense collective bargaining during the post-WWII period that set the pattern for corporate investments in their employees. Since unions today have lost so much ground, Lazonick reminds us that "[w]orkers need to fight for this type of business model—which also means that they have to fight against corporate financialization. . . . None of this happens without a labor movement that focuses on issues of corporate governance," a topic we examine in the next chapter.

In corporations that retain their financial resources and reinvest in their employees, productivity creates more stable jobs, not fewer. Equating productivity with technological job loss is a major conceptual error.

Is It the Invasion of the Kiosk Body Snatchers?

Just about every retail store is encouraging customers to check out themselves these days. It's hard to look at all those empty cash register lines without wondering what happened to the clerks, as automation allows companies to use our labor (for free) to do their tasks. But surely, given all those kiosks, we should see a major decline in grocery store jobs. The numbers, however, tell a different story.

- The Blue Wall states that have been crushed by mass layoffs also suffered significant declines in grocery jobs between 1996 and 2022: Michigan −31.1 percent; Pennsylvania −10.8 percent; and Wisconsin −11.5 percent.
- But areas that are growing economically during this same time period have experienced a vast increase in grocery jobs: California +35.7 percent; New York City +45.2 percent; and Texas +27.9 percent.[7]

These statistics strongly suggest that automation is not the key to understanding job loss for grocery store workers. Grocery employment tracks with regional economic growth, not the adoption of automation. To paraphrase Groucho Marx: Who are you going to believe? The data? Or your lying eyes?

But Surely Those Robots Killed Jobs in the Auto Industry?

These amazing machines paint, weld, assemble, and handle materials on the factory floor, all tasks once done by humans. Clearly, those welding, painting, and handling jobs in factories have been displaced. But that doesn't mean that the overall number of auto jobs has collapsed. As figure 11.1 shows, employment in the auto industry rose in the 1990s, after robots already had marched through the industry.[8] When the serious dip set in after 2000, it was due to multiple causes, including NAFTA, which made it easier to produce cars and parts in Mexico, and pressure from higher-quality imports from Japan and Europe that caused US companies to retrench. Robotics played a secondary role in that period of job contraction.

Figure 11.1. Motor vehicles and parts employment by year, 1990–2022

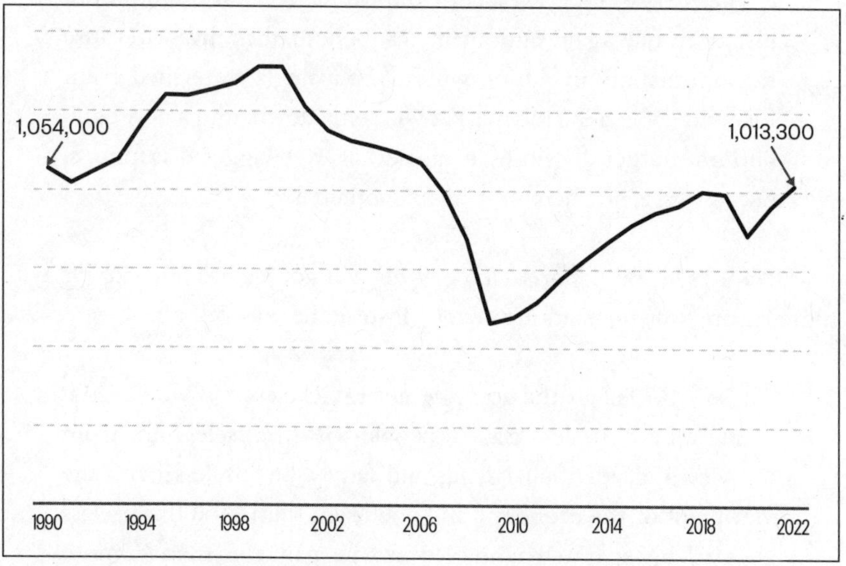

Source: Bureau of Labor Statistics [9]

Furthermore, in Japan, the world's leader in developing and deploying robotics, workers have guaranteed lifetime employment and increasing job opportunities. As one recent academic study makes clear, "[T]he decline in robot prices increased both the number of robots and employment by raising the productivity and production scale of robot-adopting industries."[10]

But What About Self-Driving Trucks?

Historian and philosopher Yuval Noah Harari also is profoundly alarmed by the power of AI. At the 2020 World Economic Forum in Davos, Switzerland, he challenged financial and political elites to face up to a brave new world inhabited by disheartened former workers. Not only will automation destroy their jobs, he said, but they also will have their data mined, their emotions monitored, their tastes manipulated, and their offspring bioengineered. Once again, the truckers take center stage:

> Suppose you are a 50-year-old truck driver, and you just lost your job to a self-driving vehicle. Now there are new jobs in designing software or in teaching yoga to engineers—but how does a 50-year-old truck driver reinvent himself or herself as a software engineer or as a yoga teacher? And people will have to do it not just once but again and again throughout their lives, because the automation revolution will not be a single watershed event following which the job market will settle down, into a new equilibrium. Rather, it will be a cascade of ever bigger disruptions, because AI is nowhere near its full potential. [11]

In Harari's vision, labor-saving devices will not lead to a better life with more leisure time for working people. Instead, he sees despair:

> Those who fail in the struggle against irrelevance would constitute a new "useless class"—people who are useless not from the viewpoint of their friends and family, but useless from the viewpoint of the economic and political system. And this useless class will be separated by an ever-growing gap from the ever more powerful elite. [12]

"Just Keep Truckin' On"

Harari and Yang are captivating storytellers. Unfortunately, they show little knowledge of the actual trucking industry. Overall, there are approximately 3.5 million truck drivers.[13] Of that, 1.64 million[14] are involved in local delivery, and 575,000 of those are self-employed.[15] About 2 million are heavy and tractor-trailer drivers.[16] Approximately half of those long-haul drivers are independent contractors.[17]

As Steve Viscelli makes clear in his excellent history, *The Big Rig: Trucking and the Decline of the American Dream*, many of those independent contractors are struggling contingent laborers, working at near poverty wages. They own their rigs, pay for their truck's insurance and maintenance, and provide for their own health and retirement benefits (if any). To make ends meet they work all the hours allowed by law, and then some.[18]

Because corporations of all shapes and sizes rely on contingent truck drivers, it's hard to imagine a rapid deployment of self-driving trucks that ends up causing mass layoffs. Contingent drivers are unlikely to unemploy themselves by buying driverless vehicles, and the thousands of firms that subcontract with independent truckers are likely to continue to find this arrangement profitable, since it is the trucker who takes all responsibility for the equipment purchases, maintenance, and benefits.

It's certainly possible that Amazon, for example, might decide eventually to replace all of its contingent drivers with automated trucks or delivery drones to drop off packages. However, in the local trucking industry, it's exceedingly difficult to imagine how to automate the delivery and installation of appliances, for example.

If automation does indeed come to truck delivery (that doesn't involve installation or intricate maneuvers of furniture and the like), it will have its hands full trying to keep up with the 11 percent expected truck driver job growth through 2031.[19] History and logic show us that although technological advances can be revolutionary, job dislocation is likely to be a slow-moving process that ripples through society rather than overwhelms it.

Can We Exorcise the Fear of Automation?

Rather than dwelling on the automation apocalypse, it pays to listen more closely to those who have studied how automation has actually affected specific industries. As one such study put it, "Compared to findings from a literature on mass layoffs, the effects of automation are more gradual and automation displaces far fewer workers, both at the individual firms and in the workforce overall."[20]

The Bureau of Labor Statistics concluded their extensive 2022 investigation of automation with this:

> Fears that automation will cause widespread job losses have been raised repeatedly in the past, which, in retrospect, usually greatly overestimated the scale of actual displacement. Recent experience and projections suggest a similar pattern may be occurring with recent developments in AI and robotics. For various reasons, technological change seems to be generally more gradual than commonly recognized. Prior waves of computing may be too familiar to receive much attention from observers of emerging trends, but their immediate effects are probably smaller than anticipated and their full impact unfolds gradually over a longer timeframe than recognized.[21]

Sure, as the financial brochures say, "past performance is no guarantee of future results." Maybe AI will finally be the technology that rapidly wipes out jobs. Let's ask ChatGPT: "Overall, the impact of AI on mass job layoffs is not straightforward and depends on various factors. While some job displacement is likely, AI also has the potential to create new jobs and enhance human capabilities."

Of course, AI could be dead wrong about AI. Maybe it's lying to us so that we don't interfere with its future conquests. Or maybe next year it will tell us that catastrophic job loss is about to eliminate most of our jobs. But look at how much our reasoning requires pure fiction. It's time to admit, at least to ourselves, that apocalyptic projections into the future are based largely on imagination, fear, and faith, not science, not economics, and certainly not history. The problem, of course, is that it is very, very difficult to challenge gut feelings based on imagination, fear, and faith.

The Problem Is Stock Buybacks, Not Automation

Nevertheless, let us attempt to undermine the sci-fi understanding of automation (as amplified by the media moguls). Let's grant, for a moment, that we won't be able to strike from our imaginations a looming world run by machines. After all, ChatGPT can now whisper sweet nothings in our ears, and robots can give us backrubs. It is totally understandable that these mind-boggling developments make it ever so easy to imagine catastrophic job destruction.

But it wasn't always so. In October 1955, a congressional committee held hearings on "Automation and Technological Change." They, like Vonnegut, sensed the nation's unease about the impact of automation. But, in those days—an era not ruled by Wall Street—they could also imagine a world in which automation benefited working people: "The prevailing workweek in manufacturing today, as is well known, is about 40 hours per week compared to about 45 in the mid-1920s and about 60 at the turn of the century. The hope is frequently expressed that the fruits of automation may permit us to reduce this still further, to 30, 32, or 35 hours per week in the not-too-distant future."[22]

Those hopes have perished. We have yet to find a current analyst who is saying: "Revolutionary automation like AI could be a terrific development for working people. These high-productivity technologies could make it possible for workers to be paid full wages and benefits while working no more than 25 hours per week. And also, working people could be liberated from the most dangerous and boring tasks!"

Instead, we live in an era where greed, not the public's welfare, rules the roost. We sense and fear that technological change will first and foremost serve financial and corporate elites, not the rest of us. We sense that the impact of automation on working people is not just a secondary consideration for the powers that be—it's not even part of the financial equation.

This is why financial maneuvers like stock buybacks and leveraged buyouts are far more dangerous to working people than automation and AI. When we see a robot or a self-checkout kiosk, we need to remind ourselves that most job destruction is engineered by the very rich and powerful to suit themselves. Those financial barons discovered that the secret to fabulous wealth isn't creating healthy, functioning companies that provide goods and services. The secret to achieving unimaginable riches is to financialize all commerce in order to siphon off as much wealth as possible.

Those who warn us about the perils of automation should review the story of Bed Bath & Beyond, which until 2022 employed 30,000 workers.

The company's officers and its major hedge fund stockholders decided long ago to milk the company for all it was worth and then some. Since 2004, the company has spent nearly $12 billion on stock buybacks to boost the price of its shares, allowing its corporate officers and major stockholders to cash out with handsome profits. The average cost of those share repurchases was $44 per share.[23] As of April 14, 2023, the company's share price was down to 24 cents! In January 2023 the company announced that more than 18,000 jobs would be lost. At the end of April 2023, it went into bankruptcy. It's possible all 30,000 jobs will soon evaporate.

The lesson here isn't that a hard-working company with hard-working employees failed in the market, losing out to online sellers like Amazon. (Clearly, it showed no interest in using the billions flowing into stock buybacks to diversify product offerings and develop a strong online presence.) The lesson here is that the company and its hedge fund looters found ways to strip out all the money they could for themselves, and then left the employees high, dry, and unemployed.

And this isn't a one-off event. Toys-R-Us met a similar fate when it closed its doors in 2018, costing more than 30,000 workers their jobs. In this case, the looting method of choice was a leveraged buyout organized by Bain Capital when Senator Mitt Romney was its CEO. After purchasing the company, Bain Capital loaded up Toys-R-Us with $5 billion in debt it couldn't service. Rest assured that before bankruptcy, Bain Capital had sucked out more wealth than it lost in equity.[24]

Labor journalist Hamilton Nolan colorfully describes the very essence of these bankruptcies: "But when you think about it a little it becomes clear that the people who fancy themselves as the captains of the ship are actually the wood-eating shipworms who are consuming the thing from inside until it sinks."[25]

Andrew Yang should note that his high-tech compatriots are also chewing on the wood. They have conducted hundreds of billions in stock buybacks while at the same time initiating hundreds of thousands of mass layoffs over the last year.

Meta/Facebook, Alphabet/Google, and Microsoft alone have announced 43,000 layoffs since the end of 2022. Yet, just before those announcements, *in the third quarter of 2022 alone,* these three firms conducted $28 billion in stock buybacks that benefited their top officers and more than 500 hedge funds that had taken large stock positions in those companies.[26] That's more than $650,000 per laid-off worker!

In the past five years, these three tech companies have conducted $383 billion in stock repurchases.[27] How much is that? Enough to pay for four years of full in-state tuition for 5.5 million students at America's public colleges and universities.[28]

The corporate media is flooded with stories about AI and how it will undermine our jobs. And yet there is simply no credible data to suggest that automation in any sector has led to, or will soon lead to, anything near this magnitude of stock buyback / leveraged buyout job destruction, especially over such a short period of time.

In addition, there is no evidence to suggest that any of these high-tech industry layoffs were connected to automation. (Wait! That's not entirely true. The layoff notices were automatically emailed to the victims.)

The equation that comes closest to capturing reality is this:

Financial looting (not automation) = mass layoffs

CHAPTER 12

Toward a Progressive Populism

Policies to Halt Mass Layoffs

"I was very progressive when I walked onto that campus. Now, I use the term 'limousine liberal.' That's how I look at them. And they are more despicable than Republicans. It's grotesque. . . . The [Oberlin College] board of directors, who set this all in motion. . . .

"I remember going to the Chairman's Twitter feed, and the whole feed was deriding Trump for this and that. And I thought, 'If Trump had gotten rid of staff like the Board did, imagine the outrage on the other side. Talk about the pot calling the kettle black!'

"It's changed my political outlook, it really has. At least the Republicans tell you they're gonna screw you. The Democrats just do it in the dark of the night. That's the way I look at it now.

"Honestly, I don't think I'll vote. I think that the political system is totally messed up. The first election that I was eligible to vote in was Clinton's final term. And I didn't miss an election. But I didn't vote in the last one. I can't vote for Joe Biden. I can't vote for Trump because I don't believe in his policies. But like, Joe Biden? That's the best that the Democrats can offer? This is absurd. This whole system is so messed up right now. We need third and fourth and fifth parties to better reflect the populace."

— Eugene McCormick, age 38,
laid off after 9 years of service

I HOPE THIS BOOK HAS MADE THE CASE THAT MAJOR CHANGES ARE needed to address mass layoffs. As a nation, it is time to decide that protecting the health and well-being of our working people should be a top priority—at least as important as quarterly increases to corporate profits.

For the past four decades, neither political party has been willing to seriously address the problem of mass layoffs. This has created a dangerous political vacuum. Working people in the United States, of all shades and ethnicities, in urban, suburban, and rural areas, desperately want stable, decent employment. Yet moves to halt or even control mass layoffs are not forthcoming from either party.

Republicans remain fully committed to economic deregulation even though that is likely to accelerate mass layoffs. At the same time, many Republican leaders seem firmly committed to re-regulating social life—eager to use the power of government to limit abortion, birth control, and LGBTQ+ rights. There also is growing Republican support for autocratic policies that include election denialism, the curtailment of voter rights, and extreme gerrymandering. Putting forth policies to curtail stock buybacks, leveraged buyouts, and mass layoffs is not on the agenda.

As our research shows, the Democrats are losing touch with the working class in large part because of a failure to address mass layoffs. There is a strong correlation between the counties that suffered the highest per capita mass layoffs and Democratic vote loss in presidential elections, especially in the more rural counties of the politically crucial Blue Wall states.

Our study also shows that the abandonment of the Democrats is *not* correlated with a rise in illiberal attitudes on divisive social issues among the white working class. In fact, the data suggest that the bulk of the working class nationwide support LGBTQ+ rights, legalization of undocumented immigrant workers, fairness for women and minorities, and bans on assault rifles.

This makes for an encouraging prospect: A new progressive populism could develop and spread among working people. We saw the first sparks during Occupy Wall Street, although it's unclear how much of this message reached the working class. The desire for economic justice was spread further during the Sanders presidential campaigns, which resonated with working people in many parts of the country. Nevertheless, when Trump received massive support in rural America, it was assumed by too many Democrats that the white working class was, and still is, a lost cause.

Given this abandonment by both political parties, there is a crying need for an independent political movement of working people that puts forth its own agenda to pressure the political and economic system to deliver stable employment—the very foundation of a decent life. Although the history of third parties in the United States is not encouraging, the epidemic of mass layoffs could give birth to a new politics that would put mass layoffs on the political agenda. That road is long and difficult, but it starts with encouraging working-class people to develop and put forth their own vision and agenda. My organization, the Labor Institute, will continue to do all it can to assist in that process.

Doing so requires that those of us who develop policies have direct engagement with working-class organizations. It requires that we actually talk with (not at) working-class people rather than writing them off as reactionary populists. And it requires that we stop talking only to ourselves. We have to share what we've learned with the people who have been directly impacted. Hard-hitting reforms need to be nurtured through a substantive dialogue between progressive policy developers and those who are personally experiencing the terrifying insecurity created by incessant financial strip-mining. The victims of mass layoffs must be part of the policy process, or the policies won't ring true. Such a dialogue could lead a progressive populist agenda that the working class embrace as their own.

What follows in this chapter is a set of substantive policy ideas that can be used to nurture such a dialogue with working-class people, especially within labor unions and immigrant worker centers.* It will be especially important to reach out to the white working-class people, who for too long have been dismissed from the progressive dialogue.

It is time to reclaim the progressive populist mantle and bring it back to its original roots—a movement that challenges financial and corporate power so that the economy serves the many and not just the few. This will be no easy task, given that Democratic Party elites think white workers are a lost cause and Republican Party elites think that white workers are ripe for illiberal exploitation. But the door is open for all who are willing to tackle layoffs of mass destruction.

This quest is particularly difficult because mass layoffs often have multiple causes, many of which are interconnected, and those causes are

---

* Immigrant worker centers are voluntary formations similar to unions that address the many problems of immigrant working people. It is estimated that there are more than 300 worker centers across the country.

multifaceted and related, and therefore confusing to untangle. The causes of mass layoffs include:

- the growth of contingent labor / gig work
- financial crashes
- leveraged (debt-financed) mergers and acquisitions
- stock buybacks
- global competition
- climate change and the move away from fossil-fuel-related industries
- the economic "war between the states," including bribes to encourage corporations to relocate
- poor management and corporate failure

It is next to impossible to tease apart these different causes of mass layoffs. What seems like bad management could easily be connected to leveraged buyouts (as was the case with Elon Musk's buyout of Twitter). What seems like job loss due to foreign competition could really be the result of stock buybacks (as was the case with Carrier). And even mass layoffs due to shifts to greener production processes could be connected to stock buybacks (as was the case with Siemens Energy).

That's why it is critical that we consider strong proposals that curb financial strip-mining—the process by which Wall Street and corporate America shift wealth away from Main Street. Financial strip-mining ties together the many causes of mass layoffs.

But we will have to go further. Fundamentally, we must question the right of employers to be the sole decision-makers in determining when mass layoffs are necessary and appropriate. And we must discuss this question directly with working people.

The first four reforms below come from Professor William Lazonick, who has probably spent more time and energy on this problem than anyone else in the country.

End stock buybacks. Using corporate money to manipulate stock is an unmitigated disaster for job stability. Before the SEC issued rule 10b-18 in

1982, few corporations resorted to stock buybacks, perhaps in fear that the SEC would accuse them of stock manipulation. As a result, in 1982 only about 2 percent of corporate profits went to stock buybacks. Today, nearly 70 percent of all corporate profits go to share repurchases to enrich share sellers. That is money *not* reinvested in workers, the company's physical plant, or the community. Now corporate executives receive most of their pay in stock options and grants, which incentivizes short-term thinking and disinvestment. And since those executives set the timing of stock buybacks, there is an irresistible incentive to use insider information to cash out. The same goes for the largest activist hedge funds, which demand more and more stock buybacks. Share buybacks also inflate the overall stock market, adding to economic instability. To avoid a sudden shock to the markets, buybacks would need to be phased out gradually. But there is no way around it: Without a dramatic reduction in stock buybacks there can be no job security.

Prohibit shareholder activists from serving on boards of directors. Hedge funds and other financial entities have invaded corporate boards to pressure for more and more stock buybacks. To silence this drumbeat for looting, corporate law should be changed to prohibit such share sellers and their representatives from serving on corporate boards. This requires reversing a series of regulations that have allowed hedge funds to easily access proxy votes and dominate boards, even when they only own a small percentage of the company's shares.[1]

Change the way top corporate officers are paid. Before the financial strip-miners took over, top corporate officials received most of their pay in salary and bonuses and only a small portion in stock options and grants. Today it is the reverse. Professor Lazonick suggests that laws and regulations be changed to remove stock-related grants from CEO compensation. It's time for CEOs to focus on the long-term task of building sustainable, innovative businesses in vibrant communities, rather than on enriching themselves through stock buybacks.

Place worker and public representatives on the board of directors. In *Investing in Innovation*, Professor Lazonick provides a compelling account of what it takes to build a successful corporation.[2] He argues that all corporations rely on three primary stakeholders making substantial investments: (1) the financial community that provides investment capital; (2) the public, via taxes to the government that fund research, education, infrastructure, and the like; and (3) the families and workers who invest in themselves and their children so that they can become productive employees. Since all three are key to creating and sustaining innovative enterprises, all three should be represented on the board of directors.

We thank Professor Lazonick for developing and describing these important reforms. The rest are from me (and many others who are working on these issues).

Public Banks

Currently, 49 states deposit tax dollars from state residents and businesses into private banks and keep the funds there until they're needed. At the end of 2021, the State of New Jersey Cash Management Fund, for example, contained $29.8 billion of taxpayer money.[3] That cash fund purchased nearly $8 billion in corporate commercial notes and $5.3 billion in bank certificates of deposits. These corporations and banks then used that taxpayer money to invest all over the world.

When local government agencies and businesses need loans from the state for infrastructure projects and the like, New Jersey doesn't use that pot of taxpayer money. Instead, it turns to Wall Street banks and insurance companies to borrow money, paying interest to their corporate financiers. In effect, taxpayers loan money to Wall Street and then Wall Street issues loans back to the taxpayers.

In one state, North Dakota, the Wall Street intermediaries are cut out of the picture. Taxpayer money goes directly into the Bank of North Dakota (founded in 1919 by the Populist movement) and then is loaned directly to local businesses and government agencies. Profits go to the taxpayer rather than to Wall Street.

Clearly, every state and large city needs their own public bank so that taxpayer money can work to develop local areas rather than to enrich financiers.

Protect Contingent and Gig Workers

Unless the wages and working conditions of contingent workers match those of full-time, salaried employees, giant warehouse firms, and other companies will replace as many employees as they can with temps. New Jersey passed legislation in 2023 to prevent temporary workers from being cheated by temp agencies. The bill calls for the right to basic information in English and the workers' native language about where they will be working, the rate of pay, their schedule, what kind of work they will be doing, and how much sick time they will get. The bill would also eliminate many of the fees that temp agencies deduct from workers' paychecks, including mandatory fees for the vans that take them to their worksites. Workers would also be guaranteed to earn at least the minimum wage after fees are deducted. (The law took effect on August 5, 2023. A federal court has refused to grant an industry request for an injunction.)[4]

Gig workers and many independent contractors should be considered employees and receive all the benefits enjoyed by regular employees.

Limit Corporate Debt

Leveraged buyouts are a calamity. Since the early 1980s, political leaders have understood that when corporations are bought with debt that is then placed on the acquired company's books, mass layoffs are sure to follow. Adding insult to injury, that debt is then tax-deductible, lowering the taxes corporations pay and depriving revenue for public services.

Take as an example the 2022 purchase of Twitter by Elon Musk for $44 billion dollars. As reported in the *New York Times* in October of that year, "Mr. Musk, the world's richest man, loaded about $13 billion in debt on the company which had not turned a profit for 8 of the past 10 years."[5] Twitter's debt payments jumped from $50 million in 2021 to about $1.5 billion in 2023.[6] To make ends meet, the staff has been reduced by 80 percent of Twitter's 7,500 employees.[7]

We need major reforms to prevent investors and corporations from buying up companies with borrowed money and then loading the debt onto those companies, often dooming them.

In 1987, Dan Rostenkowski (D-IL), then chair of the powerful House Ways and Means Committee, proposed curbing leveraged buyout tax breaks. After the House approved his bill limiting interest deductions on corporate-takeover debt, "My phones jumped off the hook from Wall Street," said Rostenkowski. "I don't want to curtail the market, but I also want those people to recognize that the taxpayer is fed up with the fact they are using their money for this ridiculous degree with which big corporations are swallowing up other corporations."[8]

The reform didn't happen. Rostenkowski said later that some people had viewed his proposed legislation as the cause of the October 1987 stock market crash. This ridiculous claim was designed to ward off any future attempts to curb the power of Wall Street.

Prevent Corporate-Focused Trade Deals

American politicians have a history of bashing Asian countries for major US job losses.

First it was Japan, in the 1980s, after it successfully competed in the US electronics and automobile markets. To show solidarity with threatened US workers in 1987, nine members of Congress stood in a circle on the Capitol grounds and smashed a Toshiba transistor radio.[9]

The Japanese did not gain access to our markets willy-nilly. They got here because our political leaders wanted to bind Japan to the West during the Cold War. Containing communism around the world trumped concerns about job losses.

Now it is the Chinese who are portrayed as trade and currency cheats who unfairly dump products into our markets. China's entry into the World Trade Organization in 2001, however, didn't happen by accident. Corporations wanted to shift production to millions of low-wage laborers in China while also gaining profitable footholds in China's vast emerging markets. Bill Clinton called it "a win-win for both countries."[10]

Unfortunately, it didn't quite work out that way. As the Economic Policy Institute reported:

> The growth of the US trade deficit with China between 2001 and 2018 was responsible for the loss of 3.7 million US jobs, including 1.7 million jobs lost since 2008 (the first full year of the Great Recession, which technically began at the end of 2007). Three-fourths (75.4 percent) of the jobs lost between 2001 and 2018 were in manufacturing (2.8 million manufacturing jobs lost due to the growth in the trade deficit with China).[11]

Nevertheless, nearly all Republicans and key Democrats (including the Clintons, Obama, and Biden) continued to support corporate-friendly trade agreements, even as the job losses mounted.

Trump and China changed the game.

Sensing the growing anger among the victims of mass layoffs, especially in the crucial Blue Wall states, Trump outflanked both parties by calling for tariffs on Chinese imports and opposing the Trans-Pacific Partnership trade deal. His attack on trade agreements may have been the key to his victory over Hillary Clinton, a free-trade advocate. Once in power, Trump slapped 25 percent tariffs on approximately $34 billion of Chinese imports.[12]

China also changed the game as it evolved into a major superpower with its own geopolitical interests. It expanded its military might while using trade deals to expand its "soft power" influence. Integrating China into the global economy did not lead to democracy there, nor did it create better bilateral relations with the United States.

For the first time since WWII, economic nationalism is spreading through the Democratic Party's leadership. The Biden administration, with support from many progressives, is providing subsidies for US manufacturers to produce in the United States, and it is attempting to prevent the export of key technologies to China. The Biden administration is also maintaining many of the Trump tariffs and expanding controls on high-tech sectors in the name of national security.

It is absolutely necessary to negotiate fairer and more balanced trade with China, including tariffs when necessary. It is very dangerous, however, to use the threat of China to achieve a more progressive agenda around domestic investment.

Please forgive the preachy tone, but no matter how hard we try to avoid attacking the Chinese people, no matter how carefully we put our concerns about China's trade policies, no matter what concrete achievements we can point to, attacking China will inevitably lead to hostility against Chinese people, including Chinese Americans. Our 150-year romance with race pseudoscience has turned the Chinese—"the yellow peril"—into a separate biological "race" that can be easily attacked as "other." Chinese Americans, and all Asian Americans, are likely to pay the price for attaching US economic renewal to China bashing.

We would do better to look closely at the corporations that have moved jobs abroad to fatten their coffers. We should also be very mindful that without stringent controls, the federal subsidies we provide to corporations to keep production at home could easily turn into ready cash for stock buybacks.

When it comes to trade agreements, the interests of the American people must be separated from the interests of corporations. In all so-called "free trade" agreements, US corporations seek rules that promote their particular interests, which are not the same as worker and community interests. Using China as a foil, rather than attacking destructive corporate behaviors, lets Wall Street off the hook, and puts a target on the backs of Asian Americans.

Given that even fair and balanced global trade agreements are likely to cause some job dislocation, we need to make sure that job dislocation doesn't occur because of lurking stock buybacks and other Wall Street predatory exploits. For those who suffer mass layoffs in hard-hit areas, we need genuine job-creation programs that don't devolve into Wall Street piggybanks—which is so often the case with "public-private" partnerships. As a United Nations report shows, public-private partnerships "have often tended to be more expensive than the alternative of public procurement . . . (and) they have failed to yield 'value for money.'"[13]

How about a massive program to mitigate mass layoffs—like the one that resurrected Western Europe after WWII?

A Marshall Plan for Victims of Mass Layoffs

After WWII, the United States instituted the largest economic development program in its history to rebuild Europe. Approximately 5.2 percent of the 1948 US gross domestic product (GDP) was poured into the program, equivalent to $1.33 trillion today as a percent of 2022 GDP).[14] The Marshall Plan was named after Secretary of State George Marshall, who came up with the strategy. Marshall and other US leaders feared that Europe's war-ravaged economies created conditions that would make communism more attractive and increase the power and influence of the Soviet Union. The Marshall Plan provided the resources European countries needed to rebuild. By 1952, when the support ended, the countries receiving the funds had grown their economies beyond their prewar levels.[15]

Imagine making similar public investments to bring prosperity to regions impacted by mass layoffs. A good place to start is the $30 billion that Hillary Clinton proposed for coal country during her 2016 presidential campaign. That's a serious amount of money targeted for infrastructure development, broadband expansion, reclamation of abandoned mines, renewable energy development on federal lands, and public research and development for carbon capture and sequestration.

Her plan had a major flaw, however. It relied too heavily on tax credits and other subsidies to private developers, which were expected to produce new jobs in alternative energy and other businesses. Given the checkered record of such subsidies—and public-private partnerships in general—there is little reason to believe those subsidies would have brought a flood of new, decent-paying jobs to these hard-hit areas.

Clinton's $30 billion would have been better spent on funding the federal and state governments as employers of last resort, guaranteeing jobs at a livable wage for all those willing and able to work. Through a series of town meetings throughout the region, a list of projects based on planner and local citizen input could be created. Those projects would be designed to improve the environment, rebuild schools and roads, expand access to higher education, develop universal preschool programs, enhance public school extracurricular activities, make homes more energy-efficient, and improve access to health care. With tens of thousands of local people back at work, with real money in their pockets, and with improved roads and schools, private enterprises (other than pill mills) would certainly follow.

A similar plan is needed for low-income urban areas. It's time to stop waiting for the free-market fairy to wave its magic trickle-down wand.

How to pay for it? It will take a great deal of political will to fairly tax the vast wealth that has gushed to the top fraction of the top 1 percent. One can imagine many revenue generators, starting with a small financial transaction tax on Wall Street beyond the modest one included in the 2022 Inflation Reduction Act. Taxing the mass buying and selling of stocks, bonds, and derivatives seems like a fair way to provide jobs for the victims of mass layoffs. We can tax fossil fuel companies and put a wealth tax on those with more than $10 million in net assets. And the carried interest loophole and the tax break for capital gains should be eliminated. Methods abound. What is needed is the will and organizational strength.

Make Unionization Easier and Simpler

This is a different kind of reform. It's needed because none of the proposals listed above will succeed and endure unless worker power grows. The Protecting the Right to Organize (PRO) Act introduced in Congress in 2021 and 2022 would be a good place to start.[16]

It was not an accident that the post-WWII era of growing equality came when labor was at its peak strength in the United States. Note that as labor union density has declined, inequality has increased (see figure 12.2).

Figure 12.1. Percent of private-sector workers in unions, 1933–2021

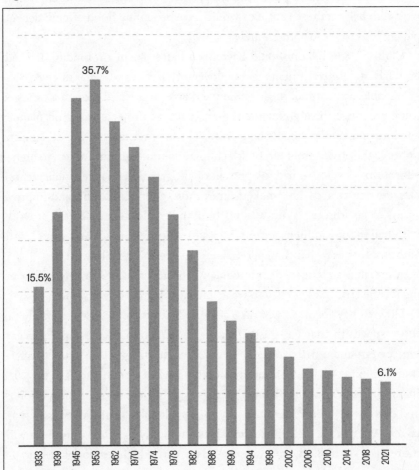

Source: unionstats.com[17]

Education: A Solution from the Man Who Hated Work and Loved Labor

The most radical proposal for addressing layoffs comes from the late Tony Mazzocchi (1926–2002), a leader of the Oil, Chemical and Atomic Workers Union, which today is part of the United Steelworkers. Based on his own hatred of dangerous, repetitive, mind-dulling, degrading, and environmentally destructive work, he argued for a straightforward solution: Let the corporations destroy all the jobs they want but force them to pay to make

Figure 12.2. Union membership and share of income going to the top 10%

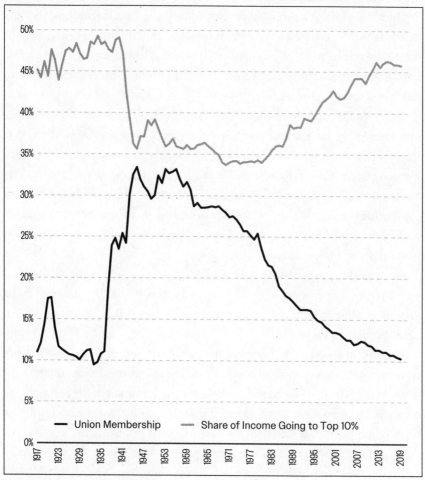

Source: Economic Policy Institute[18]

the workers whole until they find another job of their choosing. By making workers whole, Mazzocchi meant full pay and benefits, along with covering tuition for higher education or technical training for as long as it takes.

He really did hate traditional work: "Work is shit," he would say. "That's why I became a labor bureaucrat."

Because he represented tens of thousands who worked with the most dangerous substances on Earth—from fossil fuels to asbestos to plutonium, Mazzocchi saw a monumental jobs-versus-environment clash on the horizon. He recognized that these hazardous substances had to be eliminated from production to protect the exposed workers, the surrounding communities, and the environment.

Over the years, his proposal developed into the Just Transition program, which is now a core concept in planning for climate change. It is part of the 2015 Paris Climate Agreement (COP 21) and has taken legislative form, including measures in Washington State and California to provide funds for dislocated fossil fuel workers.[19]

Many intellectuals found Mazzocchi's original conception of Just Transition impossibly impractical and far too costly. That didn't stop Mazzocchi from engaging in a massive dialogue about it with thousands of workers, spanning more than two decades. He pushed his idea directly to the workers he represented—oil, chemical, and atomic workers. He argued for it at labor conventions, encouraged countless workshops in which it was discussed, pushed for it within the environmental community, and took on all comers who said it was impossible.

He would always return to the GI Bill of Rights. It was the GI Bill that paid Mazzocchi's tuition after he returned from WWII. He learned to fix dentures, while receiving a living wage from the GI Bill. Why not do that again for dislocated workers?

Mazzocchi's proposal, however, has encountered significant resistance from working-class people. They *want* to work, and most desperately want to avoid mass layoffs. To be sure, if layoffs can't be stopped, they would welcome a Just Transition that protected their economic well-being until new work could be found. And many would welcome economic support so that they could go back to school to pick up new skills. However, they would rather not see their existing jobs destroyed, their lives upended, and their communities harmed.

We need to continue a Mazzocchi-like mass educational dialogue on a wide range of policy reforms addressing layoffs of mass destruction. And we need the labor movement to lead the charge.

———

Until the unleashing of Wall Street during the Reagan revolution, unions were a major force in our political economy, counterbalancing corporate and financial power. Core industries like oil, steel, coal, rubber, long-haul trucking, and automobiles were highly unionized. Negotiations in those industries set the wage levels for much of society. And the political power of those mass organizations kept the pressure on government for worker-oriented policies like progressive tax rates, a rising minimum wage, and significant social welfare programs.

As historian Michael Merrill points out, there have been four great labor struggles in US history:

1. The struggle against royal power, which was replaced by the power of a new constitutional democracy during the American Revolution.
2. The battle against slave-owner power, which after the Civil War was replaced by the power of free labor.
3. The battle against corporate power, which was tamed by government regulation and union/worker power on the job, culminating in union rights victories during the 1930s through the 1960s.
4. The fourth great battle is happening right now: The battle against financial power, with the outcome very much in doubt.[20]

Not only are we coming up short against financial power and the greed it promotes, but the battle has taken a dangerous turn away from democratic norms, both here and abroad. The purported connection that binds capitalism and democracy is splintering before our very eyes. While the "fucking bond traders" are poised to ruin countries that dare protect working people, they also are perfectly willing to placate authoritarian regimes that stabilize wealth and its extraction.

To protect and promote democratic practices, a large democratic countervailing force needs to confront autocratic financial power. Labor organizations are among the few civic entities with that capacity. In most unions, the members are not self-selected as they would be in, for example, an environmental organization. Instead, they are chosen by the employer. That means that while the members share a common work experience, they do not necessarily share political and social attitudes. And this can be a great strength. For labor organizations to function, they must provide common educational programs that promote discussions vital to a healthy democratic society. Democratic practices within unions are at least as important as those found anywhere else in society.

Day-to-day union activities that improve collective worker well-being also help combat the polarization and authoritarian impulses that are ripping our nation apart. For generations, labor unions have been trusted sources of working-class information, which helped balance the output of pro-corporate media. The decline of union membership over the past four decades has likely created more space for the spread of misinformation, conspiracy theories, and authoritarian messaging. The decline of the labor movement has certainly created more space for the movement of wealth from the many to the wealthiest among us.

To be sure, labor organizations are not utopian democracies. They face continual struggles to preserve and enhance internal democratic norms so that the rank and file has a meaningful voice in directing union policies. But most unions have free and fair elections for their leaders, from the local shop steward to the national union president. Hedge funds do not. Private equity firms do not. Wall Street investment banks do not. Corporations do not. Philanthropic foundations do not. Universities do not. And even most civic nonprofit organizations have few internal democratic practices.

Where do citizens gain a working knowledge of democracy if not in labor unions? Where else do we learn concretely that democracy can enhance our well-being?

Working people have fought and died to win union recognition. Working people have fought and died to promote union democracy. Now, working people need to fight again to save unions and halt the carnage of mass layoffs and the deterioration of democracy. We all need a large and growing mass labor movement. There is no way around it.

Learning from the Powell Memo

As we discussed in chapter 6, Louis F. Powell Jr. wrote a highly influential memo for the US Chamber of Commerce in 1971 arguing for a long-term investment by corporate leaders in a wide variety of academic, media, and political institutions in order to forge a powerful defense of free enterprise.

It took time, money, and patience. But in little more than a decade, corporate entities took control of the national debate, eventually turning both political parties into proponents of some form of trickle-down economics. Of course, their speed was enabled by their authoritarian structure. It will take us longer because democracy, for good reasons, will slow us down.

Progressives tend to be impatient. We see suffering and injustices and feel compelled to respond immediately. What good are long-term efforts to end stock buybacks when Black men and women are being gunned down by the police? Why talk about workers on the board of directors when tens of thousands of contingent workers can't even get a permanent job? Why waste time constructing a pie-in-the-sky Marshall Plan for those left behind when the planet is burning up right now?

It is easy to say we should do both. Doing so, however, is difficult for organizations that are overwhelmed with urgent and immediate struggles. It's already challenging for civic organizations to serve these needs, raise funds, and keep their staffs from burning out. There's just not enough time also to focus on the big picture and long-term agendas. It seems wasteful to spend valuable resources on talking about major reforms that are so far out of reach. But that's what we'll have to do if we want to stop mass layoffs from tearing us apart.

It's not just thinking and talking that we need to do. We also need to fight. No mass layoff should go unchallenged. Each and every time, we should expose the financial predation that precipitated it. We should make elected leaders, even those we support, squirm when they fail to intervene.

To wage this struggle, we must prepare for short-term failures—many of them. Corporations, and even nonprofit colleges, have all the power they need to kill jobs whenever they choose. Each time it happens, however, they create a teachable moment. We can ask more and more people to square up to the cruelty and heartlessness of mass layoffs. We also need to believe, as the Populists of the late 19th century did, that education will make a difference—that even our failures bring us one step closer to building a mass movement strong enough to take on financial power.

Now is the time to build a progressive populist agenda. We believe working people are hungry to discuss how to stop mass layoffs and how to bring more justice and fairness to our economy. Our analysis strongly suggests that the working class—of all races and ethnicities—is open both to progressive economic populism *and* progressive social populism. Getting from here to there requires that we engage with these workers, rather than writing them off as the Schumer Democrats have done.

Not only is progressive populism possible—it is a must.

There is no alternative.

A Challenge to Oberlin College

"It's different when you enjoy being where you're at. Other jobs, you walk in and do what you got to do to get your paycheck and you go home. Oberlin was different. And I think a lot of it had to do with the relationships you formed working at the college, whether it's with your coworkers, whether it was with your union reps, down to students. It was just different. . . . It was more of a home feeling . . . as opposed to just a job." —Marsha Rae Douglas, laid off at age 38, after 5 years of service

MY PUBLIC CRITIQUE OF MASS LAYOFFS AND THE CORPORATIZATION of Oberlin College is not written to harm the school. Rather, I want to help prevent the administration and board from inflicting more harm on the college's cherished values. It has been a privilege to have attended Oberlin and to see our son graduate from there as well. Surrounded by so many gifted students and faculty, we learned that a good life should include a commitment to enhancing justice and fairness.

Oberlin has the opportunity, once again, to live by these core values. It is time to change how colleges (and corporations) are governed. Workers could and should be viewed as vital stakeholders. Not only should they be treated with respect, but they should be empowered to help guide their institutions. Contemporary German history shows us that corporations, large and small alike, can thrive with workers holding half the seats on their board of directors. Why not nonprofit colleges as well?

Just as when Oberlin broke new ground by admitting women and Blacks in the 1830s, it could now make history by building a model governing structure that would ensure mass layoffs would never again be used so indiscriminately.

The attack on its working people is not the first time Oberlin lost its way. In the 1880s, the college succumbed to rising white supremacy in the North by enforcing segregation in its dining halls and by allowing discrimination by fellow students, and even by some faculty.[1] This flew in the face of its abolitionist traditions. It eventually returned to its roots, becoming a safe haven for students of all genders, races, ethnicities, and creeds.

Oberlin could recover from its gratuitous violation of worker rights by becoming the first college in the nation to place worker representatives on its board of directors. It could develop a model communitarian structure in which all the members of its board would be elected representatives of the college's stakeholders—faculty, students, alumni, support staff, and blue-collar workers, as well as members from the community. So many of us want to believe the courage to imagine a better world is still alive in the college's DNA.

A new model of democratic governance is desperately needed as our society moves ever more rapidly toward autocratic corporatism. A new model also would validate what Oberlin's laid-off workers already know—that there's a better way to treat working people. It's time for Oberlin to again lead the way by building a democratic model that improves how we all work and live together.

Many thanks to all who are already traveling down this road, and a warm welcome to those who will soon join us. Most of all, many thanks to the Oberlin workers who inspired this book and so graciously allowed us to share their stories. You are helping to build a better world.

ACKNOWLEDGMENTS

EVEN THOUGH WRITING IS A LONELY ADVENTURE, THIS BOOK WAS A collective journey, as well.

The germ of the idea grew from the struggle at Oberlin College when its callous administration laid off 113 unionized food service and janitorial workers during the pandemic. We alumni formed a steering committee that included Kelly Grote '89, Cassandra Ogren '02, Susan Phillips '76, and Kris Raab '89 in an unsuccessful effort to reverse that destructive decision. Nevertheless, we raised tens of thousands of alumni dollars for the displaced workers.

Susan, who had spent her career at the United Food and Commercial Workers International Union, had been funding a sizable Oberlin student social justice internship program. After the layoffs, she pulled her support from the college in protest, and continued the internships through our Labor Institute. The program now places approximately 15 students in unions and labor-oriented organizations each summer. Several have worked directly on this book.

Constant Lundsgaard, our first Oberlin intern in 2021, did admirable research on the Mylan/Viatris shutdown in Morgantown, West Virginia. In the summer of 2022 (and then some) Oberlin interns Brandon Denton, Izzy Sanchez-Foster, Elijah Freiman, and Carson Glew interviewed many of the Oberlin workers who were let go and then produced a compelling documentary report, "It's All About the Dollar: Financialization and Mass Layoff at Oberlin College" (which can be found at https://sites.google.com/oberlin.edu/its-all-about-the-dollar/introduction).

A special thanks goes to the Oberlin workers who poured out their hearts in these interviews. (Names in quotation marks are pen names used by the workers for fear of retribution. Last names are also omitted by request.) Thank you to "Curtis Thompson," Diane, Eugene McCormick, Geoff, Jack Kubicki, Jeff Burns, "Jonathan Barton," Joseph Bennet, Lori, Marsha Rae Douglas, Mary, Michele, Patricia Baker, "Susan Carroll," Ted Hovanitz, and Vince Gancos.

The Oberlin tragedy focused my attention on the broader question of the causes and impacts of mass layoffs. Our Labor Institute political economy team (Kris Raab, Peter Kreutzer, and me) took on the challenge. We were soon joined by Carissa Gaudron, then an economics master's student from John Jay College of Criminal Justice.

Somewhere along the line, Peter found the Bureau of Labor Statistics' mass-layoff database that covered the years from 1996 to 2012. Peter then connected that database with demographic, geographic, and election results so that we could begin the long march of finding out whether mass layoffs had political impact, especially in largely white, rural counties. After careful analysis over many months, we found significant connections. I then knew we had a story to tell.

This led us directly into "populism" and the argument that the decline of the Democratic vote share really was a function of the alleged growing illiberal attitudes of the white working class in those key states. We asked: Is it really true that racism, sexism, homophobia, and xenophobia within the white working class, not economic insecurity, are moving these workers away from the Democrats?

To find answers Peter patiently responded to hundreds of my queries as he searched voter surveys that track social issue questions over long periods of time. It was grueling work as we struggled to make sense out of hundreds of thousands of survey responses.

What we found shocked us. Overall, the white working class was getting more liberal, not more right-wing, on many divisive social issue questions. How could that be when all the world was labeling these folks as racist populists?

Kris hammered us with more questions that had to be answered. Carissa searched for more studies and connected us to Princeton professor Jared Abbott, who coordinates the Center for Working Class Politics, a network of academics who are investigating similar issues.

Jared thought what we had found was promising but feared it lacked sufficient statistical rigor to move key Democratic pollsters, academics, and the like. He generously gave his time to help us deploy more advanced tests.

Next, Cyrus Cappo, also a John Jay grad student, deployed his skills to conduct some of those tests. Our basic finding was confirmed: Mass layoffs are a statistically significant cause of the decline of the Democratic presidential county vote between 1996 and 2012 in the three Blue Wall states.

Numbers are instructive, but how did this play out in the real world of mass layoffs?

John Shinn, secretary-treasurer of the United Steelworkers, came to our aid by connecting us to the local union leaders involved with two factory shutdowns that we examined in more detail, in Olean, New York, and Morgantown, West Virginia. John also hooked us up with Dirk Linder, from IG Metall in Germany, so that we could learn more about layoffs in Germany. Dirk then gave generously of his time via two Zoom calls as he walked us through how the Siemens layoffs were thwarted in Germany. It was an eye-opening encounter that changed the trajectory of the book. We then knew for certain that mass layoffs in highly advanced economies are not inevitable.

Next our editorial team swung into action. Did the story hold together? Was it interesting and worth the read? Did the arguments, facts, and references hold up?

As the sole writer I had to take incoming fire from all directions. Kris peppered the manuscript with comments as did my significant other, the labor economist Sharon Szymanski. Peter, a gifted writer (and fantasy baseball pro, no less), ran alongside me, providing edits on the fly, which helped enormously. David Dembo not only provided research updates but also poured over the draft, from the footnote formats to advanced research.

Then Jim Young, co-executive director of the Labor Institute, dug in to provide incredibly insightful and detailed critiques, chapter by chapter. He gave me the courage to ditch awkward sections and greatly strengthen others. And moments before the manuscript was due, labor activist and Labor Institute board member Mark Dudzic found a few more soft spots that Jim and I missed. Many thanks.

Meanwhile, as I disappeared into writing mode, fellow staff members Rodrigo Toscano and Arturo Archila continued their fine work on our health and safety programs. We had promises to keep, and they kept them. Many thanks. Also, my deepest appreciation to Manuela Goitein, our business manager, who expertly holds our entire show together.

A special and profound thanks also to Bill Lazonick who has patiently mentored me for years on stock buybacks and corporate looting and who provided invaluable comments on this book. I'm deeply honored and moved by the time and effort he put into the manuscript.

I'm also truly fortunate to work with Laura McClure, the editing magician. Somehow, she is able to improve the writing without losing the voice or taking it over. She is a remarkable talent, and I'm ever grateful for her friendship and expertise.

To turn all of this into a published book, my agent Bill Lee joined the "we." His guidance, thoughtfulness, and intelligence strengthened the effort. His belief in the book's message also provided encouragement all along the way.

And to be sure, many thanks to Margo Baldwin and the Chelsea Green Publishing team. They've always believed in my work and brought their insight, energy, and excellent skills to it. We're very fortunate to have them on board. I'm profoundly appreciative of the talent and commitment of Matthew Derr, the developmental editor, whose hard work and guidance have been invaluable. And a very special thanks to Rebecca Springer for her superlative copy editing, fact checking, and substantive suggestions.

The most crucial "we" involves my family. In a very real way, I'm trying to live up to the high standards of excellence set by our daughter Lilah and son Chester in their academic work. And most of all I'm truly fortunate to share decades of love with my partner, Sharon—a love that truly melts "I" into "we."

NOTES

Introduction. The Destructiveness of Mass Layoffs

1. See *The Downsizing of America: New York Times Special Report* (New York: Times Books, 1996) and Louis Uchitelle, *The Disposable American: Layoffs and Their Consequences* (New York: Vintage, 2007).
2. Roger Lee, "Layoffs Tracker," https://www.layoffs.fyi.
3. Oberlin College and Conservatory, "Oberlin History," https://www.oberlin.edu/about-oberlin/oberlin-history.
4. US Census Bureau, "Quick Facts, Oberlin City, Ohio," US Census Bureau, https://www.census.gov/quickfacts/fact/table/oberlincityohio/INC110.
5. National Institute for Occupational Safety and Health (NIOSH), "NIOSH Study Examines Relationship Between Employment Status, Healthcare Access, and Health Outcomes," Centers for Disease Control and Prevention, November 18, 2021, https://www.cdc.gov/niosh/updates/upd-11-18-21.html.
6. Sandra J. Sucher and Marilyn Morgan Westner, "What Companies Still Get Wrong About Layoffs," *Harvard Business Review*, December 8, 2022, https://hbr.org/2022/12/what-companies-still-get-wrong-about-layoffs.
7. National Vital Statistics System, "Provisional Drug Overdose Death Counts," Centers for Disease Control and Prevention, https://www.cdc.gov/nchs/nvss/vsrr/drug-overdose-data.htm.
8. Employment and Training Administration, "Rapid Response Services for Workers," US Department of Labor, https://www.dol.gov/agencies/eta/layoffs/workers.
9. The American Presidency Project, "1984 Democratic Party Platform," UC Santa Barbara, https://www.presidency.ucsb.edu/documents/1984-democratic-party-platform.
10. Eli Yokley, "Republicans Are Outperforming Their 2018 Margins Among Voters of Color," *Morning Consult Pro*, November 2, 2022,

https://pro.morningconsult.com/trend-setters/republicans
-outperforming-2018-margins-among-voters-of-color.

Chapter 1. White Working-Class Blues: Who Is the White Working Class and Why Are the Democrats Abandoning Them?

1. Les Leopold, "Winning Back the Working Class: A Time of Reckoning for Progressives," *Moyers*, Economy & Work, November 17, 2016, https://billmoyers.com/story/winning-back-working-class-time-reckoning-progressives.

2. "Inventing Black and White," Facing History & Ourselves, August 11, 2017, https://www.facinghistory.org/resource-library/inventing-black-white.

3. For an excellent account of the Populist movement, see Lawrence Goodwyn, *The Populist Moment: A Short History of the Agrarian Revolt in America* (Oxford: Oxford University Press, 1978).

4. John Bodnar, Roger Simon, and Michael P. Weber, *Lives of Their Own: Blacks, Italians, and Poles in Pittsburgh, 1900–1960* (Champaign: University of Illinois Press, 1983), 240.

5. Population Estimates Program, "Quickfacts: Race," US Census Bureau, https://www.census.gov/quickfacts/fact/note/US/RHI625221.

6. Image from Pittsburgh Urban League Archive, 1925. Reprinted in Bodnar et al., *Lives of Their Own*. Misspellings in original.

7. Stanley B. Greenberg, "The Democrats' 'Working-Class Problem,'" *American Prospect*, June 1, 2017, https://www.greenbergresearch.com/his-thinking/2017/5/25/dems-working-class-problems.

8. US Census Bureau, "Census Bureau Releases New Educational Attainment Data," February 24, 2022, https://www.census.gov/newsroom/press-releases/2022/educational-attainment.html.

9. Maryam Mohsin, "10 Small Business Statistics You Need to Know for 2023," *Oberlo*, January 28, 2023, https://www.oberlo.com/blog/small-business-statistics.

10. William R. Emmons, Ana Hernández Kent, and Lowell R. Ricketts, "The White Working Class: National Trends, Then and Now," Federal Reserve Bank of St. Louis, September 24, 2019, https://www.stlouisfed.org/en/on-the-economy/2019/september/white-working-class-national-trends-then-now.

11. To check our findings, we also used the occupational definitions developed by Professor Daniel Oesch of the University of Lausanne, Switzerland, for 12 of our 23 social issue questions. Workers in service, clerical, and production jobs were assigned working-class status. Our education/income definition and Oesch's working-class categories produced almost identical results. Daniel Oesch, "Contemporary Class Analysis," European Commission, JRC Working Paper Series on Social Classes in the Digital Age, European Commission, January 2022, https://joint-research-centre.ec.europa.eu/system/files/2022 -01/jrc126506.pdf. (Special thanks to Jared Abbott of the Center for Working Class Politics for helping us with the Oesch codes.) Also, when comparing 2018 and 1996 survey results on 12 social issues questions for the white working class and the managerial/professional class, the overall mean difference is 0.3 percent. The standard deviation of the 48 observations is 1.6 percent.

12. American National Election Studies, "2020 Time Series Study, Full Release [dataset and documentation]," July 19, 2021, https://election studies.org/data-center/2020-time-series-study.

13. Political strategist and Clinton political advisor James Carville, 2006, https://quotefancy.com/quote/1125310/James-Carville-Pennsylvania -is-Philadelphia-and-Pittsburgh-with-Alabama-in-between.

14. Jim Geraghty, "Chuck Schumer: Democrats Will Lose Blue-Collar Whites but Gain in the Suburbs," *National Review*, July 28, 2016, https:// www.nationalreview.com/corner/chuck-schumer-democrats-will-lose -blue-collar-whites-gain-suburbs.

15. Domenico Montanaro, "Hillary Clinton's 'Basket of Deplorables,' in Full Context of This Ugly Campaign," NPR, September 10, 2016, https://www.npr.org/2016/09/10/493427601/hillary-clintons-basket -of-deplorables-in-full-context-of-this-ugly-campaign.

16. The American Presidency Project, "Comprehensive Employment and Training Act Statement on the Level of Public Service Jobs Under the Program," UC Santa Barbara, March 14, 1978, https://www.presidency .ucsb.edu/documents/comprehensive-employment-and-training-act -statement-the-level-public-service-jobs-under.

17. Ben Smith, "Obama on Small-Town Pa.: Clinging to Religion, Guns, Xenophobia," *Politico*, April 11, 2008, https://www.politico.com/blogs

/ben-smith/2008/04/obama-on-small-town-pa-clinging-to-religion-guns
-xenophobia-007737.

Chapter 2. Mingo Capitalism: How Wall Street Destroyed Jobs in West Virginia, Pennsylvania, Michigan, and Wisconsin, and How That Cratered Support for the Democrats

1. "Is Mingo County the Best West Virginia County for Your Business?" West Virginia Demographics, https://www.westvirginia-demographics .com/mingo-county-demographics.
2. Lorraine Boissoneault, "The Coal Mining Massacre America Forgot," *Smithsonian Magazine*, April 25, 2017, https://www.smithsonianmag .com/history/forgotten-matewan-massacre-was-epicenter-20th-century -mine-wars-180963026.
3. West Virginia Office of Miners' Health Safety and Training, "1995 Production and Employment by County," https://minesafety.wv.gov /wp-content/uploads/2020/12/1995prodempl-1.pdf.
4. US Election Atlas, "2020 Presidential General Election Data Graphs - West Virginia," https://uselectionatlas.org/RESULTS/datagraph. php?fips=54&year=2020; "1996 Presidential General Election Data Graphs - West Virginia," https://uselectionatlas.org/RESULTS/data-graph.php?fips=54&year=1996.
5. West Virginia Office of Miners' Health Safety & Training, "2020 Coal Production and Employment by County," https://minesafety .wv.gov/PDFs/Annual%20Reports/2020%20Spreadsheets/2020%20 %20Prod-Employment%20by%20Cnty.pdf.
6. "Full Rush Transcript Hillary Clinton Part//CNN TV One Democratic Presidential Town Hall," CNN Press Room, March 13, 2016, https:// cnnpressroom.blogs.cnn.com/2016/03/13/full-rush-transcript-hillary -clinton-partcnn-tv-one-democratic-presidential-town-hall.
7. Chris McGreal, "Why Were Millions of Opioid Pills Sent to a West Virginia Town of 3,000?" *Guardian*, October 2, 2019, https://www.theguardian .com/us-news/2019/oct/02/opioids-west-virginia-pill-mills-pharmacies.
8. McGreal, "Why Were Millions of Opioid Pills."
9. National Center for Health Statistics, "Drug Overdose Mortality by State," Centers for Disease Control and Prevention, https://www.cdc.gov/nchs/ pressroom/sosmap/drug_poisoning_mortality/drug_poisoning.htm.

10. In 2021, there were 10 deaths among 61,402 coal miners nationally. Mine Safety and Health Administration, "Coal Fatalities for 1900 Through 2022," US Department of Labor, https://arlweb.msha.gov/stats/centurystats /coalstats.asp.

11. "A 'Freedom Budget' for All Americans: A Summary," A. Philip Randolph Institute, January 1967, https://www.prrac.org/pdf/Freedom Budget.pdf.

12. Mike Wessler, "Updated Charts Provide Insights on Racial Disparities, Correctional Control, Jail Suicides, and More," Prison Policy Initiative, May 19, 2022, https://www.prisonpolicy.org/blog/2022/05/19 /updated_charts.

13. Susan Okie, "The Epidemic That Wasn't," *New York Times*, January 26, 2009, https://www.nytimes.com/2009/01/27/health/27coca.html.

14. Evan Osnos, "When Wall Street Came to Coal Country: How a Big-Money Gamble Scarred Appalachia," *Guardian*, September 14, 2021, https://www.theguardian.com/environment/2021/sep/14/wall-street -coal-country-hedge-funds-coal-mining-appalachia-west-virginia.

15. Osnos, "When Wall Street Came to Coal Country."

16. Osnos, "When Wall Street Came to Coal Country."

17. Osnos, "When Wall Street Came to Coal Country."

18. "Securities Exchange Act of 1934," August 10, 2012, https://www.nyse .com/publicdocs/nyse/regulation/nyse/sea34.pdf.

19. William Lazonick, *Investing in Innovation: Confronting Predatory Value Extraction in the U.S. Corporation* (Cambridge: Cambridge University Press, 2023), https://doi.org/10.1017/9781009410700.

20. Compiled by Matt Hopkins (Academic-Industry Research Network) using Standard & Poor's ExecuComp data on the highest-paid executives and the proportions of their total compensation in the form of realized gains from stock options and stock awards.

21. Office of the Under Secretary of Defense for Acquisition and Sustainment, Defense Pricing and Contracting, "Contract Finance Study Report," Department of Defense, April 2023, 39, https://www.acq.osd .mil/asda/dpc/pcf/docs/finance-study/FINAL%20-%20Defense%20 Contract%20Finance%20Study%20Report%204.6.23.pdf.

22. Taylor Kuykendall, "Peabody Energy Accelerating Highly Active Share Buyback Program," *S&P Global Market Intelligence*, July 31, 2019,

https://www.spglobal.com/marketintelligence/en/news-insights
/trending/W8-1q9vEH3NN-j1vL0hrNA2.

23. Arch Coal, "Arch Coal, Inc. Announces Stock Repurchase Agreement with
Monarch Alternative Capital" (news release), ARCH, December 11, 2017,
https://investor.archrsc.com/2017-12-11-Arch-Coal,-Inc-Announces
-Stock-Repurchase-Agreement-with-Monarch-Alternative-Capital.

24. US Bureau of Labor Statistics, "Mass Layoff Statistics," Department of
Labor, https://www.bls.gov/mls.

25. William Lazonick, "Investing in Innovation: Confronting Predatory
Value Extraction in the U.S. Corporation," Academy-Industry Research
Network, Working Paper #22-09/01, September 26, 2022, https://
theairnet.org/melseerg/2022/10/Lazonick-Investing-in-Innovation
-20220926.pdf.

26. Lenore Palladino and William Lazonick, "Regulating Stock Buybacks:
The $6.3 Trillion Question," Roosevelt Institute Working Paper, May
2021, https://rooseveltinstitute.org/wp-content/uploads/2021/04
/RI_Stock-Buybacks_Working-Paper_202105.pdf.

27. "All Employees: Manufacturing in Michigan," updated September 20,
2023, https://fred.stlouisfed.org/series/MIMFG; "All Employees:
Manufacturing in Pennsylvania," updated September 20, 2023, https://
fred.stlouisfed.org/series/PAMFG; "All Employees: Manufacturing in
Wisconsin," updated September 20, 2023, https://fred.stlouisfed.org
/series/WIMFG.

28. WARN is the Worker Adjustment and Retraining Notification Act, a
federal requirement from the Department of Labor. Each state has to
record these layoffs. Michigan Department of Technology, Management
& Budget, "Michigan Labor Market Information: WARN Archive,"
https://milmi.org/WARN/archive#warn2022; Pennsylvania Department of Labor & Industry, "WARN Notices," https://www.dli.pa.gov
/Individuals/Workforce-Development/warn/notices/Pages/default
.aspx; and Wisconsin Department of Workforce Development, "2022
Layoff Notices and Updates Filed with DWD," https://dwd.wisconsin
.gov/dislocatedworker/warn/default.htm?year=2022.

29. Using the Ordinary Least Squares (OLS) method of regression analysis,
we calculated the effect that changes in a one-unit increase in total
layoffs per capita has on the percentage of the Democratic vote, while

holding other variables constant across the 222 counties under examination (because it is a time series panel $n = 1,086$). These are called *fixed effects*, and they allow statisticians to isolate the effect exclusively from layoffs on the populations in the regression. For this model, we assume that for all counties in the dataset, changes in demography, income, union density, or other factors remain constant across counties from 1996 to 2012. The multiple regression results confirmed a highly significant inverse relationship between the layoff variable and the Democratic vote share under these conditions. It is important to note that the US Bureau of Labor Statistics stopped collecting mass-layoff data under the Obama administration in 2012. So our results show how mass layoffs caused cracks in the Blue Wall four years before it collapsed into the Trump column in 2016.

Chapter 3. White Working Class Woke? Increasing Liberalism on Divisive Social Issues

1. The ANES survey shows a slight decline in the Black working-class Democratic votes in presidential elections, from 97.1 percent in 1996 to 93.8 percent in 2020. However, the percent of those who identified as Democrats increased slightly, from 78.4 percent to 80.6 percent (though this is within the margin of error). For Hispanic working-class voters the declines were more substantial. The Hispanic Democratic presidential vote declined from 77.8 percent to 66.0 percent between 1996 and 2020, while Democratic Party identification fell from 66.7 percent in 1996 to 50.6 percent in 2020. The number of Asian Americans is too small to separate out the working class from the managerial class.

2. American National Election Studies, "SDA 4.1.4: Tables: American National Election Study 1948–2016—Cumulative," accessed July 12, 2023, https://sda.berkeley.edu/sdaweb/analysis?dataset=nes2016c; and American National Election Studies, "SDA 4.1.4: Tables: ANES 2020 Time Series Full Release," accessed July 12, 2023, https://sda.berkeley.edu/sdaweb/analysis?dataset=nes2020full.

3. American National Election Studies, "SDA 4.1.4: Tables: American National Election Study 1948–2016—Cumulative"; and (2020) V202065x gives a slightly different answer: Democrats 31.5 percent, Republicans

42.7 percent: American National Election Studies, "SDA 4.1.4: Tables: ANES 2020 Time Series Full Release."

4. Justin Gest, *The White Working Class: What Everyone Needs to Know* (New York: Oxford University Press, 2018), 22.

5. For a basic explanation of confidence intervals, see Adam Hayes, "What Is a Confidence Interval and How Do You Calculate It?" *Investopedia*, April 24, 2023, https://www.investopedia.com/terms/c/confidenceinterval .asp, and "A Basic Explanation of Confidence Intervals," US Census Bureau, last updated October 8, 2021, https://www.census.gov/programs -surveys/saipe/guidance/confidence-intervals.html.

6. ANES and GSS surveys at https://sda.berkeley.edu/archive.htm; CES survey at https://yougov.crunch.io. Data filtered using Labor Institute definition of white working class.

7. CES: "In the election for US President, who did you vote for [If reported voting]." Presidential preferences filtered by Labor Institute definition of the white working class.

8. CES. Data filtered by Labor Institute definition of white working class.

Chapter 4. Are You a Reactionary Populist? How Social Attitudes of the White Working Class Are Similar to Those of Other Classes and Ethnic Groups

1. As of late 2022, according to "United States Population 2023 (Live)," World Population Review, https://www.worldpopulationreview.com /countries/united-states-population.

2. Stephen Ansolabehere, Brian F. Schaffner, and Sam Luks, "CES Common Content, 2018," Harvard University, 2019, https://doi.org/10.7910 /DVN/ZSBZ7K; data accessible at https://sda.berkeley.edu/sdaweb /docs/cces2018/DOC/hcbkx01.htm.

3. "CES 2018: Common Content CC18_422a."

4. "CES 2018: Common Content CES CC18_422e."

5. "CES 2018: Common Content CES CC18_422h."

6. American Immigration Council, "Who and Where the DREAMers Are, Revised Estimates" (fact sheet), October 16, 2012, https://www.american immigrationcouncil.org/research/who-and-where-dreamers-are -revised-estimates.

7. "CES 2018, Common Content: CES CC18_322b."

Chapter 5. The Use and Abuse of Populism:
The Mischaracterization of White Working-Class Politics

1. Stephen Ansolabehere, Brian F. Schaffner, and Sam Luks, "CES Common Content: CES 318a," Harvard University, 2019, https://doi.org/10.7910/DVN/ZSBZ7K; data accessible at https://sda.berkeley.edu/sdaweb/docs/cces2018/DOC/hcbkx01.htm.

2. Elaine Kamarck and Alexander Podkul, "The 2018 Primaries Project: The Demographics of Primary Voters," *Brookings*, October 23, 2018, https://www.brookings.edu/research/the-2018-primaries-project-the-demographics-of-primary-voters.

3. Paul Krugman, "Making America the Opposite of Great" (opinion), *New York Times*, January 5, 2023, https://www.nytimes.com/2023/01/05/opinion/america-kevin-mccarthy-great.html.

4. Anahi Van Hootegem et al., "Work Is Political: Distributive Injustice as a Mediating Mechanism in the Relationship Between Job Insecurity and Political Cynicism" *Political Psychology* 43, no. 2 (May 26, 2021): 375–96, https://doi.org/10.1111/pops.12766.

5. A. Mughan, C. Bean, and I. McAllister, "Economic Globalization, Job Insecurity and the Populist Reaction," *Electoral Studies* 22, no. 4 (December 2003): 617–33, https://doi.org/10.1016/S0261-3794(02)00047-1.

6. L. Guiso, et al., "Economic Insecurity and the Demand of Populism in Europe," *Journal of Economic Literature* (August 2023), https://www.heliosherrera.com/populism.pdf.

7. Andrew Wroe, "Political Trust and Job Insecurity in 18 European Polities," *Journal of Trust Research* 4, no. 2 (October 2014): 90–112, https://doi.org/10.1080/21515581.2014.957291.

8. Andrew Wroe, "Americans Don't Trust Government Because They Feel Economically Insecure" (blog post), London School of Economics, September 29, 2015, https://eprints.lse.ac.uk/75749/1/blogs.lse.ac.uk-Americans%20dont%20trust%20government%20because%20they%20feel%20economically%20insecure.pdf.

9. Yi Che et al., "Did Trade Liberalization with China Influence US Elections?" *Journal of International Economics* 139 (November 2022), https://doi.org/10.1016/j.jinteco.2022.103652.

10. Anthony Mughan and Dean Lacy, "Economic Performance, Job Insecurity and Electoral Choice," *British Journal of Political Science* 32, no. 3 (July 2002).

11. Mike Lux, "A Strategy for Factory Towns," *American Family Voices*, February 22, 2023, https://www.americanfamilyvoices.org/post/a-strategy-for-factory-towns.

12. As quoted in Goodwyn, *The Populist Moment*, 164.

13. Michael Kazin, *The Populist Persuasion: An American History* (New York: Basic Books, 1995), 73.

14. Kazin, *The Populist Persuasion*, 144.

15. Thomas Frank, *The People, No: A Brief History of Anti-Populism* (New York: Metropolitan Books, 2020).

16. Seymour Martin Lipset, "Democracy and Working-Class Authoritarianism," *American Sociological Review* 24, no. 4 (August 1959): 482–501, https://doi.org/10.2307/2089536.

17. Michael Paul Rogin, *The Intellectuals and McCarthy: The Radical Specter* (Cambridge, MA: MIT Press, 1969), 84.

18. Rogin, *The Intellectuals and McCarthy*, 276.

19. Theda Skocpol and Vanessa Williamson, *The Tea Party and the Remaking of Republican Conservatism* (New York: Oxford University Press, 2012), 23.

20. Robert Pape, "American Face of Insurrection: Analysis of Individuals Charged for Storming the US Capitol on January 6, 2021," Chicago Project on Security and Threats, January 5, 2022, https://cpost.uchicago.edu/publications/american_face_of_insurrection.

Chapter 6. Before Greed Was Good: The Unwinding of Post–World War II Working-Class Prosperity

1. Federal Reserve Bank of St. Louis, https://fred.stlouisfed.org.

2. For a history of the impact of the Cold War on American domestic policies, see Gary Gerstle, *The Rise and Fall of the Neoliberal Order: America and the World in the Free Market Era* (Oxford: Oxford University Press, 2022).

3. Stan Luxenberg, "Lifetime Employment, U.S. Style," *New York Times*, April 17, 1983, https://www.nytimes.com/1983/04/17/business/lifetime-employment-us-style.html.

4. Bruce Nussbaum, "The End of Corporate Loyalty?" *BusinessWeek*, August 4, 1986, 42.

5. Nussbaum, "The End of Corporate Loyalty," 43.

6. William Lazonick, "Profits Without Prosperity," *Harvard Business Review*, September 2014, https://www.hbr.org/2014/09/profits-without -prosperity.

7. This section draws on my previous books on financialization: *The Looting of America: How Wall Street's Game of Fantasy Finance Destroyed Our Jobs, Pensions, and What We Can Do About It* (White River Junction, VT: Chelsea Green, 2009), *How to Make a Million Dollars an Hour: Why Hedge Funds Get Away with Siphoning Off America's Wealth* (New York: Wiley, 2012), and *Runaway Inequality: An Activist's Guide to Economic Justice* (New York: Labor Institute, 2018).

8. Robert W. Crandall, "Extending Deregulation: Make the U.S. Economy More Efficient," Brookings Institution, 2007, https://www.brookings .edu/wp-content/uploads/2016/06/PB_Deregulation_Crandall.pdf.

9. Patrick Bayer and Kerwin Kofi Charles, "Divergent Paths: A New Perspective on Earnings Differences Between Black and White Men Since 1940" (working paper no. 2018-45), Becker Friedman Institute for Economics at UChicago, July 2018, https://bfi.uchicago.edu/wp-content/uploads /WP_2018-45_0.pdf.

10. David Vine, "Where in the World Is the U.S. Military?" *Politico Magazine*, July/August 2015, https://www.politico.com/magazine/story/2015 /06/us-military-bases-around-the-world-119321.

11. Kimberly Amadeo, "Vietnam War Facts, Costs, and Timeline," *The Balance*, March 29, 2022, https://www.thebalancemoney.com/vietnam-war -facts-definition-costs-and-timeline-4154921.

12. Eduardo Porter, "Black Workers Stopped Making Progress on Pay. Is It Racism?" *New York Times*, June 28, 2021, https://www.nytimes.com /2021/06/28/business/economy/black-workers-racial-pay-gap.html.

13. Milton Friedman, "A Friedman Doctrine—The Social Responsibility of Business Is to Increase Its Profits," *New York Times*, September 13, 1970, https://www.nytimes.com/1970/09/13/archives/a-friedman-doctrine -the-social-responsibility-of-business-is-to.html.

14. Herbert Mitgang, "GM Challenged on 'Responsibility,'" *New York Times*, May 17, 1970, https://www.nytimes.com/1970/05/17/archives /gm-challenged-on-responsibility-gm-meeting-to-vote-on.html.

15. William Lazonick writes that "the demands of Campaign GM for safer and less-polluting cars were demands that GM engage in automobile

innovation. . . . What Friedman called 'pure and unadulterated socialism' proved to be the innovative future of the automobile industry!" William Lazonick, "The Claims of the Community: Modern Corporations Should Serve Communities Too," *Boston Review*, October 1, 2019, https://www .bostonreview.net/forum_response/william-lazonick-claims-community.

16. Pew Research Center, "Public Trust in Government, 1958–2022," June 6, 2022, https://www.pewresearch.org/politics/2022/06/06 /public-trust-in-government-1958-2022.

17. Thomas Young, "40 Years Ago, Church Committee Investigated Americans Spying on Americans," *Brookings*, May 6, 2015, https://www .brookings.edu/blog/brookings-now/2015/05/06/40-years-ago-church -committee-investigated-americans-spying-on-americans.

18. Louis F. Powell Jr., "The Memo," *Powell Memorandum: Attack on American Free Enterprise System*, August 23, 1971, https://scholarlycommons.law .wlu.edu/powellmemo/1.

19. For an excellent history of trucking, see Steve Viscelli, *The Big Rig: Trucking and the Decline of the American Dream* (Oakland: University of California Press, 2016).

20. World Inequality Database, accessed January 3, 2023, https://wid.world /data.

21. Michael C. Jensen, "Eclipse of the Public Corporation," *Harvard Business Review*, September/October 1989, https://hbr.org/1989/09/eclipse -of-the-public-corporation.

22. CEO pay from "CEO Compensation Survey," *Forbes*, April and May issues, 1971–2014; Equilar/*New York Times*, "Equilar/*New York Times* 200 Highest-paid CEOs," 2015–2019 and 2021; Equilar/AP CEO Rankings, 2020–2021; earnings for workers from US Bureau of Labor Statistics, "Employment, Hours and Earnings from the Current Employment Statistics Survey (National)," https://data.bls.gov.

Chapter 7. After Greed Was Good: How Wall Street Looting Normalized Mass Layoffs

1. Jacob Weisberg, "The Road to Reagandom," *Slate.com*, January 8, 2016, https://www.slate.com/news-and-politics/2016/01/ronald-reagans -conservative-conversion-as-spokesman-for-general-electric-during-the -1950s.html.

2. Mark Erlich and Jeff Grabelsky, "Standing at a Crossroads: The Building Trades in the Twenty-First Century," *Labor History* 46, no. 4 (2005), https://doi.org/10.1080/00236560500266241.

3. US Bureau of Labor Statistics, "Extended Mass Layoff Initial Claimants for Unemployment Insurance by County Residency, by Race/Ethnicity, Gender, and Age, Private Nonfarm Sector, Annual Totals, 1995–2012" (database), https://www.bls.gov/mls/cntyic.xls, with summary calculations by the Labor Institute.

4. "New Street Capital Inc.," Encyclopedia.com, https://www.encyclopedia.com/books/politics-and-business-magazines/new-street-capital-inc.

5. Kenneth Robinson, "Savings and Loan Crisis, 1980–1989," Federal Reserve History, https://www.federalreservehistory.org/essays/savings-and-loan-crisis.

6. Federal Reserve Bank of St. Louis.

7. Sebastien Canderle, "Modern Private Equity and the End of Creative Destruction," CFA Institute blog, May 13, 2020, https://blogs.cfainstitute.org/investor/2020/05/13/modern-private-equity-and-the-end-of-creative-destruction.

8. David A. Vise and Steve Coll, "After 8 Years, a Chance to Return to the Fray," *Washington Post*, February 8, 1989, https://www.washingtonpost.com/archive/politics/1989/02/08/after-8-years-a-chance-to-return-to-the-fray/8efa11a2-a4a6-45ba-8f52-5c7528f07ce4.

9. In a note from Professor Lazonick to the author in a March 2, 2023, email, "Rule 10b-18 gives a company's senior executives a 'safe harbor' against manipulation charges if the OMRs executed on any single trading day are no more than 25% of the average daily trading volume (ADTV) of the stock over the previous four weeks. Today, for many companies this safe harbor can amount to hundreds of millions of dollars per day—trading day after trading day (in the case of Apple the safe harbor ADTV 'limit' is billions of dollars per trading day). Moreover, there is no presumption of manipulation if the company does buybacks on any single trading day that exceed the safe harbor ADTV (because the SEC had not adopted prior rules to define the amount of OMRs that would be deemed 'manipulation.') And without a special investigation of daily OMRs for a specific company at a specific time (which the SEC has rarely if ever done under Rule 10b-18), the SEC does not even know

the daily OMRs because companies are not required to disclose those data. For that reason, we call Rule 10b-18 'a license to loot.'"

10. Ronald Ostrow, "E.F. Hutton Guilty in Bank Fraud: Fined $2 Million in Scheme Similar to 'Check Kiting'," *Los Angeles Times*, May 3, 1985, https://www.latimes.com/archives/la-xpm-1985-05-03-mn-11827 -story.html.

11. Massive amounts of money can also be moved to share sellers through dividend recapitalizations. Cerebus, the private equity fund that controls the Albertsons grocery chain, made the company borrow $1.5 billion in order to provide a $4 billion dividend just before its proposed merger with Krogers. This was more than 50 times the size of its usual dividend. See Joe Nocera, "The Kroger-Albertsons Merger Spotlights a Popular Private Equity Tactic," Dealbook newsletter, *New York Times*, December 17, 2022, https://www.nytimes.com/2022/12/17/business /dealbook/kroger-albertsons-merger-private-equity-tactic.html.

12. William Lazonick, Mustafa Erdem Sakinç, and Matt Hopkins, "Why Stock Buybacks Are Dangerous for the Economy," *Harvard Business Review*, January 7, 2020, https://hbr.org/2020/01/why-stock -buybacks-are-dangerous-for-the-economy.

13. Compiled by Matt Hopkins (Academic-Industry Research Network) using S&P's ExecuComp data.

14. S&P Compustat, compiled and corrected by Mustaffa Erdem Sakin.

15. William Lazonick, "The Scourge of Corporate Financialization: Income Inequity, Employment Instability, Productive Fragility," Institute for New Economic Thinking, August 21, 2023, https://www.ineteconomics .org/perspectives/blog/the-scourge-of-corporate-financialization -income-inequity-employment-instability-productive-fragility.

16. Calculations by Öner Tulum of the Academic-Industry Research Network based on the S&P Compustat database.

17. William Lazonick, "Profits Without Prosperity," *Harvard Business Review*, September 2014, https://www.hbr.org/2014/09/profits -without-prosperity.

18. Allan Sloan, "Corporate Killers: Wall Street Loves Layoffs, but the Public Is Scared as Hell. Is There a Better Way?" *Newsweek*, February 26, 1996, https://www.wolfgangs.com/vintage-magazines/newsweek/vintage -magazine/OMS793479.html. Also in 1996, the *New York Times*

published a seven-part series (March 3–9, 1996) and a book version, *The Downsizing of America: Millions of Americans Are Losing Good Jobs. This Is Their Story* (New York: Crown Publishing, 1996).

19. Anne E. Polivka, "A Profile of Contingent Workers," *Monthly Labor Review*, October 1996, https://www.bls.gov/opub/mlr/1996/article/profile-of-contingent-workers.htm.

20. Staffing Industry Analysts, "The U.S. Gig Economy—2022 Edition," September 23, 2022, https://www2.staffingindustry.com/Research/Research-Reports/Americas/The-US-Gig-Economy-2022-Edition.

21. "The Contingent Labor Imperative: How Agile Enterprises Succeed in a Modern Workforce Model," MBO Partners, August 2022, https://www.mbopartners.com/state-of-independence/contingent-labor-report.

22. BLS (US Bureau of Labor Statistics): Anne E. Polivka, "A Profile of Contingent Workers," *Monthly Labor Review*, October 1996, https://www.bls.gov/mlr/1996/10/art2full.pdf; GAO (Government Accountability Office): Charles A. Jeszeck, "Contingent Workforce: Size, Characteristics, Earnings, and Benefits," GAO-15-168R, April 2015, https://www.gao.gov/assets/gao-15-168r.pdf; SIA (Staffing Industry Analysts), "Number of US Contingent Workers Totals 51.5 Million; Temps Assigned by Staffing Firms at 8.5 Million: SIA Report," August 2021, https://www2.staffingindustry.com/Editorial/Daily-News/Number-of-US-contingent-workers-totals-51.5-million-temps-assigned-by-staffing-firms-at-8.5-million-SIA-report-58836.

23. Total federal drug control spending is expected to reach over $45 billion in 2023. This does not include the billions in state and local drug enforcement. See Statista Research Department, "Total Federal Drug Control Spending in the United States from FY 2012 to FY 2024," *Statista*, March 21, 2023, https://www.statista.com/statistics/618857/total-federal-drug-control-spending-in-us.

24. "Offenses," US Federal Bureau of Prisons, Statistics, https://www.bop.gov/about/statistics/statistics_inmate_offenses.jsp.

25. Data from 2015 and 2016 from Josh Katz, "Drug Deaths in America Are Rising Faster than Ever," *New York Times*, June 5, 2017 , https://www.nytimes.com/interactive/2017/06/05/upshot/opioid-epidemic-drug-overdose-deaths-are-rising-faster-than-ever.html; prior years from

National Center for Health Statistics, National Vital Statistics System, and CDC/NCHS, National Vital Statistics System, "Data Brief 81: Drug Poisoning Deaths in the United States, 1980–2008."

26. E. A. Carson and R. Kluckow, "Correctional Populations in the United States, 2021—Statistical Tables," US Bureau of Justice Statistics, February 2023, https://www.bjs.ojp.gov/library/publications/correctional -populations-united-states-2021-statistical-tables.

27. CEO pay from CEO compensation surveys, *Forbes*, April/May issues, 1971–2011 and *"New York Times*/Equilar 200 Highest-Paid CEO Rankings,"* 2012–2021; worker earnings based on US Bureau of Labor Statistics, "Pay & Benefits," http://www.bls.gov/data/#wages.

Chapter 8. Halting Mass Layoffs—A Bridge Too Far for the Democrats? How Joe Biden, Chuck Schumer, and Bernie Sanders Refused to Intervene

1. Bob Woodward, *The Agenda: Inside the Clinton White House* (New York: Simon & Schuster, 1994).

2. "Capital returns" includes buybacks and dividends. Stone Fox Capital, "United Technologies: No Longer a Bargain," *Seeking Alpha*, March 21, 2016, https://www.seekingalpha.com/article/3959961-united -technologies-no-longer-bargain.

3. Dividend Channel Contributor, "United Technologies Popular Amongst Latest 13F Filers," *Forbes*, April 29, 2015, https://www.forbes.com /sites/dividendchannel/2015/04/29/united-technologies-popular -amongst-latest-13f-filers-2.

4. Reymerlyn Martin, "Were Hedge Funds Right About Buying United Technologies Corporation (UTX)?" *Insider Monkey*, March 26, 2019, https://www.insidermonkey.com/blog/were-hedge-funds-right-about -buying-united-technologies-corporation-utx-730847.

5. Canadian Press, "As Trump Claims to Have Saved Carrier Jobs, Details Are Hazy," *Lethbridge News Now*, November 30, 2016, https://lethbridge newsnow.com/2016/11/30/as-trump-claims-to-have-saved-carrier -jobs-details-are-hazy.

6. Bryan Gruley and Rick Clough, "Remember When Trump Said He Saved 1,100 Jobs at a Carrier Plant?" *Bloomberg*, March 29, 2017, https://www

.bloomberg.com/news/features/2017-03-29/remember-when-trump
-said-he-saved-1-100-jobs-at-a-carrier-plant.

7. Tony Cook, "Trump Campaigned on Saving Jobs at Indianapolis'
Carrier Plant: This Is What It's Like Now," *Indystar*, October 30, 2020,
https://www.indystar.com/story/news/politics/2020/10/30/trump
-campaigned-saving-jobs-carrier-what-its-like-there-now/6010437002.

8. Nelson D. Schwartz, "Trump Sealed Carrier Deal with Mix of Threat and
Incentive," *New York Times*, December 1, 2016, https://www.nytimes
.com/2016/12/01/business/economy/trump-carrier-pence-jobs.html.

9. Gruley and Clough, "Remember When Trump Said He Saved 1,100 Jobs?"

10. Steven Greenhouse, "Op-Ed: The Story Behind Trump's Tweet Attack
on Chuck Jones of the United Steelworkers," *Los Angeles Times*, December 8, 2016, https://www.latimes.com/opinion/op-ed/la-oe
-greenhouse-trump-steelworker-tweet-20161208-story.html.

11. Les Leopold, "The Hypocrisy of Corporate Welfare: It's Bigger Than
Trump," *Common Dreams*, December 9, 2016, https://www.common
dreams.org/views/2016/12/09/hypocrisy-corporate-welfare-its
-bigger-trump.

12. Robert Harding, "Cuomo: New York Reaches Agreement with Alcoa
to Preserve 600 Jobs in Massena," *Auburn Citizen*, November 25, 2015,
https://auburnpub.com/blogs/eye_on_ny/cuomo-new-york-reaches
-agreement-with-alcoa-to-preserve-600-jobs-in-massena/article_ca
814874-92be-11e5-85e0-136822f6f663.html.

13. Alcoa, "Alcoa's Massena Operations Celebrates Its 120th Anniversary"
(news release), June 18, 2022, https://www.alcoa.com/global/en
/what-we-do/aluminum/stories/releases?id=2022/06/alcoas-massena
-operations-celebrates-its-120th-anniversary-.

14. Bernie Sanders 2020 campaign video, "Siemens Shutdown," posted
to Facebook, May 25, 2019, https://www.facebook.com/watch/?v
=2229341903822653.

15. Siemens Energy, "Share Buyback 2020–2021" (report), https://www
.siemens-energy.com/global/en/company/investor-relations/share
/share-buyback/share-buyback-2020.html.

16. Rick Miller, "Schumer Left Out of Loop on Siemens Layoffs," *Olean
Times Herald*, February, 6, 2021, https://www.oleantimesherald.com

/news/schumer-left-out-of-loop-on-siemens-layoffs/article_64fb9949
-a246-58e8-b2fa-3c546c2e95de.html.

17. Rick Miller, "County to Forgive $2 Million Loan If Cimolai-HY LLC
Creates 200 Jobs," *Olean Times Herald*, December 14, 2022, https://
www.oleantimesherald.com/news/county-to-forgive-2-million-loan-if
-cimolai-hy-llc-creates-200-jobs/image_10f07f67-32c4-503d-97d6-9b8a6a
61414d.html.

18. Barbara Humpton, "The Infrastructure Law Supports Bold Action. Now
Let's Get to Work" (press release), Siemens, November 15, 2021, https://
new.siemens.com/us/en/company/press/siemens-stories/ceo-perspective
/the-infrastructure-bill-supports-bold-action-now-lets-get-to-work.html.

19. US Government Accountability Office, "COVID-19: Agencies Are Taking
Steps to Improve Future Use of Defense Production Act Authorities,"
December 16, 2021, https://www.gao.gov/products/gao-22-105380.

20. Federal Trade Commission, "FTC Reaches Record Financial Settlement to Settle Charges of Price-Fixing in Generic Drug Market" (press
release), November 29, 2000, https://www.ftc.gov/news-events/news
/press-releases/2000/11/ftc-reaches-record-financial-settlement-settle
-charges-price-fixing-generic-drug-market.

21. Amber Phillips, "How a Senator's Daughter Became CEO of the
Company at the Center of the EpiPen Controversy," *Washington Post*,
August 24, 2016, https://www.washingtonpost.com/news/the-fix/wp
/2016/08/24/how-a-senators-daughter-became-ceo-of-the-company
-at-the-center-of-the-epipen-controversy.

22. Brielle Ferdinand, "Heather Bresch Realized over $113 Million as Mylan
CEO," *Equilar*, November 20, 2020, https://www.equilar.com/blogs
/490-mylan-ceo-resignation.html.

23. Calculations provided by William Lazonick.

24. All direct quotes from Bill Hawkins come from an interview conducted
on August 16, 2022, by Elijah Freiman, a Labor Institute Oberlin summer intern.

25. Katharine Eban, "'We Can't Reach Him': Joe Manchin Is Ghosting the
West Virginia Union Workers Whose Jobs His Daughter Helped
Outsource," *Vanity Fair*, July 23, 2021, https://www.vanityfair.com
/news/2021/07/joe-manchin-is-ghosting-the-west-virginia
-union-workers.

26. Our Revolution, "Invoke the Defense Production Act to Halt Decommissioning of the Viatris Pharmaceutical Plant" (open letter to President Biden), July 21, 2021, https://static1.squarespace.com/static/62f41050584 b40607baef690/t/637e36700bf37d3c77c619db/1669215858062/LETTER _Mylan_sign_on.pdf.
27. Sandra J. Sucher and Marilyn Morgan Westner, "What Companies Still Get Wrong About Layoffs," *Harvard Business Review*, December 8, 2022, https://hbr.org/2022/12/what-companies-still-get-wrong-about-layoffs.
28. Alec MacGillis, "Tim Ryan Is Winning the War for the Soul of the Democratic Party" (opinion), *New York Times*, October 21, 2022, https://www.nytimes.com/2022/10/21/opinion/tim-ryan-democrats -midterms-ohio.html.

Chapter 9. There Is Another Way: How a Major Capitalist Democracy Avoids Mass Layoffs

1. Ewan McGaughey, "The Codetermination Bargains: The History of German Corporate and Labour Law," Law, Society and Economy Working Papers, London School of Economics and Political Science, October 2015, http://eprints.lse.ac.uk/61593/1/The%20codetermination%20 bargains%20the%20history%20of%20german%20corporate%20and%20 labour%20law.pdf.
2. "Germany: The Economy—1890–1914," *Britannica*, https://www .britannica.com/place/Germany/The-economy-1890-1914.
3. McGaughey, "The Codetermination Bargains."
4. "Germany, The Economy," *Britannica*.
5. "Germany, The Economy," *Britannica*.
6. David P. Conradt, "Social Democratic Party of Germany," *Britannica*, https://www.britannica.com/topic/Social-Democratic-Party-of-Germany.
7. McGaughey, "The Codetermination Bargains."
8. At the Potsdam Conference at the end of WWII, Berlin was divided into four zones—American, French, British, and Soviet. In 1949, the American, French, and British zones merged into West Berlin, a part of the new West Germany.
9. McGaughey, "The Codetermination Bargains."
10. Laszlo Goerke and Yue Huang, "Job Satisfaction and Trade Union Membership in Germany," GLO Discussion Paper no. 1135, Global Labor

Organization GLO, Essen, 2022, https://www.econstor.eu/bitstream /10419/261792/1/GLO-DP-1135.pdf.

11. All Dirk Linder quotes are from a recorded Zoom interview with the author on November 1, 2022.

Chapter 10. TINA's Last Dance? Facing the Fatalism of Mass Layoff Capitalism

1. Barnaby J. Feder, "Mrs. Thatcher Tests the Miners," *New York Times*, August 28, 1983, https://www.nytimes.com/1983/08/28/business/mrs -thatcher-tests-the-miners.html.

2. Francis Fukuyama, "By Way of an Introduction," in *The End of History and the Last Man* (New York: Free Press, 1992).

3. Joseph Schumpeter, *Capitalism, Socialism and Democracy* (London: Allen & Unwin, 1954), 83.

4. Woodward, *The Agenda*.

5. Louis Uchitelle, "The Bondholders Are Winning; Why America Won't Boom," *New York Times*, June 12, 1994, https://www.nytimes.com /1994/06/12/weekinreview/ideas-trends-the-bondholders-are-winning -why-america-won-t-boom.html.

6. President William Clinton, "Remarks at the Paul H. Nitze School of Advanced International Studies," March 8, 2000, https://www.govinfo .gov/content/pkg/WCPD-2000-03-13/html/WCPD-2000-03-13-Pg487 -2.htm.

7. Thomas L. Friedman, "How China Lost America," *New York Times*, November 1, 2022, https://www.nytimes.com/2022/11/01/opinion /china-united-states-trade-economy.html.

8. Jonathan Rée, "Opium of the Elite," *London Review of Books* 45, no. 3 (February 2023): 5, https://www.lrb.co.uk/the-paper/v45/n03/jonathan -ree/opium-of-the-elite.

9. William Lazonick, "Investing in Innovation: A Policy Framework for Attaining Sustainable Prosperity in the United States," Working Paper Series inetwp182, Institute for New Economic Thinking (April 2022), https://doi.org/10.36687/inetwp182.

10. Ian Smith, "What Does the Public Think of Federal Employees?" *FedSmith*, March 23, 2022, https://www.fedsmith.com/2022

/03/23/what-does-public-think-of-federal-employees; and Pew Research Center, "Americans' Views of Government: Decades of Distrust, Enduring Support for Its Role," June 6, 2022, https://www.pewresearch.org /politics/2022/06/06/americans-views-of-government-decades-of -distrust-enduring-support-for-its-role.

11. Institute for Crime and Justice Policy Research, "World Prison Brief," October 2021, accessed January 3, 2023, https://www.prisonstudies. org/highest-to-lowest/prison_population_rate.

12. Franklin Roosevelt, "Second Bill of Rights, 1944," Bill of Rights Institute, https://www.billofrightsinstitute.org/activities/franklin-roosevelt -second-bill-of-rights-1944.

Chapter 11. Isn't Automation *the* Problem?

1. Kevin Dixon, "W Grove and the Rise of the Machines," *We Are South Devon*, December 8, 2020, https://wearesouthdevon.com/w-grove -and-the-rise-of-the-machines.

2. "I, Robot (short story)," Wikipedia, https://en.wikipedia.org/wiki /I,_Robot_(short_story).

3. The Fix Team, "The October Democratic Debate Transcript," *Washington Post*, October 16, 2019, https://www.washingtonpost.com/politics /2019/10/15/october-democratic-debate-transcript.

4. Andrew Yang, "Yes, Robots Are Stealing Your Job" (opinion), *New York Times*, November 14, 2019, https://www.nytimes.com/2019/11/14 /opinion/andrew-yang-jobs.html.

5. Michael J. Hicks and Srikant Devaraj, "The Myth and the Reality of Manufacturing in America," Center for Business and Economic Research, June 2015, https://projects.cberdata.org/reports/MfgReality.pdf.

6. All quotations in this chapter from William Lazonick are from an email to the author on April 24, 2023.

7. Federal Reserve Bank of St. Louis, "All Employees: Retail Trade: Grocery Stores" for each of these states, https://fred.stlouisfed.org/categories /27281.

8. Federal Reserve Bank of St. Louis, "All Employees, Motor Vehicles and Parts," https://fred.stlouisfed.org/series/CES3133600101.

9. "All Employees, Motor Vehicles and Parts."

10. Daisuke Adachi, Daiji Kawaguchi, and Yukiko U. Saito, "Robots and Employment: Evidence from Japan, 1978–2017," *Journal of Labor Economics*, October 25, 2022, https://doi.org/10.1086/723205.
11. World Economic Forum, "Read Yuval Harari's Blistering Warning to Davos in Full," January 24, 2020, https://www.weforum.org/agenda/2020/01/yuval-hararis-warning-davos-speech-future-predications.
12. World Economic Forum, "Read Yuval Harari's Blistering Warning."
13. Jennifer Cheeseman Day and Andrew W. Hait, "Number of Truckers at All-Time High," US Census Bureau, June 6, 2019, https://www.census.gov/library/stories/2019/06/america-keeps-on-trucking.html.
14. US Bureau of Labor Statistics, "Heavy and Tractor-Trailer Truck Drivers," *Occupational Outlook Handbook*, 2022, https://www.bls.gov/ooh/transportation-and-material-moving/heavy-and-tractor-trailer-truck-drivers.htm.
15. Day and Hait, "Number of Truckers at All-Time High."
16. BLS, "Heavy and Tractor-Trailer Truck Drivers."
17. Booker Transportation, "What Percentage of Truckers Are Owner Operators," August 6, 2022, https://bookertrans.com/what-percentage-of-truckers-are-owner-operators.
18. Viscelli, *The Big Rig*.
19. US Bureau of Labor Statistics, "Delivery Truck Drivers and Driver/Sales Workers," *Occupational Outlook Handbook*, 2022, https://www.bls.gov/ooh/transportation-and-material-moving/delivery-truck-drivers-and-driver-sales-workers.htm.
20. James Bessen et al., "Automatic Reaction—What Happens to Workers at Firms That Automate?" Working Paper No. 19-2, Boston University School of Law, 2019, https://scholarship.law.bu.edu/faculty_scholarship/584.
21. Michael J. Handel, "Growth Trends for Selected Occupations Considered at Risk from Automation," *Monthly Labor Review*, US Bureau of Labor Statistics, July 2022, https://www.bls.gov/opub/mlr/2022/article/growth-trends-for-selected-occupations-considered-at-risk-from-automation.htm.
22. "Automation and Technological Change: Hearings before the Subcommittee on Economic Stabilization of the Joint Committee on the Economic Report," Congress of the United States, October 1955, https://www.jec.senate.gov/reports/84th%20Congress/Automation

%20and%20Technological%20Change%20-%20Hearings%20%2875
%29.pdf.

23. Allan Sloan, "Bed Bath & Beyond: How Stock Buybacks Undermined the Company," *Yahoo Finance*, January 11, 2023, https://news.yahoo .com/bed-bath-beyond-how-stock-buybacks-undermined-the-company -154202427.html.

24. Adam Lewis, "Toys R Us Creditors Sue Former Bain Capital, KKR Execs," *Pitchbook*, March 13, 2020, https://pitchbook.com/news /articles/toys-r-us-creditors-sue-former-bain-capital-kkr-execs.

25. Hamilton Nolan, "Executive Pay Is the Skeleton Key," *How Things Work*, June 16, 2023, https://www.hamiltonnolan.com/p/executive -pay-is-the-skeleton-key.

26. Insider Monkey Team, "15 Companies That Are Buying Back Their Stock," *Yahoo Finance*, December 29, 2022, https://finance.yahoo.com /news/15-companies-buying-back-stock-005623362.html.

27. Data can be found at https://ycharts.com.

28. Estimate based on tuition data found at Victoria Yuen, "The $78 Billion Community College Funding Shortfall," Center for American Progress, October 7, 2020, https://www.americanprogress.org/article/78-billion -community-college-funding-shortfall.

Chapter 12. Toward a Progressive Populism: Policies to Halt Mass Layoffs

1. For more details, see William Lazonick, "Investing in Innovation: Confronting Predatory Value Extraction in the U.S. Corporation," The Academic-Industry Research Network, working paper (October 26, 2022), 43–46, https://theairnet.org/investing-in-innovation-confronting -predatory-value-extraction-in-the-u-s-corporation.

2. Lazonick, "Investing in Innovation," 43–46.

3. Division of Investment, Department of the Treasury, State of New Jersey Cash Management Fund, "Financial Statements, Management's Discussion and Analysis and Supplemental Schedule," June 30, 2021, https://www.nj.gov/treasury/doinvest/cmf/CMFStatementsFis-cal2021.PDF.

4. Diane Geller and David Sprong, "New Jersey Temporary Workers' Bill of Rights to Take Effect August 5," *JD Supra*, August 1, 2023, https://

www.jdsupra.com/legalnews/new-jersey-temporary-workers-bill
-of-1733828.

5. Lauren Hirsch, "Can Elon Musk Make the Math Work on Owning Twit-ter? It's Dicey," *New York Times*, October 30, 2022, https://www.nytimes
.com/2022/10/30/technology/elon-musk-twitter-debt.html.

6. Luc Olinga, "Elon Musk Has a Huge Twitter Debt Bill," *TheStreet*,
January 19, 2023, https://www.thestreet.com/technology/elon-musk
-has-a-huge-twitter-debt-bill.

7. Andrew Tarantola, "80 Percent of Twitter's Full-Time Staff Has Evapo-rated Under Musk," *Engadget*, February 6, 2023, https://www.engadget
.com/80-percent-of-twitters-full-time-staff-has-evaporated-under-musk
-234247201.html.

8. Albert B. Crenshaw and Tom Kenworthy, "Rostenkowski Hill May Curb
LBO Tax Breaks," *Washington Post*, December 7, 1988, https://www
.washingtonpost.com/archive/business/1988/12/07/rostenkowski-hill
-may-curb-lbo-tax-breaks/5c4fcc72-65db-4ea5-88fb-10caacae9feb.

9. T.R. Reid, "Boycott Toshiba Computers, But Don't Let Congress Force
You," *Washington Post*, July 13, 1987, https://www.washingtonpost
.com/archive/business/1987/07/13/boycott-toshiba-computers-but
-dont-let-congress-force-you/a6130b8a-7be4-4737-8150-adc74e53443b.

10. President William Clinton, "The Clinton-Gore Administration: Working
to Open China's Markets to America's High-Tech Industries," Clinton
White House Archives, March 1, 2000, https://clintonwhitehouse5
.archives.gov/textonly/WH/Work/030200.html.

11. Robert E. Scott and Zane Mokhiber, "Growing China Trade Deficits
Cost 3.7 Million American Jobs Between 2001 and 2018," Economic
Policy Institute, January 30, 2020, https://www.epi.org/publication
/growing-china-trade-deficits-costs-us-jobs.

12. Evelyn Cheng, "China Announces Retaliatory Tariffs on $34 Billion Worth
of US Goods, Including Agriculture Products," CNBC, June 15, 2018,
https://www.cnbc.com/2018/06/15/china-announces-retaliatory-tariffs
-on-34-billion-worth-of-us-goods-including-agriculture-products.html.

13. Jomo KS et al., "Public-Private Partnerships and the 2030 Agenda for Sus-tainable Development: Fit for Purpose?" DESA Working Paper No. 148,
Department of Economic and Social Affairs, United Nations, February
2016, https://www.un.org/esa/desa/papers/2016/wp148_2016.pdf.

14. The Marshall Plan provided approximately $17 billion in aid to Europe when the US gross domestic product was $258 billion. German Marshall Fund, "The Spirit of the Marshall Plan," https://www.gmfus.org/spirit-marshall-plan.
15. History.com Editors, "Marshall Plan," *History*, November 1, 2022, https://www.history.com/topics/world-war-ii/marshall-plan-1.
16. AFL-CIO, "What Is the PRO Act?" https://www.aflcio.org/pro-act.
17. Barry T. Hirsch, David A. Macpherson, and William E. Even, "Union Membership, Coverage, and Earnings from the CPS," March 22, 2023, http://unionstats.com.
18. Lawrence Mishel and Jessica Schieder, "As Union Membership Has Fallen, the Top 10 Percent Have Been Getting a Larger Share of Income," Economic Policy Institute, May 24, 2016, https://www.epi.org/publication/as-union-membership-has-fallen-the-top-10-percent-have-been-getting-a-larger-share-of-income.
19. For more on Mazzocchi, see Les Leopold, *The Man Who Hated Work and Loved Labor: The Life and Times of Tony Mazzocchi* (White River Junction, VT: Chelsea Green Publishing, 2007).
20. Les Leopold, "6 Reasons Why Trump Is Too Weak to Save American Jobs," *Salon*, March 10, 2017, https://www.salon.com/2017/03/10/6-reasons-why-trump-is-too-weak-to-save-american-jobs_partner.

Postscript: A Challenge to Oberlin College

1. Cally Waite, "The Segregation of Black Students at Oberlin College After Reconstruction," *History of Education Quarterly* 41, no. 3 (Autumn 2001): 344–64, https://www.jstor.org/stable/369200.

INDEX

ABOUT THE AUTHOR

A GRADUATE OF OBERLIN COLLEGE and Princeton University's School of Public and International Affairs, Les Leopold co-founded the Labor Institute, a nonprofit organization that provides research and educational programs on occupational safety and health, the environment, and political economics to unions, worker centers, and community groups. He serves as the Labor Institute's executive director and is leading a national education campaign for workers to reverse runaway inequality and halt mass layoffs. Les's other books include *Defiant German, Defiant Jew: A Holocaust Memoir from Inside the Third Reich* (Amsterdam Publishers, 2020); *Runaway Inequality: An Activist's Guide to Economic Justice* (Labor Institute Press, 2018); *How to Make a Million Dollars an Hour: Why Hedge Funds Get Away with Siphoning Off America's Wealth* (John Wiley and Sons, 2013); *The Looting of America: How Wall Street's Game of Fantasy Finance Destroyed Our Jobs, Pensions, and Prosperity, and What We Can Do About It* (Chelsea Green Publishing, 2009); and *The Man Who Hated Work and Loved Labor: The Life and Times of Tony Mazzocchi* (Chelsea Green Publishing, 2006).

the politics and practice of sustainable living

CHELSEA GREEN PUBLISHING

Chelsea Green Publishing sees books as tools for effecting cultural change and seeks to empower citizens to participate in reclaiming our global commons and become its impassioned stewards. If you enjoyed *Wall Street's War on Workers*, please consider these other great books related to economics and policy.

DOUGHNUT ECONOMICS
Seven Ways to Think Like a
21st-Century Economist
KATE RAWORTH
9781603587969
Paperback

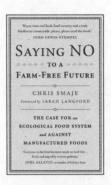

SAYING NO TO A FARM-FREE FUTURE
The Case for an Ecological Food System
and Against Manufactured Foods
CHRIS SMAJE
9781915294166
Paperback

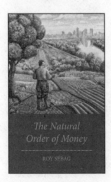

THE NATURAL ORDER OF MONEY
ROY SEBAG
9781915294227
Hardcover

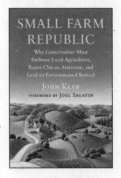

SMALL FARM REPUBLIC
Why Conservatives Must Embrace
Local Agriculture, Reject Climate Alarmism,
and Lead an Environmental Revival
JOHN KLAR
9781645022190
Paperback

For more information,
visit **www.chelseagreen.com.**

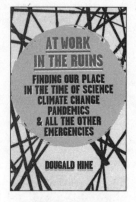
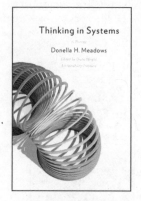
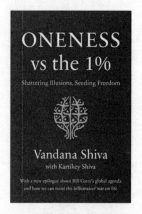
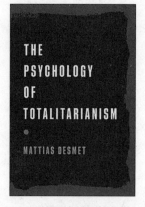